SERVANT LEADERS OF THE PEOPLE OF GOD

An Ecclesial Spirituality for American Priests

Robert M. Schwartz

PAULIST PRESS
New York/Mahwah

Library of Congress Cataloging-in-Publication Data

Schwartz, Robert M. (Robert Morris). 1941–
    Servant leaders of the people of God: an ecclesial spirituality
for American priests/by Robert M. Schwartz.
        p.   cm.
    Includes bibliographical references.
    ISBN 0-8091-3106-4
    1. Catholic Church—United States—Clergy—Religious life.
I. Title.
    BX1407.C6S38   1990
    248.8'92—dc20   89-36765
                                                                 CIP

Published by Paulist Press
997 Macarthur Boulevard
Mahwah, New Jersey 07430

Printed and bound in the
United States of America

Contents

Dedicated with love and gratitude to
the people of God in
the archdiocese of Saint Paul and Minneapolis;
to
Margaret and Aaron,
parents who gave me life and faith;
to
the ecclesial community
which shared a hunger for holiness and justice;
to
the presbyterate,
friends and witnesses to a servant ministry;
to
Archbishop John Roach,
beloved pastor and credible leader.

May Jesus Christ be praised!

Acknowledgements

Expressing gratitude is difficult, not because little is due, but because there are too many to thank and no adequate words to convey it. I am deeply grateful for the love and support of many.

First I wish to thank my family. They have supported me in many ways over the years, but I was particularly touched by their letters, pictures, calls, gifts and visits during my studies abroad when much of this book was written.

I have been blessed by the people of the archdiocese of St. Paul and Minneapolis. I have found it difficult to survive apart from parish life, so richly have I been loved, supported and challenged by those I came to serve, who in turn have ministered to me. I also owe a debt of gratitude to the St. Paul Seminary School of Divinity community and to the novitiate community of the Sisters of St. Joseph. They have challenged me to a broader vision of the church.

Archbishop Roach and the priests of the archdiocese have trusted me with the gifts of fellowship and leadership. I have grown because I have been empowered to do so by a vibrant presbyterate. I am grateful for the nine years I was privileged to serve at the Center for Growth in Priestly Ministry. My desire to write on ordained ministry has its origin in my experiences there.

The National Organization for Continuing Education of Roman Catholic Clergy has a very special place in my heart. As president of that organization I was challenged to be more than I had imagined possible. I could never repay the debt I owe to so many at NOCERCC for giving me so much.

It has been my joy to serve as a facilitator at three Collegeville Assemblies of the National Conference of Bishops. I have grown in my appreciation of the bishops as I have seen them in action. I am grateful for that opportunity. I am also thankful for the ready response of so many bishops to my request for homilies and other material. Msgrs. Daniel Hoye and Colin MacDonald deserve special mention, as does Fr. Robert Sherry. Without their help my task would have been more difficult.

Fr. Philip Rosato, S.J., who directed my research and the original thesis, pushed me hard, always giving encouragement and support. I profited immensely from his excellent direction. Thanks, too, to Fr. John Navone, S.J., whose enthusiasm for this work brought me peace and joy.

The priests of the Casa Santa Maria offered me friendship and assistance. Too many to mention by name, I wish to say thanks to all in acknowledging those who helped in the final preparation of the original text: Tom Mullin, Bill Zwiefka, Ed Montero, Tom Beggane, Rick Gabuzda and Tom Spitzmueller. Also thanks to Bill McDonough for bibliographical suggestions. Fr. Al Bitz and Msgr. Andrew Cusack were largely responsible for getting the ear of a publisher.

Friends give freely what money can't buy. The Lord has been very good to me in my friends. I am blessed indeed!

Introduction

by Joseph Cardinal Bernardin, Archbishop of Chicago

The 25th anniversary of the close of the Second Vatican Council is an appropriate moment to assess its impact on the church and the extent to which we have appropriated its teaching and implemented its intended renewal. It is also a fitting time to identify the tasks which still lie before us.

Among their ecclesiological concerns, the Council Fathers strengthened our understanding of the role of bishops and highlighted the vocation and ministry of the laity in the church and in the world. So, conciliar teaching has had a significant impact on both bishops and laity. However, those whose daily lives and ministry have perhaps been most affected by the Council and subsequent renewal have been *priests*. While the Council—and, subsequently, the U.S. bishops—have had much to say about the priesthood, there has not been a comprehensive synthesis of that teaching.

We all owe Father Robert Schwartz a great debt of gratitude for his generous investment of time and talent in developing a masterful summary of conciliar and episcopal teaching on the priesthood.

After setting the historical and cultural context of the U.S. presbyterate in the last quarter century, Fr. Schwartz presents a comprehensive review of the ontological, ecclesial, sociopolitical, and eschatological dimensions of the priesthood in the conciliar documents. He demonstrates that the theology of the priesthood is quite complex and embraces inevitable tensions—for example, between ontological and functional understandings of priestly identity and ministry. He also helps explain why living in accord with that teaching is often difficult, requiring ongoing conversion and growth.

The author then surveys the teaching of the National Conference of Catholic Bishops and that of a broad cross section of U.S. bishops. What emerges in these two chapters (6 and 7) is both a realization of its consistency with conciliar teaching and an appreciation of the broad consensus about such essential issues as priestly identity, role, and spirituality.

Father Schwartz concludes with a helpful analysis of this episcopal teaching in light of the conciliar documents and points out several challenges for further reflection, dialogue, and articulation.

Priests—both diocesan and religious—and bishops will profit greatly from this splendid book. Those ordained before the Council will appreciate the balanced, insightful discussion of how and why our understanding of the priesthood has shifted in the past twenty-five years without at all diminishing the essential role of the presbyterate in the church. Those who were ordained in the 60's—who prepared for priestly ministry during the Council itself—will find here both clarity and helpful perspective to illuminate their experience of that exciting, and confusing, decade.

Those ordained since the Council, as well as those preparing for ordination during this post-conciliar era, will see here a thorough presentation of conciliar teaching on the priesthood. Indeed, this book deserves a special place in bibliographies for seminary courses in ecclesiology and/or the theology of the priesthood.

This book will also be beneficial for women religious, religious brothers, and lay people who want to understand more clearly the diversity of complementary roles within the ecclesial community and the specific contribution of priests. Indeed, as Father Schwartz points out in the last chapter, unless priests are correctly understood and lovingly supported by those they serve, their ministry will be ineffective.

My hope is that all who read this book will also be affected by Father Schwartz's love for the priesthood and his care for his fellow priests.

Introduction

by Most Rev. John A. Marshall,
Bishop of Burlington

In 1972, the year of my ordination as a bishop, I can recall the joy, the hope, the inspiration which so many priests experienced from reading and studying *Spiritual Renewal of the American Priesthood*. There was reason to expect that this presentation of the elements of an experiential spirituality would give rise to other treatises on the same subject. Since then much has been written but few, if any, major works on the spiritual life have developed the basic themes of *Spiritual Renewal of the American Priesthood* in such a way that our understanding and, therefore, our practice of the spiritual life in the modern American context has been greatly enhanced.

Servant Leaders of the People of God is a challenging explanation of the spiritual life, which builds upon the foundation which had been outlined in *Spiritual Renewal of the American Priesthood*. Father Robert Schwartz accepts the fact that priestly spirituality for our times must be realized in a willingness to live out our personal lives in terms of the death-resurrection mystery of our Lord and Savior Jesus Christ. But he points out further, and explains ever so clearly, that there can be no separation of a priest's spirituality from his ministry: "Ministry to the needs of this world and proclamation of the kingdom are so fused that they cannot be separated in an authentic Christian spirituality."

A priest grows in holiness only as he develops an ever more Christlike concern for, and service to, God's people. And in order to exercise compassion of this kind for the spiritually and materially poor he must be a man of persevering prayer; he must derive spiritual sustenance from the scripture; he must live a sacrificial lifestyle of poverty, chastity, and obedience, which canot be done without deep devotion to the eucharist. In order to be like Christ, the priest must be with Christ. Only then can the priest act *in persona Christi*, minister appropriately to the least of his brethren, and grow in holiness.

Reading *Servant Leaders of the People of God,* one cannot help but think of St. Vincent de Paul as a model of the spirituality described in this book. It is not Father Schwartz's intention, however, to go back into history searching for a model. Rather, he would wish to inspire each priest to study the spiritual life and ministry of Jesus, to pray about the means whereby he can be one in mind, in heart and in ministry with the Lord, and then live out once more in human history the death-resurrection mystery as priests are called to do. He would have us make our own words the words of St. Paul:

> The life I live now is not my own;
>   Christ is living in me.
> I still live my human life,
>   but it is a life of faith in the
>   Son of God,
>   who loved me and gave Himself for me.
> I will not treat God's gracious gift as
>   pointless (Gal 2:20–21).

1.

The American Priest
in Context

Issues Inviting a Response

The Second Vatican Council brought change, growth and turmoil to the Catholic Church. While still adolescent in its historical development, the church in the United States was propelled into adulthood by the dislocation and restructuring which has marked the years following the council. An ecclesial community still young in its journey found energy in the challenge of the council and for the first time began to sense its proper place in the total church. Less defensive about being both Catholic and American, the American Catholic sought to integrate both of these treasured identities. Thus, the invitation of the council to renewal and the emerging maturity of a young ecclesial community came together in the post-conciliar period. After more than twenty years the face of American Catholicism is undeniably different. In few places is the difference experienced as profoundly and with as much expectation and tension as in the lives of American priests.

Since the close of the Second Vatican Council the American bishops have responded to the spiritual needs of priests in the United States in a variety of ways. This study articulates the direction for the spiritual growth of American priests emanating from Vatican II and the magisterium and pastoral practice of their bishops within the context of two major tensions within church life in the United States: ecclesial leadership set against ecclesial membership, and service to humanity set against witness to the kingdom. The special contribution which the bishops make lies in the way in which they integrate these contrasting realities, presenting them as interrelated dimensions of an authentic presbyteral spirituality.

Even though the focus of the council is far-reaching and much broader than the sacrament of orders, yet the conciliar documents examine this sacrament in many contexts and affirm that it is essential to an authentic articulation of the nature and mission of the church. The theological understandings and the pastoral directives of the council provide the setting for the American bishops in providing pastoral leadership for the church in the United States.

The task of this first chapter is to paint a picture of the current situation in the American church using broad strokes so as to better understand the challenge facing priests in responding to the summons of the council as articulated in the magisterium of the bishops of the United States. This will be done in terms of four classical themes in the spiritual life: identity, asceticism, activity, and goal. While each of these themes is essential, they have been defined in diverse ways and integrated with more or less success in the history of the church. In response to the insights and preferences of a given age, there have been significant swings of the pendulum which have had important effects on the concrete shape of presbyteral spirituality in a particular period. A long tradition offers these four themes to American priests as both gift and challenge. Accordingly, they provide a logical framework for this initial chapter and a necessary backdrop for those that follow.

I. The Distinctive Identity of Priests Today

In 1983 a noted religious sociologist told a national conference on church vocations: "I submit that the twentieth century Roman Catholic model of Christian ministry has come to an end . . . what is eroding is the socio-historical *model* of Christian ministry which reached its zenith in the mid-twentieth century."[1] Dr. Schoenherr points out the current challenge both to identifying all ministry with the ordained, and to the hierarchical structure of church authority. He concludes that the traditional understanding of ministry as restricted to a "clerical elite" is unacceptable to a growing number of Catholics.[2]

In a survey of attitudes among the clergy, older priests reported some interesting changes relative to the priesthood as they experience it: the respect which comes to the priestly office has declined, and the security which results from responding to a divine call has diminished. The survey concludes: "Apparently the ontological nature of the priesthood has diminished a bit in importance."[3] Andrew Greeley reports that the clergy continue to have a great crisis in morale which flows, at least in part, from the belief that the priesthood is no longer important to the religious life of the laity.[4]

Yet, in the midst of this apparent uncertainty, Dr. Schoenherr affirms that "the priesthood will remain the core of the ministry."[5] He bases this opinion on the centrality of the eucharist in the Catholic tradition, and on the general agreement among social scientists that sacrificial ritual is the foundation of organized religion. The further development of primary professions in the modern world will also bolster ordained ministry. He ends with an important addendum: "A Catholic ministry in which the primacy is still the priesthood is only possible if it is complemented by full participation of religious and lay ministers."[6]

Profound questions are being asked about the identity of priests in all segments of the American church. These inquiries touch not only on the role of the ordained, but also on the style in which their ministry is exercised. In the contemporary world the moral laxity of the clergy in general is seldom a subject of criticism. Furthermore, ecumenical dialogue has enlightened or resolved a number of interfaith issues which made an unprejudiced assessment of the clergy difficult. The central area of concern about priests, therefore, is a deeper one which is much harder to articulate: Is their way of being and acting a valid reflection of the master who came to serve, and not to be served?

This is a particularly pertinent question in the Catholic tradition, for, as will be shown in Chapter 2, the council documents describe the priest as an effective sign of Christ's leadership as head of his body, the church. Since the very concept of headship is repulsive in a democratic society if it is not understood and lived out as Christ exemplified it, this suggests a transformation of radical proportions in the ordained based on prayerful openness to that which the Spirit of God alone can accomplish.

In every age Christians have been influenced, even seduced, by the prevailing secular lifestyle and worldly modes of exercising authority. Long remembered are those who have withstood the seduction, for the likeness of the master is easily seen in the lives of Mother Teresa of Calcutta, Pope John XXIII, and St. Francis of Assisi. The imprint of the gospel, appropriated in prayer and action, makes these and others the subject of awed fascination in a world of very secular values. Inasmuch as authentic prayer, appropriate identity and effective activity go hand in hand, they are the crucial requirements for the credible exercise of ordained ministry.

The importance of an evangelical lifestyle is magnified because modern society refuses to accord the church the authority of previous ages. Contemporary theology also regards the role of the church differently, as Karl Rahner emphasizes: "The world is penetrated and filled with God's grace. The sacraments are certainly events of this grace . . . yet this must not be understood as though the world were otherwise profane and without grace."[7] Attention has shifted from the church as the center of God's saving plan to the church as the servant of redeemed humanity. And so the function of ministry has changed as well, since it is no longer seen as "taking grace" to people as if for the first time, but as fostering grace already at work in them. Consequently, in a church seeking to renew itself in the image of Christ, there is tension between a focus on the ordained and the power they have in a priest-centered community, and ecclesial ministers and the service they give in a people-centered one. Previous understandings about clerical lifestyle and privilege enter into this tension.[8]

A little history gives a helpful perspective on why servant-leadership is a particular challenge today. Because the beginning of the American seminary system was largely the gift of the French church, the first attempts at priestly formation on American soil grew from the tradition spawned there in the wake of the Council of Trent and the upheavals of the French Revolution. In reaction to the theological deviations of reformers and the excesses of revolutionaries, the typical French seminary favored simple, clear and correct teaching on Catholic dogma, without creative innovation. In response to the laxity of the clergy, it emphasized the moral and spiritual formation of future priests within a structure which controlled activity and guaranteed conformity to a higher level of moral and spiritual life.[9]

For very good reasons order, discipline, orthodoxy and conformity were given prominence. An almost rigid dedication to correct ways of thinking and appropriate ways of acting seldom yielded extraordinary priests, but the products of these seminaries were a vast improvement over the generality of the clergy. The desperate state of affairs can be seen in the lament of St. Vincent de Paul: "The Church is going to ruin in many places on account of the evil life of her priests; it is they who are ruining and destroying her . . . and the depravity of the ecclesiastical state is the chief cause of the ruin of God's Church."[10]

Although the United States was far from this milieu geographically, the situation in Europe had a profound influence on the formation of the American clergy, as John Tracy Ellis testifies in the historical study of priesthood in the United States commissioned by the National Conference of Catholic Bishops. He maintains that there is a direct relationship between the origins of the seminary system and many of the presuppositions in American Catholicism. As evidence he offers the fact that with the single exception of the distinctive thrust of the Vatican II document on religious freedom, American theology has come directly from Europe with its methods of teaching and its philosophical and theological framework as well.[11]

Accordingly, the focus of the spiritual life imparted in the early American seminaries was largely a result of the concerns of the period, reflecting European insights. The Third Council of Baltimore emphasized the development of priestly virtues thought to be especially lacking in that age, namely humility, obedience and the respect owed to superiors. Moreover, seminarians were to be on guard against an "immoderate love of their own freedom" and a dislike for rules, for the bishops saw nothing as more contrary to a true priestly spirit.[12]

These virtues were further underscored in reaction to the widening gulf between the church and the world flowing from the Enlightenment and the struggles for political emancipation, as well as from later concern about modernism and Americanism. The revival of Thomism as the uniform theological discipline offered apparent security in a world which had lost its equilibrium. As a result, little flexibility or experimentation was allowed in seminary classrooms, nor was that which was distinctively American easily admitted.[13]

Although the church in the United States has been enriched by a European perspective in reading the gospels and has built well on that foundation, it has been slow to claim aspects of its own experience which also throw light on the mystery of Christ. For example, in interacting with the dominant culture, adequate attention has not been given to the significance of religious values and symbols in American life. Unlike most European countries, the United States does not have a large secular sector in its culture; the portion of the population which is anti-religious or anti-clerical is not over ten to twenty percent.[14] In fact, when asked to indicate the importance of God in their lives on a scale of one to ten, the combined total for all Americans was 8.21, higher than every country in Europe, and significantly more than most.[15] The fact that South Africa is the one country in the world ranking higher on this scale suggests that there is more involved in an authentic response to the gospel than this question measures, yet it also points out a significant fact: "The core values of the American people are religiously based and, more specifically, based upon biblical, Judeo-Christian, religion."[16]

Just as the American church made a significant contribution to the discussion of religious liberty at the council, so, too, its extraordinary experience with other Christian bodies can contribute to a renewed image of the priest which is both more sensitive to the gospel in imaging the servant-headship of Christ, and more attentive to the fundamental equality of all the faithful in inviting their participation.[17] While in need of enrichment from the universal church, the American experience has much to offer to prayerful reflection on the meaning of authentic leadership in the image of Jesus.

In the ferment which produced the council and in the years that lie beyond it, the whole church has undergone a profound change of perspective. Since Christians now have the ability to stand back and observe the historical process in a way which no other generation has enjoyed, it is possible to be self-critical against a much broader background. This historical consciousness frees priests from the prospect of being trapped by their immediate history, culture or surroundings, and enriches them with a new breadth of human experience, for now it is possible to fathom the experience of the early church and that of other historical periods and geographical areas. This historical, trans-cultural and trans-global experience has produced a new self-understanding in priests, as well as renewed rites and fresh energies in the American church.[18]

Inasmuch as prayer is one of the major activities which deepen both an authentic self-understanding and a vivid consciousness of the demands of the gospel, it is a crucial concern in the spiritual life. In recent years, the prayer life of the American priest has changed radically. The research document on the sociology of the priest commissioned by the American bishops reported that in the wake of the council 42 percent of American priests prayed the entire breviary daily. Private prayer or meditation was a part of the daily life of 69 percent of priests over 55, and 38 percent of those ages 26 to 35.[19] A look at the age spectrum suggests that prayer practices continue to change in the direction favored by the younger clergy.

In a very short period of time, the almost universally observed practice of praying the entire breviary daily "under pain of serious sin" has changed dramatically, indicating that obligation alone is no longer regarded as a compelling reason to pray by most priests. In a book of reflections on the same survey Andrew Greeley proposes that obligatory prayer was faithfully discharged in a tightly structured church which could invoke penalties on those who do not pray; but in a more fluid church where people have lost their fear of penalties imposed by canon law or moral theology, the obligation to pray out of fear of serious sin is without force.[20] He locates the source of the problem in the imposition of obligations without adequate intellectual development; in a church which no longer functioned out of obligation and in which no rationale had been given the bottom fell out.[21]

Charles E. Curran takes up the same theme: "There is no doubt that prayer requires some type of discipline. When all discipline had been brought about through external means of sanctions, then true education had not been accomplished."[22] The result is that many priests have abandoned traditional forms of prayer without putting anything else in their place in the hope of finding something more meaningful. The situation is a potentially dangerous one, since shallowness, a lack of perception of what is most real, an absence of sensitivity to the presence of God, and a lack of reverence for life are often the by-products of not praying.

Prayerful reflection, in its many forms, gives substance to Christian belief by renewing disciples in the image of Christ. Therefore, this experience of God, emerging from the core of human existence, is essential to Christian identity.[23] It is here, at the center of their being, that priests are more deeply conformed to Christ, the servant-head of the church. Prayer, then, clarifies both their identity as presbyters and their mission in the ecclesial community.

After the council, religious priests moved quickly in clarifying the distinctive charism of each religious community. This resulted in a noticeable enrichment of the American church; it also intensified a question which is as old as the church itself: Is there a distinctive spirituality for diocesan priests, or do they simply adopt the spirituality of some spiritual giant, one that appeals to them, and make it their own? The lack of a well-developed spirituality in a strictly presbyteral context has lent urgency to this inquiry.

In fact, it has generated an even deeper question: What is the relationship between ministry and spirituality? At least part of the answer lies in a proper understanding of both as components of an interrelated whole. Thus, as ministry is more and more seen to be interpersonal, prayer, too, is understood in these terms. Communion with God, the communion of the eucharist, and the communion of saints all point to the relational nature of grace, permeating prayer and ministry and uniting them. Since those who do not experience communion cannot be a source of it for others, growth in relationships through both prayer and ministry is a priority for presbyteral spirituality if the ordained are to be effective servants of the graced life of the church.[24]

Although a busy parish often challenges a personal decision to pray, guaranteeing time for it by setting priorities, handling interruptions and dealing with lack of organization is a skill which preserves the roots of ministry from atrophy due to lack of adequate nourishment. Among all the choices which a priest has to make, the decision to pray or not to pray has crucial importance.[25]

Prayer, identity and maturity are mutually interrelated dimensions of presbyteral spirituality which will be even more closely associated with effective ministry in the future. In making suggestions for the 1971 Synod of Bishops on the ministerial priesthood, a hearing in Episcopal Region VII reported that as time goes on priests will need to be more fully mature human beings with deep spiritual conviction and dedication, combined with sensitivity and flexibility in dealing with people and problems. In other words, they will have to demonstrate self-confidence, competence, vision, initiative, creativity and a special ability to communicate with those they serve.[26]

In the psychological study of priests commissioned by the American bishops, a key finding establishes an overriding context: "The priests of the United States are ordinary men. Many of their conflicts and challenges arise precisely because they are ordinary men who may have to live as though they were not ordinary at all."[27] While the report makes no startling discoveries, it does point to psychological underdevelopment as a basic problem: "A large proportion of the priests in this cross-sectional sample, as in any cross-sectional sample of American men, has not developed to full maturity."[28] The underdeveloped person has not passed through all the stages of growth which lead to what is recognized as mature, adult behavior; thus, he is often involved in relationships that are distant and stylized—unrewarding both for himself and for others involved.[29] This finding suggests that the relational aspects of prayer may be seriously affected by lack of human development, as may effective involvement in the communion of the church.

The inability of many priests to recognize their own talents and gifts may have a spiritual dimension associated with not having taken a long and loving look at the real in contemplation.[30] Consequently, many spend more time worrying about failure and weakness than being thankful for their giftedness and success. The result is a lowering of self-esteem which alienates them from self, from others and from God.[31]

The study conducted by the American bishops concludes very pointedly: "The priests of the United States are clearly adequate in their function; they could be far more effective personally and professionally if they were helped to achieve greater human and religious maturity."[32] Thus, the distinctive identity of presbyters as those exercising the office of Christ, the shepherd and head, is, on one hand, the result of sacramental ordination; on the other, it is related to both regular prayer and psychological development. These are factors, then, which the bishops must consider in developing the ontological dimension of the teaching of Vatican II on priestly spirituality.

II. The Ecclesial Context of Presbyteral Asceticism

The demand for service in today's church is constant, generating tension between ministry and the traditional practices of asceticism. Not only has this tension focused attention on the kind of asceticism to which priests are called today, but, more importantly, it has made a separation of ministerial activity and spirituality untenable. That which was also true in a slower paced world becomes an absolute necessity in a church of diminished numbers of priests and increased expectations: asceticism and ministry must be related to one another.

Another look at American history will help locate some of the reasons why ministerial activity and asceticism are so often seen to be in conflict. While the decrees of the Third Council of Baltimore gave great attention to seminaries, they often viewed the theological and formational task undertaken there as separate from the pastoral experience of the church. Accordingly, the work of the seminary professor was to be so totally focused on the seminary and the "glory and increase of theological knowledge" that it was to be committed only to priests who would give themselves wholeheartedly to the matter, not permitting themselves to be distracted by undertaking work outside the seminary.[33] These decrees capture an understanding of the relationship of theology to the pastoral consciousness of the church and of the seminary to the ministerial activity of the ecclesial community which has had enduring influence.

While seminary formation was surely aimed at producing priests who could face the practical challenges of parish life, it was clearly far removed from it in both intellectual and spiritual attitude.[34] Hence, seminary professors were to teach by word and example; yet, in listing the qualities desirable in rectors and other teachers, pastoral experience was not mentioned. A gulf arose between the seminary and the parish, theology and pastoral practice, spirituality and ministerial experience, making a notable contribution to the milieu in which American priests struggle to establish a viable spirituality.

Many priests were formed in a tradition which tended to see spirituality focused on discipline and theology focused on dogmatic statements. Spiritual exercises were usually understood as laudable private additions to one's schedule. These propensities were easily coupled with the rugged individualism and the intellectual fundamentalism native to the American environment, producing a spirituality which was concrete, pragmatic, orthodox and active.[35] It was also most often solitary and nourished outside the normal course of daily events, although it was expected to have an effect on them. As a synthesis proper to its own time, this approach to spirituality proved to be successful and served the American church well.

Yet, the appreciable distance between many traditional practices of spirituality and the activities of ministry has produced a restlessness in priests seeking more integration among various aspects of life, broader insights into the Catholic tradition, and fuller psychological development. An important thrust of contemporary spirituality, then, is to transcend the stereotypes of American culture and the compartmentalization of earlier formation, in order to be nourished by a fuller understanding of the human person, the experience of ministry, and more familiar contact with a worldwide church.[36]

Ministerial activity can be both a blessing and a dilemma, as is evident in the very success of the American church, an energetic community which expresses its vitality through active parishes, schools, hospitals and numerous other institutions and programs. Since an immigrant church made urgent demands on priests, the active orientation of the American clergy has sometimes led to a questioning of the depth of their spirituality. Amid the pressures of a typical parish today the same question is often posed by priests themselves.

Religious life in the United States has taken on a more active character as well; thus, in the rush to respond to pastoral needs, the distinctive charisms of particular institutes were often compromised in order to answer a pressing demand for parish ministers. The benefits of the involvement of religious priests in countless parishes and institutions are monumental; yet religious have found it necessary to seek a better balance between apostolic activity, on one hand, and the prayer, community life and specific gifts proper to each institute, on the other.[37] The challenge is to blend the traditional charisms and the apostolic way of life in a way which is faithful to both and true to the American experience.

Because diocesan and religious priests now know one another better through presbyteral gatherings fostered by the council, they have begun to challenge one another to a renewed understanding of priestly spirituality in which the presbyteral mission itself is a primary concern. Thus the relationship between ministry and spirituality is a common concern forging new bonds of understanding and cooperation among American priests.

Today, there is widespread agreement that ministry is more than a necessary burden or a way to practice mortification; it is the centerpiece of the priest's distinctive call to holiness.[38] Accordingly, the proclamation of the gospel, the eucharist, the liturgy and the sacraments are the primary sources and expressions of pastoral charity. The activities which prepare for this ministry and the pastoral care which flows from it complete the distinctive spirituality of the priest.[39] This ecclesial synthesis lies at the heart of contemporary literature on presbyteral spirituality.[40]

An authentic presbyteral spirituality is focused on the life-giving relationship of Christ to the church.[41] Since within that relationship priests have an essential role, their greatest ascetical challenge may well be to lead from center stage, with real authority, without making themselves the focus of attention. The test of their spirituality is the ability to remain the "best man" at the Lord's wedding feast, for to steal attention for oneself is to ruin the celebration. Remaining the crucial yet uncelebrated enabler of another's feast is asceticism at its heights.[42]

As ecclesial persons priests must deal with many temptations to flee their environment: too many liturgies, prayer forms that don't seem to fit the active life, living in the midst of people while remaining alone and lonely, persistent pressure and countless expectations. Contemporary asceticism challenges the ordained to seek for holiness in this very milieu, because it is in the ministry itself, especially in the liturgical celebrations of the church and the relationships which flow from them, that the spirituality of the priest is to be found.[43] Consequently, it is at moments of serving others that the Holy Spirit is powerfully present for the sanctification of the minister as well. In mediating the activity of the Spirit, priests also experience the transforming presence of the One whose herald and servant they have become in presbyteral ordination.[44]

This focus on priestly ministry itself as the forum for presbyteral spirituality is part of a broader reappraisal of the relationship of the world, the body and human activity to the experience of God. Richard McBrien sums up the importance of Teilhard de Chardin for post-conciliar spirituality by saying: "The great mystery of Christianity is not that God appears (epiphany), but that God shines through the universe (diaphany). Our prayer therefore, is not that we might see God 'as He is in Himself' but that we might see God in all things."[45] This movement from a more negative to a more positive attitude toward the world and human experience is reflected in many recent spiritual writers. Thomas Merton insisted that spirituality means more than abandoning all things and emptying oneself of images and desires, because it is through union with humanity that life is penetrated by the love of God. In this union God is discovered, his mercy is experienced, and liberation from self-concern is received.[46] The belief that God is present in the universal struggle to find him led Merton to dialogue with the religious traditions of the east, a venture that resulted in his early death. Matthew Fox takes up the same theme, insisting that the focal issue in spirituality is not the redemption of the soul, but the redemption of the world. Since human beings are so much in the world and the world so much in them, healing one is healing the other.[47]

Because insights into the Hebraic roots of Christianity and contributions from the human sciences have led to a renewed focus on the humanity of Christ in a fittingly human approach to salvation, the incarnation is given more significance in contemporary spirituality. In his groundbreaking classic *Holiness Is Wholeness,* Josef Goldbrunner sought to end the warring between body and soul, posed as two opposing entities, by finding in the incarnate one a wholeness which includes the bodily and the spiritual.[48]

True spirituality is to be found in the midst of a fully human life and not apart from it, because God has chosen not only to create human nature, but also to work through it. Authentic disciples, then, will seek to be part of God's historical, developmental and transcendent presence in the midst of humanity's journey, since the practices of the spiritual life must always respect the way that God relates to human nature.

Theologians, priests, religious and laity were invited to contribute to a number of the regional meetings preparing for the 1971 Synod of Bishops. While the results affirmed the traditional areas of priestly asceticism (prayer, daily mass, the sacrament of penance, self-denial, and poverty, among others), they also proposed that new understanding was needed. Episcopal Region VII suggested: "In view of current disenchantment with older forms of prayer and spiritual exercises, bishops and priests should place priority on personal and united efforts to determine and encourage modern asceticism and prayer."[49]

What is meant by "modern asceticism"? Some of the other regions make recommendations which are more concrete. Region VIII highlighted the quality and availability of service rendered to the people of God, since they found true asceticism to be rooted in the eternal, yet manifested in the temporal activities of priestly ministry.[50] Region IV reported that they had considered priestly asceticism from a number of angles and then discovered that the very process in which they were involved—studying, exploring and penetrating the ministry—was a form of asceticism demanding time, effort, direction and self-control. This same region had noted earlier that there was too little performance accountability expected of bishops and priests at a time when society demands such assessment of others.[51] Region X seems to pull the new emphasis together: "The unique call to the priests of our times is to struggle as leaders for renewal of the Church and society, both spiritually and socially, and it is within this context of struggle that the priest develops his spirituality."[52]

The demands of ministry, then, are their own form of asceticism: living life deeply and creatively, accepting its joy and pain, seeking to find God in all things, receiving whoever comes with gentleness and concern. Priests are called to an asceticism which not only seeks to discipline the body, but, even more, strives to strengthen Christian insight and commitment, thereby heightening the capacity for ministry.[53] Asceticism, then, is doing what one does in the name of Christ and in service to his people with all the faith, love and skill that can be mustered. In today's church doing what one is called to do, doing it well, and doing only that, is the core asceticism around which all other spiritual exercises must be ordered.

Since the appropriate context for presbyteral spirituality is service to church and society, priests involved in parish ministry have special importance, being called to live among baptized Christians pursuing secular vocations in very ordinary circumstances. As pastors, they must live with the ambiguity of the world, challenging, embracing and tolerating it, while always refusing to reject it by an existence apart.[54] Pastoral ministry in the midst of the world reveals that God is the source and goal of the secular journey.

Both the ecclesial and secular settings of priests in the United States, while challenging, have very positive features. Not only is religion a national value with 95 percent claiming belief in God,[55] and 91 percent expressing a religious preference, but 68 percent of Americans say that they are, in fact, members of a church or synagogue. In the average week 40 percent of the adults in the United States attend religious services,[56] and even among the "unchurched," close to three in four say that they pray.[57] More encouraging yet is the 1985 finding that 51 percent of American adults were more interested in religion now than they were five years ago.[58] Surprisingly, a Gallup survey concludes that the best description of religion in the United States is "stability," since "basic religious beliefs, and even religious practice, today differ relatively little from the levels recorded 50 years ago."[59] In contrast, during the same half century, a rather sharp decline in basic religious beliefs has occurred among Europeans. Perhaps even more startling is the fact that during the disillusionment of the 1970's public confidence in organized religion was higher than in the seven other major institutions surveyed.[60] The Catholic Church offers an equally positive picture: 28 percent of Americans are Catholics, a numerical increase of almost 20 percent since 1940. Currently, almost 33 percent of the teenagers in the country say that their religious preference is Catholic.[61] Furthermore, the laity are convinced that priests are important, even though they may not always give them high marks on performance.[62] While highly educated Catholics are three times more likely to see priests as rigid or backward-looking, and five times more likely to see them as "stuffy" than the less educated, even here the overall impression of priests is a positive one.[63] In rating the way the clergy handle parish ministry, "an astonishing 88 percent approved of the job their priests were doing."[64] Similarly, 50 percent of parishioners see their priests as "very understanding" and another 37 percent as "fairly understanding" of the practical problems of the laity. Finally, 29 percent rated sermons as excellent, and another 44 percent as good, while two Catholics in three expressed either "a great deal" or "a lot" of confidence in their church, and 85 percent reported an overall positive lifetime religious experience.[65] In brief, the total environment in which priests are called to minister is more friendly than they may believe.

Yet, there are negative factors as well. While Sunday mass attendance has declined from 74 percent in 1958 to 53 percent in 1985, 78 percent of the laity still attend mass at least once a month, indicating a fair amount of faithfulness to the structures of Catholic life in a society which has difficulty with commitment.[66] Still, the reasons for involvement in the church may have changed dramatically, since many Americans value individual autonomy to the point of finding it very difficult to discover their deepest meaning through tradition and community. *Habits of the Heart: Individualism and Commitment in American Life* comments: "Most of us imagine an autonomous self existing independently, entirely outside any tradition and community, and then perhaps choosing one."[67] The authority which people ascribe to religion has changed as well, with many paying more attention to the subjective than the objective, to the relative rather than the absolute, to the individual over the group, and to the secular in place of the sacral.[68] As a result, Americans have moved toward seeing identity as a private matter, giving rise to an "invisible religion" which is often at odds with the "official religion" to which they belong.[69]

Furthermore, "there is evidence of a tendency to view religion as useful for some personal or social end rather than as an expression of devotion to God alone."[70] Hence, the strongest value commitments among Americans are to family, career, a high standard of living, and good health. Inasmuch as other commitments, including religious ones, are instrumental to these, "most Americans see religion as an assist in making decisions, attaining worldly success, gaining wealth and health and achieving security and happiness."[71] The church may be utilized, then, to serve privatized needs, with evangelization and a social or prophetic ministry given much less priority.

Not only do priests minister in this milieu, but they themselves are a part of it. One of the most challenging questions in the American church is why priests, who are highly valued by those they serve, continue to resign from active ministry or hesitate to recruit others to take their place. Andrew Greeley comments: "Paradoxically, it would appear that precisely at a time when the preaching and counselling abilities of priests are most important to Catholics, priests themselves have little regard for the importance of their work."[72] While the reasons that priests leave are complex,[73] the fact that they do is a common experience. National data on the diocesan clergy shows that 20 percent of them leave within five years of ordination and that by the time of their twenty-fifth anniversary almost half will have resigned.[74]

There is evidence that those who resign are relatively more "liberal" than those in their ordination class who remain; thus, "as the oldest members of the clergy retire or die and the youngest either resign or mellow with age and increased responsibilities, the overall pattern of beliefs and values will reflect a retreat toward more conservative ground."[75] Consequently, priests will become a more homogeneous group, on the one hand, and less open to innovation, on the other. Richard Schoenherr says that the demographic transition toward a smaller and older group of priests is so strong that to turn it around in a short period of time would take drastic, if not unrealistic, changes.[76]

All of this has a serious impact on the way priests experience parish ministry. Moreover, the manner in which they handle insights into the contemporary situation has a direct relationship to their spirituality, and thereby to their effectiveness. For example, 50 percent of U.S. parishes are currently staffed by one person, the pastor. This can be either energizing or depressing, depending on the style of the priest involved.[77] Even when there is more than one priest available in a parish, studies show that the occupational satisfaction of associate pastors is at the level of semi-skilled workers.[78] While the morale of priests rose between 1970 and 1985, it did so less among the young.[79] With so many younger priests leaving ministry, their overall less than enthusiastic reaction to the concrete experience of the priesthood must be taken seriously. Yet, in the midst of an extended period of clergy disillusionment, the latest Gallup survey comments: "The ten-to-one approval rating of parish priests is really quite remarkable."[80] Astounding, too, is the unusually high ratings which the church received for treatment of the role of lay people at the same time that the laity are pressing for greater responsibilities.

Since the council relates presbyteral spirituality to an existential setting—the family of God as a community fired with a single ideal —this concrete, interpersonal dimension of priestly life must be taken quite seriously as the milieu in which priests grow into that which they were ordained to be.

III. Presbyteral Service to Church and Society

Spirituality has always struggled to define the nature of the sacred and the secular, their relationship to one another, and the role of the church and its ministers in both: Are these separate or co-extensive realities? Granted that there is no autonomy from God, what kind of independence does the "world" have in relationship to the church, and how are the political and ecclesial spheres interrelated? Most basically, what is the relationship between nature and grace? These are important questions for priests, for they are ordained as ministers of the sacred, sent to serve a world which both demands and deserves that its sovereignty be respected.

To understand the relationship between Catholicism and American society, it is necessary to consider again the historical forces which shaped present realities. The Catholic Church in the United States has an extraordinary heritage; drawn together from many lands and cultures, it has been enriched by the Celtic, Germanic, Slavic and Latin strains of European Catholicism, as well as by blacks, Hispanics and members of the eastern rites. Nurtured far from the protection or interference of governments long involved in church affairs, American Catholicism has grown in an environment which is officially neutral on religious matters, yet often unofficially Protestant in its outlook.[81]

As communities of immigrants in foreign surroundings, American Catholics learned to cherish the religious traditions which gave them identity and security. They built parishes, schools and other institutions to protect what they cherished, and gave sons and daughters in great numbers to staff them. The resulting intimacy between church institutions, the priests and sisters who staffed them, and the American Catholic laity has been deep and friendly. The reciprocal closeness of the church and the life of the people is a characteristic which greatly influences the nature of the American church.

Thus, the American church truly belongs to the people, since it enjoys both the broad support and the willing participation of the lay community. The American priest, even with the most clerical of personalities, is not far removed from happenings in the lives of the laity. Friendly banter and exchange between parish priest and parishioners is taken for granted in even the most structured of environments. Although clericalism does exist in American Catholicism, isolation does not. Priests and lay people are involved in a remarkable dialogue which shows itself in how the ordained act, where they live, how they dress and the way in which they see themselves.

Because American priests live their spirituality in intimate relationship with the people they serve, distinctions between clergy and laity are often less clear, accentuating the tension between those who emphasize the distinctiveness of priests as those having a special role, and those who call attention to the equality of all the baptized in the life of the church. This tension has great influence on the way in which priestly spirituality is perceived. Furthermore, the emphasis in the council on the role of the laity affirmed an already existing insight and intensified the discussion. In many ways, the tension between lay identity and the identity of the ordained has been healthy and creative. In any event, it is the omnipresent background against which conversation about the ministry and spirituality of priests takes place in the American church.[82]

Recently, the role of women in church and society has influenced the discussion of priestly ministry in a special way in the United States,[83] with one in four Catholics saying the church does a poor job in responding to this issue. While many women do not believe that the church responds well to the needs of women in general, they are three times more likely to be satisfied with the way they are treated in their own parish. Surprisingly, slightly more men than women say the church is doing a poor job in handling the needs of women. Even though the Gallup survey concludes that it would be too strong to assert that Catholic women, as a group, are angry with their church, there is no doubt that discussions of both the distinctive role of the ordained and justice in the church move rapidly to this issue.[84]

From the very beginning, the immigrant status of Catholicism in the United States intertwined the clergy and laity, the sacred and secular, and the church and society in an experience with few barriers or divisions, thereby mixing together people and issues held farther apart in other cultural expressions of the church. It also created a community of builders, of people concerned about daily service to human needs. Cardinal Gibbons, the youngest bishop to attend the First Vatican Council and one of the giants of the American church, said quite bluntly that what is most important and instructive for the priest as an ambassador of Christ, after a knowledge of the Bible, is the study of humanity.[85]

This has been an enduring theme of the American bishops, since involvement in human issues has characterized their ministry to the present day. Their pastoral letters on war and peace and on the American economy, along with the one being written on the role of women, are but a continuation of a basic instinct, more freely expressed now because of greater self-confidence in the American environment.[86]

Consequently, the addressing of apparently secular realities from the perspective of gospel values is a traditional, if at times controversial, aspect of the American Catholic experience. The orientation of the American church toward basic issues within contemporary society has fostered the application of Christian values to the daily arena of human activity in an effort often shared with the Protestant and Jewish religious communities. Priests, then, have learned to work in a broader community of human and religious values which has produced a practical ecumenism oriented toward joint action for social change.[87]

A preference for action has marked the American experience from its earliest days. And so Archbishop John Ireland of St. Paul proclaimed: "To sing lovely anthems in Cathedral stalls, wear coats of embroidered gold . . . while the world outside is dying of spiritual and moral starvation, that is not the religion we need today."[88] Sometimes even to the detriment of the community, theological reflection and contemplative prayer have taken second place to getting things done for people. Accordingly, although schools have been an important part of the task, until recently their purpose has been more functional than creative. Likewise, the American Catholic seminary has traditionally been a place to learn the basic truths, not to extend, develop or challenge them, since the purpose of its educational program was to form good and moral priests who could teach the core message and build the necessary institutions for a rapidly expanding church. The goal was neither saint, scholar, nor prophet, but a priest of practical skills, moral uprightness and orthodox faith, able to face the concrete issue of survival in an often hostile environment.

Since choices were usually made in light both of an alien society and the diverse mixture of peoples that made up the immigrant Catholic community, involvement in justice issues was more a matter of self-defense than prophetic utterance. In fact, in order to counterbalance the disparate origins and cultures of American Catholics, now subjected to an environment which prided itself on its ability to absorb newcomers, the church in the United States leaned heavily on psychological and social conformity to a clear and rigorously enforced definition of Catholicism. As a result, good administration and clear legislation were more important than extensive theological knowledge, daring prophetic resolve or profound contemplative insight. This often led to a preference for canonical and supervisory skills over theological and spiritual development in the daily life of the American church.[89]

Yet in spite of its self-protective stance, the church in the United States has been deeply influenced by the broader cultural context of the secular world which often operates as if it were without religious values. Not only have most of the major philosophers of the past century been atheists, but the central fact of the modern history of the western world, from the end of the middle ages until the present, is a decline of religion which has continued almost unabated in spite of momentary religious revivals. During this period, human consciousness has undergone a profound change of outlook which penetrates to the deepest levels of psychic life. This must never be forgotten, because for the believer religion is not so much a theological system in which to put faith, as it is a complex system of meanings and understandings which surround an individual from birth to death, making sense of all and providing rituals so that life can be negotiated and transcended.[90] In downplaying the significance of religion, then, contemporary society has also lost the broader human understandings associated with it.

Perhaps the disassociation of religion from basic understandings about life can be seen most clearly in the deterioration of a moral consensus in society. Here, the influence of secularization is unmasked as a fact of modern life. A consideration of the place of religion in literature, art, theater and films leads to much the same conclusion. Thus, it is not surprising that television directors and writers interviewed in the book *The View from Sunset Boulevard* dismissed all religion as irrelevant, and none of them could recognize the influence of religious values in his or her own life. Consequently, in treating the great concerns of human life—love, death, relationships, success and failure—reference is seldom if ever made to religion, God or immortality.[91]

Even though Americans attend church services more often than their European counterparts, it would appear that religious values penetrate no more deeply into the working consciousness of American society. Furthermore, since religion is often interpreted as a way to enhance individual well-being, not as a response to moral imperatives based on higher truths, it may be that in America, too, the day is rapidly approaching when believers, in the traditional sense, will find themselves at the fringes of society.[92]

Because the civilization in which American priests minister revolves around interlocking networks of productivity, profit and efficiency, there is a temptation for them to substitute action for faith and teaching for proclamation, thereby devaluing personal presence, receptivity and worship.[93] In this setting, the very concept of the priesthood as an essential service to society is threatened inasmuch as the transcendent vision and sacramental ministry priests offer are seen as having little value, representing an outmoded institution with archaic rituals and moral norms. Coming to an accurate appreciation of the normative values of society may be an invitation to conversion for presbyters and laity alike, for then they are challenged both to pursue more authentic values and to seek out their proper role as servants in church and global community.

Vatican II generated a mood of optimism regarding a fresh approach to contemporary society, since at the close of the council prospects for renewal seemed unlimited. In the intervening years many of the clergy have moved from euphoria to frustration. It may be that the optimism of the 1960's was a bit romantic and naive, even giving birth to a triumphalism of renewal, coinciding with the enthusiasm of American society in its war against poverty and quest for racial justice. As a result, many priests put themselves at the service of the community with uncommon passion. In fact, renewal has been slow to happen, a reality which is difficult to accept in a culture of instant success.[94]

In the renewed quest to serve church and society, many priests find themselves stretched between what was, what is, and what is yet to be. They often feel isolated from both bishops and people by a lack of understanding and an inability to communicate. Furthermore, the secularization of western culture has deeply affected the relationship between priests and the people they seek to serve, the very spirit of the times being opposed to any effort by the church to constrict the moral conduct of its members on either the personal or the social levels.[95] In response to this challenge to the traditional way of exercising authority, Pope Paul VI called for dialogue within the church and between it and the world community in his encyclical *Ecclesiam Suam*. Nonetheless, many priests find themselves torn between a more direct approach to authority and the dialogical stance endorsed by the pope.[96]

Yet, in spite of these obstacles, the Catholics of the United States are amazingly responsive to the teaching of the church on justice issues. Perhaps the best example is the 1983 pastoral *The Challenge of Peace: God's Promise and Our Response*. Before this document on war and peace was released, 34 percent of both American Catholics and Protestants thought too much money was being spent on weapons and defense. A year later, after its release, the percentage of Protestants opposing current levels of spending in this area remained the same, while the number of Catholics doing so moved to 54 percent—a change of twenty points, or about 10 million people. This leads Andrew Greeley to comment: "There are probably no teachers in the world with more potential power than American Catholic bishops . . . when the laity and the hierarchy . . . are in effective communication with one another."[97]

This responsiveness is further documented in *The American Catholic People*. In May of 1983 Catholics were evenly divided on whether a course detailing the dangers of nuclear war should be required for all high school students. A year later 58 percent thought it should be required and 38 percent said it should not, while Protestants remained evenly divided.[98] More importantly, there has been an evolution in the Catholic community, among bishops and laity alike, from the "hawkish" position held in the 1950's to a strong "dovish" position today. Thus, in a survey seeking reaction to a 1981 United Nations resolution forbidding the sale of arms by one nation to another, Catholics supported the embargo by a margin of 22 percentage points (56–34 percent) and Protestants by 9 (49–40). This leads the authors to conclude: "The breadth and depth of Catholic dovishness is one of our most important findings in this volume."[99]

But this harmonious relationship between the bishops and the laity does not end with the nuclear issue, since American Catholics are in agreement with their leaders on the basic themes of the economic pastoral as well: "Given a choice, they would spend more for

butter and less for guns—and they would cut military spending before cutting social spending to reduce the national deficit."[100] It is
impressive, indeed, to see that Catholics, by and large, have not
abandoned the poor as they themselves have moved into the middle
class and beyond. In fact, white Catholics are generally more sensitive to the concerns of blacks and other minorities than white Protestants, and even nudge their own church leaders a bit by giving them
low marks on meeting the needs of these groups.[101]

Nevertheless, the acceptance of official church teaching is not
universal in scope, since in the area of sexual morality Catholics have
generally not been responsive. Two examples make this clear: While
adherence to the official teaching on birth control had already
eroded prior to *Humanae Vitae,* it did not stop doing so afterward.
Thus, in 1963 over half of American Catholics disapproved of the
use of artificial means of birth control, while at present only a little
more than 10 percent do.[102] Secondly, in 1969, 72 percent viewed
premarital sex as morally wrong; by 1985 only 33 percent did so. In
this period of time Catholics moved from being slightly more likely to
disapprove of sexual activity outside of marriage than Protestants to
considerably more likely to approve.[103] The one exception to this
pattern is abortion; here the attitude of Catholics has changed little
since the council. Hence, 65 percent of American Catholics reject
abortion on demand.[104] While the majority reject abortion in general, they do not do so absolutely inasmuch as they would allow it in
some circumstances, a position which is unacceptable to the magisterium, as well as to both pro-life and pro-choice lobbies.[105]

From all of this, it is obvious that both the ecclesial community
and the larger society which priests are ordained to serve are very
complex, each having positive and negative aspects. An appreciation
of the practical-social dimension of presbyteral life has great importance, then, since the spirituality enunciated by the council is meant
to empower priests to serve the family of God by assembling and
leading it in fulfillment of its mission to the world.

IV. The Kingdom as the Goal of Priestly Spirituality

While productivity and success are important values gleaned
from the American culture, priests must integrate them into a way of
life based on the paschal mystery, that is, on a kingdom which is truly
operative in the temporal, but capable of fulfillment only beyond
earthly limits. Being stretched between secular culture and faith
values, discernment is an ever important skill for the priests. How do

they draw their insight and strength from a spiritual experience which is embodied in earthly realities?

Although most priests work among people who make constant, often mundane, demands on them, the response they give must both come from and lead to the God who transcends present concerns. The task inherent in the presbyteral mission involves correlating daily life with the in-breaking of the kingdom, and present activity with its future fulfillment. This responsibility invites priests to a deeper integration of ministry and prayer, an association which has been strengthened as the ordained have become more a part of a global community, sharing the insights of liberation theology and hearing the stories of fellow priests, lay people and religious returned from diocesan or community missions. In a paradoxical way, the impossibility of the human situation often calls forth the resources of faith in remedying the present, at the same time that it reveals life's true goal.[106]

It is more and more difficult to defend a prayer life held separate from earthly realities, because the world as it is speaks so eloquently of the need for God. The reverse is also true: a genuine life of prayer elicits a strong witness to the power of God through action on behalf of justice and peace. Just as love of God and love of neighbor are complementary aspects of the Christian life, so too are prayer and social action; when separated neither is authentic.[107] An appropriate spirituality demands prayerful involvement in the concrete realities of daily life, expressing the power of the kingdom in action.

The relationship between daily life and the kingdom is unclear for many priests formed in a seminary system which imparted abstract spiritual principles, true and universal, to be adapted and applied to individual situations, since life itself seemed to be no more than an accidental, changeable, element; the principles were the truths of the spiritual life.[108] Contemporary spirituality begins with concrete life experience, the life of the priest—even this particular priest—and seeks to find within this experience the activity of God calling to holiness.[109] It is necessary to attend to principles derived both from each person's experience and from the tradition of the church, but the focus is not on them, but on life itself.[110] The ministry and life situation of the priest provides the opportunity to experience the kingdom of God.

The kingdom manifests itself in presbyteral ministry primarily as pastoral charity embodying the values of the gospel.[111] Pastoral charity, then, is both the root and the foundation of priestly spirituality.

Therefore, the role of the Christian pastor is the key to understanding priests and the special service which they offer to the ecclesial and secular communities as ministers of reconciliation with God and neighbor.[112] Growth in the pastoral charity of Christ, as a concrete manifestation of the kingdom of God, is the immediate goal of presbyteral spirituality.

Priestly ministry both effects the kingdom, here and now, and points to its fulfillment in the future. As such, it straddles the present and the hereafter; sensitivity to the emphasis given to each and the balance between the two is a constant concern of an appropriate spirituality. To what extent, then, do priests concern themselves with the temporal issues of the church and society as an expression of the total transformation which has already been realized in Christ?[113] On the other hand, to what degree do they focus attention on a life beyond this one as witnesses to a kingdom which is to be revealed when Christ comes again, or at least after death?[114]

Judgments in this area have profound pastoral repercussions, for they often present themselves as tensions between social action and contemplation, between preparing people for the present life and for a future heaven. The pastoral situation is often emotionally charged as well, since in reaction both to a church whose spiritual, liturgical and architectural design was to lift people out of this world, and to charges that religion is a dream lulling people into inaction with the promise of future glory, the emphasis has recently moved to a more socially oriented understanding of the church. The result has been a deeply felt polarization in which people label themselves and others as conservatives or liberals, proponents of the old church or the new. Most noteworthy may be the popular opinion that it is necessary to make a choice between these two ways of approaching the Christian life. Lack of balance and deep-seated divisions are common, providing fertile ground for heresy on both the right and the left.

In the wake of a council which emphasized the need to see the incarnation as the model for church life and response to the modern world as a Christian responsibility, a reaction has developed. Whether it is merely recalcitrance or a healthy invitation to balance is yet to be seen. Vatican II is far enough in the past, though, that many realize that some contemporary problems are connected with the relationship between incarnational and transcendent ways of approaching discipleship. Charles Curran comments: "The sixties suffered from the theological disease of an acute case of collapsed eschaton."[115] Consequently, the promise of renewal was often interpreted as imminent entry into eschatological perfection. The lack of sustained theological reflection on the transcendent in the post-con-ciliar period, the stress on immanence, and an overly optimistic focus on quick success and ready answers in the first blush of renewal have led to a hunger for a broader based spirituality.

Yet the road to balance does not lie in the past, but in reclaiming the full heritage of the church in the light of contemporary insights. Sexuality is a case in point. Recently, the significance of sexuality in both the broad and the more specific senses has become prominent in formulating a positive approach to spirituality. James Nelson writes in *Embodiment* that the body is an instrument of communion, a true language: "The body is not merely the necessary physical sub-structure through which the spoken and written word must come. . . . The body can be word itself—as Christians recognize in Jesus Christ, the Word made flesh."[116] And so sexuality bears within it a deep desire for communion with others and with God. It is the energy which both sustains family, friendship and community in the present life and impels disciples toward union with God in hope of future fulfillment.

Strangely enough, clearer insight into the role of human sexual-ity has led some to a more ready understanding of transcendence. Accordingly, in bringing together the psychological insights of Carl Jung and the mystical experience of St. Teresa of Avila John Welch underlines the fact that her spiritual journey is expressed in terms of masculine and feminine: "Teresa uses a universal image for the union of human and divine, the spiritual marriage. The close, per-sonal relationship between a man and a woman in marriage is some indication of the nature of the prayer experience in the last dwelling place."[117] The steady growth of contemplative prayer fraternities among priests, such as *Jesus Caritas,* and the multiplication of individ-ually directed retreats point to a hunger for unitive, personal prayer which is rooted more deeply in human sexuality. This experience, too, affirms that in times of profound reflection the immanent and transcendent meet, offering the strength and insight of a more bal-anced whole.

Celibacy certainly enters into the heart of this discussion in the contemporary church.[118] At the outset, it is apparent that many Catholics do not link celibacy very closely with the value they place on their priests; thus, a smaller number would have problems ac-cepting the return of married priests to active ministry than would object to the clergy living away from the rectory. The fact that 75 percent of American Catholics say they could accept a change to a married clergy needs to be considered in assessing the perceived value of celibacy.[119] While a majority of American priests would prefer to see celibacy optional, most affirm that in all likelihood they would continue to choose celibacy for themselves.[120] There is evidence, though, that the desire to marry is an important reason both for resignations from active ministry and for the decline in the number of those entering the seminary.[121]

The connection between celibacy and the priesthood is being questioned in the American church. This indicates, among other things, that both a more cogent theology of celibacy and a more convincing witness to its religious significance needs to be offered for the benefit of priests and laity alike. The basic premises need to be looked at; for example, is celibacy meant to enhance availability and the ability to serve, or is it a transcendent witness to a future way of life? Or, better yet, can either of these understandings, incarnational or transcendent, bear the burden of a life commitment to celibacy alone? On one hand, a secularized society easily turns celibacy into an incomprehensible burden in the same way that it dismisses sacraments as interesting but meaningless symbols, since it views a life oriented toward absolute truth as too abstract, or just plain irrelevant.[122] On the other, society is intrigued by celibacy, since, being more than a helpful adjunct to a life of service, it witnesses to the communion with God and future hope for which the modern world yearns.

To be effective, though, celibacy must be healthy; that is, it must be lived as a positive reality. The psychological underdevelopment of many American priests, previously noted, is a special concern, since those lacking sufficient maturity often live celibacy as if it simply meant to remain unmarried. Seldom does it reflect a higher degree of religiously motivated dedication.[123] In fact, the opposite may even be true. Celibacy may evolve into a self-centered lifestyle having more in common with the freedom of bachelorhood than with the commitments of a dedicated person. In this way a lack of human maturity robs celibacy of both its incarnational and its transcendent value in the life of the church. Since, in this situation, much of a priest's energy goes into living with non-integrated celibacy and sexuality, that which remains for meaningful service is significantly reduced.[124] Thus, a promise which is meant to point to the gospel may actually draw energy away from serving it.

The effort to come to a balanced understanding of the role of the incarnational and the transcendent in presbyteral spirituality has led to a reappraisal of the lifestyle appropriate to priests. A renewed appreciation of human intimacy and involvement in the concerns of the community has led many priests to reevaluate the traditional expressions of transcendence and separation from the world embodied in recent clerical culture. Yet, the challenge remains the same: to be in the world, but not of it, to have deep roots in the present while being drawn into the future, to take the temporal seriously while not making it the total reality. An appropriate balance is far from a merely theoretical concern, as is seen in the sobering consequences of treating the relationship between the immanent and transcendent as abstract and unimportant. The way in which priests see these realities will determine the sources from which they draw energy and the direction in which they focus their activity.

A sound understanding of the relationship between the temporal and the transcendent is also necessary to properly articulate the social teaching of the church, since service to the poor is also a realization of the kingdom of God. There is a temptation in the American setting to divorce explicit religious motivation from the marketplace. While the same good people who partake in the eucharist may also be involved in "social work," their secular occupation is usually limited to fulfilling a need for food, shelter or education, and not extended to satisfying a hunger for reconciliation with God and eternal life.[125] The result is not only a diminution of the benefits which the needy derive, but also a lessening of the impetus and energy which the kingdom is able to impart to those who serve it. This does not suggest that there is no difference between evangelization and social action, only that the relationship between them is more profound than contemporary forms capture.[126]

A lack of proper integration of the eschatological dimension of Christianity into justice ministry can also be found in a tendency to use the gospel to buttress philosophical arguments relative to social causes rather than the reverse. In addition, excessive dependence on ideas about the kingdom and an underdeveloped appreciation of the power which it imparts imposes severe limitations on social action. A number of contemporary women theologians offer real liberation from an overly cerebral approach to faith, allowing the church to move beyond correct understandings about the kingdom to a deeper sensitivity to the graced life-force which rouses people to action. Accordingly, Rosemary Haughton and Monika Hellwig give great attention to compassion as a participation in the being of God.[127]

While using all available human resources, an authentic spirituality guarantees that activity is empowered by the gospel and sustained by it in a way which witnesses to the kingdom and leads to its full realization. The eschatological dimension of presbyteral spirituality safeguards this dynamism, seeing to it that priestly ministry leads in Christ, through the Spirit, to the Father.

This, then, is a brief overview of the major issues which affect the spirituality of American priests. It is this concrete situation which invites a response from the magisterium in charting a path for the future.

2.

Participants in Christ
the Head of the Church

The Sacramental Dimension of Priestly Spirituality

The Catholic tradition affirms that the ministerial priesthood is a distinctive, essential, and effective sign of Christ the head building up and leading his body, the church. In the mind of the Second Vatican Council, those in ordained ministry serve the church "in the person of Christ" and as successors to the ministry of the apostles. A specific group of individuals, the twelve chosen by Christ, link Christ's headship to a continuing sacrament of leadership in the church.

This correlation of Christ, the twelve and ordained ministry is essential to an authentic understanding of the sacrament of orders. In restating the traditional teaching, Vatican II affirms that although ordained ministry is rooted in the sacraments of initiation, it derives from a special sacramental celebration. In doing so, it highlights the distinctive ontological foundation of the ministry of the apostles and insists that this ontologically distinct ministry continues in the sacrament of orders.[1]

Vatican II maintains that there is a difference in the very being of the ordained, and not only a change in their ecclesial function.[2] This metaphysical language presents its own difficulties in articulating the faith of the church in a community no longer accustomed to think in these categories. In using it the council seeks both clarity of thought and a mode of expression which respects traditional philosophical categories; at the same time it places the ontological aspect of its teaching within a broader conceptual framework. At first glance, what is being proposed may seem foreign to the values which a democratic society cherishes. There is no doubt that misunderstanding of the ontological difference predicated of ordained ministry has led to clericalism on the one hand, and unfortunate attempts to build a church structure without clergy on the other. A precise understanding of the ontological dimension of ordained ministry as proposed by the council is crucial to the development of a priestly spirituality which is authentic for ordained ministers and beneficial to the Christian community.

The sacramental viewpoint which underlies the theology of the church articulated by the council supports its ontological affirmations about ordained ministry. Therefore, just as redemption is mediated through the humanity of Christ, and the church continues to be an instrument of salvation, so, too, ordained ministry is a distinctive sacrament of God's saving presence. Vatican II teaches that Christ continues his servant ministry as head of the church through the words and actions of the ordained.[3] These specially deputed ministers are empowered to mediate the activity of Christ, the head, in his care for the church, which is his body. It is to this sacramental understanding of the ministry of priests that this chapter is directed.

So as not to distort the ontological affirmations of Vatican II about the special character of ordained ministry, but to understand them in their proper setting, the entire conciliar teaching on the sacrament of orders must be carefully considered. This will be done in the course of the next four chapters. This larger context is necessary if presbyteral spirituality is not to close in on itself.

At the outset, it is clear that the council challenges priests to root their spirituality in a proper understanding of their distinctive participation in the mystery of Christ and the church. For this to happen priests must allow the Spirit to move them out of themselves, as it were, and into a new set of relationships. This movement to a relational vision of the church, and away from an institutional one, is evident in the structure of *Lumen Gentium*. The decision of the council fathers to begin with statements about Christ and the people of God was no accident, but a carefully chosen approach to the life and faith of the church.[4] This relational understanding of the ecclesial community has many implications for the ordained and, as will be shown, is a recurring theme in the council's presentation of priestly spirituality.

The distinctive and unifying goal of the council is to proclaim Christ, his identity in relation to the church, and the meaning of the participation of the church in him. *Lumen Gentium* opens with the proclamation that "Christ is the light of humanity." It then states that Vatican II intends to bring the light of Christ, which visibly shines out from the church, to all: "Since the church, in Christ, is in the nature of sacrament—a sign and instrument, that is, of communion with God and of unity among all men—she here purposes . . . to set forth, as clearly as possible, and in the tradition laid down by earlier councils, her own nature and universal mission."[5]

From the beginning Vatican II makes the decisive choice to treat two pivotal issues in terms of the whole church. The first is participation in the priesthood of Christ. The second is the call to holiness.[6] In considering the first of these, *Lumen Gentium* states: "The baptized by regeneration and the anointing of the Holy Spirit are consecrated to be a spiritual house and a holy priesthood.''[7] This is immediately clarified by a statement on the ministerial priesthood. As will be shown, the council views both forms of priesthood as sharing in the priestly character of the church as a whole.[8] It is in this context that Vatican II affirms that the ordained participate in the priestly identity of the church in a distinctive and essential way.[9]

The priesthood of the ordained exists not only in relationship to the priesthood of Christ, but also to that of the baptized; thus the ministerial priesthood is related to the priestly character of the baptized by its very nature. Ordained priests are meant to be effective signs of the communion which exists between Christ the head and the members of the church. Hence, a private priestly spirituality is impossible, because priests are by definition christic and ecclesial persons.

In considering the second pivotal issue, the call to holiness, the council boldly states: "It is therefore quite clear that all Christians in any state or walk of life are called to the fullness of Christian life and to the perfection of love. . . ."[10] There is diversity in the church and distinction of roles, but there is not a higher and lower level of spirituality, an elementary level of morality for some and a more exalted level for others.[11] Jesus preached holiness of life to each and every one of his disciples without distinction.[12]

Priests are called to holiness, since their mode of life is of crucial importance to the ecclesial community they serve. They are called to the one holiness of the church, in the midst of the church and for the benefit of the church. Their holiness exists for the service of an ecclesial body called to the same sanctity.[13] In *Presbyterorum Ordinis* the council states the ecclesial context of priestly spirituality quite carefully.[14] It follows, then, that a self-centered or narrowly conceived presbyteral spirituality is a theological contradiction, since a mature priestly identity transcends self and claims Christ and the church as its present preoccupation and its boast at the Lord's coming. When the ministry of the word and sacraments shall cease and the goal of pastoral guidance comes to fullness in the kingdom, Christ and the church will remain.[15] It is within this framework that the council makes its ontological statements about ordained ministry.

While the ontological dimension of priestly spirituality flows from baptism, confirmation and orders, this chapter will concentrate on the distinctive ontological character of ordained ministry arising from the sacrament of orders; the necessary ecclesial foundation for priestly ministry in baptism and confirmation will be treated in the next. Here, the ontological dimension of priestly spirituality will be approached from three perspectives: configuration to Christ the head, action in the church in the person of Christ, and service in a community of ordained ministers.

I. Christ as the Servant-Head of the Church

What does Vatican II mean when it says that Christ is the head of the church? In providing an answer the council depicts Christ as the sacrament of God, the source of the Spirit, the model of holiness, the pattern for ministry and the center of unity. In each of these characteristics of his headship Christ has no peer. As head, Christ is the only adequate, accurate and dynamic source of the church's life.

The council affirms that Christ is the first and fundamental sacrament: "He is the image of the invisible God."[16] All things were created in Christ, and it is through him that humanity has access to the very depths of God.[17] Only Christ can profess to be "the way, and the truth, and the life."[18] No other human instrument can claim to be sacrament of God's saving presence in this radical sense. Yet those in ordained ministry participate in the sacramentality of Christ in a distinctive way, giving visible expression to his servant-headship.

Since orders is a sacrament of Christ's enduring headship, priests objectively participate in the peerless reality of Christ. Yet precisely because Christ is without equal, the ordained will always experience a subjective distance between the person of Christ and their ability to witness to him. Conscious of their limitations, priests are called to a transparency which orients their lives toward the divine person they are to effectively represent. The summons to personal holiness was made stronger in the revision of *Presbyterorum Ordinis* because a number of the bishops feared that the objective ontological conformity to Christ affirmed of priests in the council documents would obscure the fact that the council also had the subjective sanctity of the ordained in mind.[19] Not only are priests ontologically conformed to Christ through ordination, but they are to grow to be more apt expressions of the one they represent through personal participation in his holiness.

The difference between the headship of Christ and the sacramental headship of those who participate in him is that Jesus alone is the focal point of humanity. All sacramental manifestations of headship in the church must point to his. Although the ordained truly mediate the saving mission of Christ, they are effective only through their participation in him; thus it is the function of priestly spirituality to constantly deepen subjective conformity to Christ in response to the permanent ontological grace conferred in ordination.

As head of his body the church, Christ gives the Holy Spirit as his first gift to those who believe.[20] This same Spirit formed Jesus in the womb of the Virgin Mary, filled his ministry and was breathed forth from the cross.[21] Through the paschal mystery, Jesus is the source of the Spirit which gives birth to the church. Although the Spirit is present in the ministry of others, he always acts to form the image of Jesus in the church. Since through participation in Christ presbyters have a special relationship to the Spirit, they too build in the image of Christ.[22] They are called, then, to the same self-concealing and other-revealing ecclesial service as the Spirit who animates their ministry; accordingly priests who project their own image rather than that of Christ have lost sight of their dynamic relationship to him.

Jesus sends his Spirit to accomplish two tasks in the church. The first is sanctification: conformity to Christ in holiness of life. The second is mission or ministry. In treating the first, the council declares: "All the members must be formed in his likeness, until Christ be formed in them. For this reason we, who have been made like to him, who have died with him and risen with him, are taken up into the mysteries of his life, until we reign together with him."[23] As head of the church Christ is model and source of holiness for his body.[24] Others participate in Christ and reflect his image in impressive ways; yet it is he alone who is the exemplar to which the church must be conformed.

Since Christ is holy, those who participate in Christ through the sacraments are made objectively holy. That which is true of every Christian has special meaning when applied to those who participate in the holiness of Christ as head of the church. An authentic presbyteral spirituality draws priests more deeply into their special identity in Christ so that they may also grow in subjective holiness. That which is affirmed as ontological truth must become existential reality so that the ordained can say with St. Paul, ". . . I have become your father in Christ Jesus through the gospel. I urge you, then, be imitators of me."[25] Priests are distinctively conformed to Christ so that they might be holy in the way that he is as head of the body, and so put that holiness at the service of the church.

Jesus was sent by the Father in the power of the Holy Spirit. The second task of the Spirit is sustaining this mission through the ministerial life of the church. Accordingly, the same Spirit is present in both head and members, transforming the entire body not only into a graced likeness of Jesus, but also into a dynamic enactment of his mission. Ministry, then, is a share in the Spirit's work of sanctification, that "we may through all things grow unto him who is our head."[26]

Since presbyters exist to serve the holiness and mission of the church, they are empowered by their ordination to unite sanctity and ministry; thus presbyteral spirituality is a call to personal holiness for the sake of mission. Inasmuch as the ordained participate in the service which Jesus constantly renders to his church as its head, an accurate understanding of the way in which Christ ministers to the church is crucial for the spiritual life of priests.

Vatican II insists that the kingdom of God is revealed principally in the Christ who came to serve and give his life.[27] Consequently, contemplation of Christ, especially as servant, is essential to the growth of priests as his sacramental image. To claim participation in the headship of Christ without the radical self-giving of the cross is to profess nonsense. Failure to choose the servant-Christ as the object of contemplation is to open oneself to the allurements of a self-centered society. Priests have the indispensable task, then, of placing themselves in the presence of Jesus crucified until he impresses himself on their minds and hearts. The perils of clericalism beset those who forget the unique manner in which Christ is head of the church. *Optatam Totius*, the document on the training of priests, strongly affirms this point.[28]

Furthermore, the council proposes Christ as the center of unity for all creation. *Lumen Gentium* explains the role of Christ by citing a passage from the gospel of John: "And I, if I be lifted up from the earth, will draw all to myself."[29] The First Eucharistic Prayer of Reconciliation paints an image of Christ in his cosmic headship: "Yet before he stretched out his arms between heaven and earth in the everlasting sign of your covenant, he desired to celebrate the Paschal feast in the company of his disciples."[30] The outstretched body of Jesus on the cross unites heaven and earth in a profound act of reconciliation.

The church shares this ministry of reconciliation as the messianic people founded by Jesus. Even though it does not presently include the whole human family, it is the seed of unity, hope and salvation for the entire human race. Being united with Christ its head, the church is an instrument of salvation for all.[31] In its ministry of reconciliation and communion the church realizes, here and now, its participation in the holiness and mission of Jesus. At the same time, the ecclesial community seeks the fulfillment of eschatological holiness when all will be one in Christ.[32] Perfect communion is the goal of the servant-headship of Jesus; thus in pursuing loving communion with Christ the head and among his members, the church is faithful to its deepest vocation and enjoys a foretaste of the kingdom.[33]

Conformity to the servant-headship of Christ enables priests to be signs and agents of reconciliation within the ecclesial community. Communion, unity, peace and love are the goals of presbyteral spirituality because they are the goals of the Lord whom priests represent. Thus, when the council teaches that the eucharist is the summit and source of the true Christian spirit, it stresses a central element of the spiritual identity of priests.[34] It is precisely by entering into the servant-sacrifice of the head and in being transformed by him in the gift of communion that priests become sacraments of reconciliation and unity in Christ, the purpose for which they were ordained.

Vatican II describes participation in the servant-leadership of Christ by locating the ordained within the framework of his threefold ministry as prophet, priest and shepherd. The council states that priests "are consecrated in order to preach the gospel and shepherd the faithful as well as to celebrate divine worship."[35] In exercising the office of Christ the shepherd presbyters assemble the family of God as a community of faith and lead it in the Holy Spirit to God the Father.[36] The office of pastor is, "in the strict sense of the term, a service"[37] given as "a spiritual power . . . whose purpose is to build up"[38] the church. The goal of pastoral leadership is the education of the faithful toward Christian maturity and the spiritual growth of the body of Christ. Since pastors are responsible for the development of the ecclesial community, they are empowered to gather it for worship, lead it through instruction and guide it in service.

Priests are to be servants of the common good. In fulfilling this responsibility, they are challenged to conform their lives to the persuasive gentleness and love of Jesus, as well as to his clarity of vision and commitment to the truth. As sharers in the servant-ministry of Christ they must renounce their own convenience, benefit or advantage for the sake of the community. The ordained are called to live the love of the good shepherd, giving their lives for those entrusted to their care. The ministry of servant-leadership pulls priests in many directions in bridging conflicts, uniting points of view, correcting error and gathering all into a community with a common life and goal. This entails a kind of discipline particularly suited to pastors— an asceticism of availability to the community and pastoral responsiveness.[39]

The council calls Christ "the great prophet" who proclaimed the kingdom in his life and by the power of his word.[40] Those in ordained ministry teach in his name and with his authority; thus as preachers and teachers of the word priests share in Christ's prophetic role in such a way that their words are "not the mere word of men, but truly the word of God."[41] Vatican II affirms that preaching the gospel is the first duty of priests. This is a strong affirmation indeed, especially in view of the fact that the priesthood was previously defined primarily in the language of sacrifice.[42] Since the power of the word forms the people of God and nourishes its growth, priests are to speak in the name of Christ and to invite people to conversion and holiness. Because they participate in the prophetic mission of Christ, the proclamation of the gospel is a duty which priests owe to everyone.[43]

Since as the Word made flesh Christ is more than a preached word, the gospel is to be pondered, internalized and made part of the very being of priests, so that, like Christ, they proclaim the gospel by the testimony of their lives. The first concern of priestly spirituality is that the ordained respond to the call to conversion and renewal offered them by the divine word present in scripture and sacrament. The prophetic role of the presbyter is to be supported and strengthened by its visible effects in their lives.

Finally, presbyters participate in Christ's servant-leadership through the ministry of sanctification, since in the sacramental actions of the ordained Christ himself acts as priest to make his people holy.[44] Through the mediation of ordained ministry he admits members to the church in baptism, leads them in worship, forgives sinners and relieves those who are sick.[45] Configuration to Christ in his priesthood places presbyters at the center of the Christian community as instruments of holiness, distinctively associated with the person of Christ in his saving work, and empowered to facilitate the sanctification of the community. This is perhaps clearest in the eucharist in which the words of institution are repeated by priests as they were spoken by Christ himself in the gospel accounts of the last supper.

The eucharist is the "source and summit of all preaching of the gospel" and "the whole spiritual good of the church, namely Christ himself."[46] The liturgy renders worship to God and achieves human sanctification with maximum effectiveness; and so all other activities of the church are directed to it. Here, presbyteral ministry finds its focus: "Sharing in the unique office of Christ, the mediator" and announcing the word to all, priests are enabled to bring the people of God to full participation in the sacred mysteries.[47]

Identification with Christ in holiness of life enables presbyters to gather the people of God effectively, to preach to them convincingly, and to lead them in prayer powerfully. Thus, the unity and harmony of the ministerial priesthood as a sharing in Christ's three-fold ministry of servant-leadership is most obvious in the eucharistic assembly.

II. Ecclesial Ministry in the Person of Christ

The phrase *"in persona Christi"* has special theological significance in understanding the teaching of the council on ordained ministry. *Lumen Gentium* uses it or its equivalent five times, *Presbyterorum Ordinis* three times, and *Sacrosanctum Concilium* once. The council uses this phrase only in the context of ordained ministry, attributing action "in the person of Christ" or identification with Christ the head of the church only to the ministerial priesthood. There was considerable discussion of this terminology in the time between the first and final versions of the text of *Presbyterorum Ordinis*.[48] The decision to use "in the person of Christ" to identify the being and mission of Christ as the head of the church with no other sacrament but orders was a deliberate choice.[49]

Vatican II insists that although the priesthood of the baptized and that of the ordained are essentially different, they are also by their very nature related to one another. "Though they differ essentially and not only in degree, the common priesthood of the faithful and the ministerial or hierarchical priesthood are nonetheless ordered one to another; each in its own proper way shares in the one priesthood of Christ."[50] Since configuration to Christ the head relates ordained ministers to the church, the next task is to consider the way in which participation in the headship of Christ defines the relationship of priests to the life of the ecclesial community. This relationship lies at the heart of the appropriate identity which presbyteral spirituality seeks to establish and nurture.

While affirming the significance of the sacraments of initiation in priestly life, *Presbyterorum Ordinis* uses the phrase "in the person of Christ" to make an ontological statement attesting to the importance of the sacrament of orders in conferring a distinctive identity on priests in the mission of the church: "Through that sacrament priests by the anointing of the Holy Spirit are signed with a special character and so are configured to Christ the priest in such a way that they are able to act in the person of Christ the head."[51] The sacraments of baptism, confirmation and orders are notable in that they embody a distinctive and enduring divine promise both to be with and to act through the persons receiving them. Thus the council affirms that there is a change in being in those receiving these sacraments, an ontological change, which is rooted in the activity of God, relating the recipients to Christ and the church in a new way.

Accordingly, Vatican II teaches that something more than a different ecclesial function is given to the ordained. There is a change in identity, an essential change in the way priests are related to Christ the head, and through the head to the church. This change in being represents the promise of God to act in and through them in a specific way for the good of the church. This is not to say that function is unimportant. The ordained are empowered and summoned to be effective signs of Christ; thus they must be functional persons without being functionaries, sacramental persons without being defenders of extraordinary status.

Both the opportunity and the challenge offered to presbyters by the ontological foundation of their ministry are very significant, since human experience makes it clear that sacraments do not attain their full effect automatically, that is, without human cooperation. There is a great difference between being baptized and being a saint, although baptism contains the promise of sainthood. There is a difference of equal proportions between being ordained and being an effective and mature sign of Christ's headship. In ordination a gift is given and a promise conferred. Priests are called to grow into the grace of this sacrament. Hence the sacrament of orders is a pledge on God's part which is yet to be fulfilled in the lives of those who have received it. Coming to full stature in Christ and growing to maturity as a participant in his headship depends on the response of the ordained to the sacramental grace they have received.

As the text of *Presbyterorum Ordinis* was being revised many bishops asked that the intimate connection between priestly ministry and presbyteral holiness be stated more eloquently.[52] Consequently, it is precisely the graced potential contained in ministry itself to which the council draws attention in speaking about the call of priests to holiness: "Since every priest in his own way assumes the person of Christ he is endowed with a special grace. By this grace the priest, through his service of the people committed to his care and all the people of God, is able the better to pursue the perfection of Christ, whose place he takes."[53] The road to spiritual growth indicated by

Vatican II is the service and care of the people of God in the person of Christ; thus priests grow in holiness by fulfilling their presbyteral mission. By acting in the person of Christ the head, priests more and more correspond to Christ and are transformed into effective participants in his headship.

Vatican II often specifies the eucharist as the setting for action in the person of Christ. "The ministerial priest, by the sacred power that he has, forms and rules the priestly people; in the person of Christ he effects the eucharistic sacrifice and offers it to God in the name of all the people."[54] An appropriate appreciation of the complex nature of the eucharistic assembly challenges priests to a broader understanding of the threefold way in which they act in the person of Christ. "It is in the eucharistic cult or in the eucharistic assembly of the faithful that they exercise in a supreme degree their sacred functions, there acting in the person of Christ."[55] In the hospitality of priests Christ gathers his people. In their prophetic word he speaks. Through their prayer of thanksgiving Christ involves all in his sacrifice to the Father and nourishes them at his table. Because each aspect of the saving work of Christ is important, not to emphasize one at the expense of the others is a true discipline demanding balance, reflection, preparation and the development of skills.

Since the eucharist is a sacramental reality, it testifies to the instrumentality of the church in making the saving presence of God visible in human history. In this light, *Sacrosanctum Concilium* assigns sacramental characteristics to the various elements of the eucharistic assembly. It affirms that Christ is present in the person of the minister, in the eucharistic species, in the scriptural word, and in the prayer and song of the community.[56] The council enunciates a dynamic understanding of the nature of sacraments; thus the ministerial priesthood is sacramental, not only in the ritual of ordination, but also in the activity of presbyteral ministry. The spirituality arising from presbyteral ordination challenges priests to be authentic signs of Christ in the fulfillment of their liturgical role.

Because the priesthood is more than a cultic function, the ordained must actively preside in the person of Christ. Vatican II insists that the ministerial priesthood makes Christ present in his leadership of the church;[57] thus the full, active participation of priests in the liturgical life of the church is a central issue for their spirituality. Conformity to rubrics and correctness of ceremony are not sufficient for the ministry the church seeks from them.[58] Conversion to Christ, especially in his servant-leadership of the church, is the sacrament of orders lived to the full; an ever deepening conformity to Christ in pastoral leadership is the distinctive feature of presbyteral spirituality.

The celebrated eucharist is the source of spiritual transformation for priests, as it is for the people they serve. "So when priests unite themselves with the act of Christ the priest they daily offer themselves completely to God, and by being nourished with Christ's body they share in the charity of him who gives himself as food to the faithful."[59] Here, the council again affirms that ministerial activity in the person of Christ more and more identifies priests with his saving mission. In manifesting the love of Christ for the faithful, priests are transformed into that powerful love. While charity and the unity of the body are the principal effects of the eucharist, the charity of Christ the pastor is the specific grace offered to those who preside.

In the process of acting in the person of Christ, whether it be in the liturgy or in an endless variety of pastoral activities, priests are offered the grace of conformity to the Christ they represent. Vatican II insists that priests grow in holiness, not in spite of ministry, but through the experience of it. The council gives an apt summary of its teaching on priestly spirituality in *Presbyterorum Ordinis:* "By adopting the role of the good shepherd they will find in the practice of pastoral charity itself the bond of priestly perfection which will reduce to unity their life and activity. Now this pastoral charity flows especially from the eucharist."[60]

III. Ordained Ministry as a Distinctive Sacramental Community

As has already been said, the council affirms both that the foundation of the church is linked to the sending of the apostles who share in the mission of Christ, and that this unique apostolic community is the source of the sacrament of orders.[61] It teaches that this distinctive apostolic ministry was a constitutive element of the church at its beginning and is a permanent principle of its existence: "These apostles he constituted in the form of a college or permanent assembly, at the head of which he placed Peter, chosen from amongst them."[62] Because their mission was to last until the end of time "the apostles were careful to appoint successors in this hierarchically constituted society."[63]

Vatican II affirms that the bishops are the heirs to the mission of the apostles, thereby fulfilling a major concern of the council: to state clearly the doctrine about bishops who, together with Peter's

successor, guide the church in the name of Christ.[64] Episcopal ordination, then, confers the grace of the Holy Spirit and a sacred character so that "bishops, in an eminent and visible way, undertake
Christ's own role as teacher, shepherd, and high priest, and act in his
person."[65]

Inasmuch as Vatican II insists that priests do not exist for themselves, but for the church, the ordering of ecclesial ministry is made
concrete in the mission of the bishop. *Christus Dominus* states: "It is
the bishops who enjoy the fullness of the sacrament of orders, and
both priests and deacons are dependent on them in the exercise of
their power."[66] It is clear that the bishops, above all, act "in the
person of Christ."[67] Thus the full sacramentality of the church is
most evident in the eucharistic celebration in which the bishop presides surrounded by his priests and all the faithful.[68]

By the very nature of their ordination priests are collaborators
with their bishop, appointed to a service which is ordered under his
authority and dependent on him.[69] Joined to the episcopal order,
priests share in the authority by which Christ sanctifies, governs and
builds up his body.[70] The identity, role and mission of priests, then,
are part of a greater whole. Therefore they are called to a shared
ministry not only as members of the church, but also as partakers of a
community of ordained ministers which is ordered in its very definition to the bishop.

Religious priests are also related to a bishop and a local presbyterate in ministerial pursuits. The council is careful to call attention to this relationship.[71] And so religious priests are challenged to
find elements of their spiritual identity in a presbyteral community
which is broader than their particular religious family or charism.[72]

It is immediately evident that collaboration and the ability to live
and work in a cooperative way must be characteristics of presbyteral
life. Collaboration involves a sharing of prayer, life and love, as well
as ministry. All of these are recommended to the bishop and presbyterate alike. Bishops are to regard their priests as "indispensable
helpers and advisors" and as "brothers and friends."[73] Priests are to
reverence the bishop and show their attachment to him in love and
obedience arising from a spirit of cooperation. All priests, and in a
special way the diocesan clergy, are reminded that faithful and generous cooperation with their bishop is a great help in their sanctification.[74]

Since collaboration and interdependence are not demeaning
attributes, they in no way militate against a basic equality between
bishops and priests. Inasmuch as the work of salvation is the result of

equal divine persons collaborating in each other's specific mission in a way which produces a unified saving action, the relational life of the Trinity is the source of the graced reality to which the church is called.[75] Grace is a sharing in the life of the Trinity which is made visible in the life of the church; thus the community arising from sacramental ordination not only participates in the saving work of the divine persons, but it also mirrors the nature of trinitarian life. The spirituality arising from shared ministry is profoundly trinitarian, then, having its source in the concrete experience of grace in ministerial relationships.

A proper understanding of the relationship which exists between priests and the bishop is shown in their willingness to represent him and, in a certain sense, to make him present in the local community which they serve.[76] Here, too, priests are called upon to be transparent to another whose ministry they typify. It is an additional claim on self-transcendence in the spiritual life of priests.

Although presbyters represent the bishop and make him present as chief pastor, the council emphasizes that priests are to be conformed to Christ, not to the bishop. *Presbyterorum Ordinis* says that by the sacrament of orders priests are configured to Christ, being constituted as servants of the head and instruments of him whom they represent.[77] There is an important difference between the way priests make Christ present and the way they represent the bishop, since the sacrament of orders is oriented to Christ and his unique headship. As sacramental persons the ordained are to lead people to Christ, model and spouse of the church.

Just as priests must step aside so that the people they serve may be espoused to Christ, so they must also make room for other members of the presbyterate. The needs of the apostolate are many and the talents of any individual are limited. No priest is sufficiently endowed to carry out even his own limited mission alone or in isolation.[78] In fact, priests are not called to minister alone, but as members of a presbyterate. The imposition of hands by all priests present at the ordination liturgy is testimony to entrance into a presbyteral community.[79]

Vatican II draws attention to the presbyterate as a sacramental reality in the life of the local church. By gathering around the bishop in liturgy, advising him individually and through a presbyteral council, and providing a wide spectrum of ministerial talents and services, the presbyterate witnesses to holiness while seizing opportunities for corporate ministry and mutual support among priests. This community of apostolic charity and brotherhood is recommended to priests with special urgency by the council.

Charity, common prayer and wholehearted cooperation are the characteristics ascribed to the presbyterate. Its goal is twofold. First of all the relationships among priests witness to "that unity with which Christ willed his own to be perfected in one, that the world might know that the Son had been sent by the Father."[80] The presbyterate is a witness to the nature of the church as sign of unity, love and peace.

Secondly, the presbyterate exists for the upbuilding of the body of Christ. It is this servant community under the leadership of the bishop which forms the ongoing sacrament of the headship of Christ. The presbyterate is not an accidental addition to the ministry of the bishop, since both the bishop and his presbyterate are essential to what the sacrament of orders symbolizes and hopes to effect. Accordingly, the council views priests as "providential cooperators of the episcopal order"[81] and as the "spiritual crown" of the bishop.[82]

The inference is that no individual, not even the bishop, is an adequate sign or instrument without the amplification of other ministers. Corporate ministry is a necessity for the sake of the church. The spiritual challenge given to priests is to envision themselves as completed in the ministry of others. Consequently, common prayer, joint planning and shared activity are expressions of a sacramental and spiritual community which is greater and more effective than any one of its members. Herein is born a spirituality of the presbyterate which stands against personal isolation and individualism because these deny a trinitarian understanding of grace, a communal perception of the church, and insight into the corporate nature of presbyteral ministry.

The council teaches that the visible structure of ordained ministry, which it calls hierarchical, is a concrete expression of the care of Christ for his church. It insists that this tangibly structured community of ministers is not separate or distinct from the church of grace endowed with spiritual gifts, but is an expression of it. In this regard, comparison is made to the mystery of the incarnation: as the human nature of Jesus serves the divine Word, so the visible structure of the church serves the Spirit of Christ, who fills it with life in building up the body.[83] Using the image of the sheepfold, *Lumen Gentium* states that the sheep, ". . . although watched over by human shepherds, are nevertheless at all times led and brought to pasture by Christ himself, the good shepherd and the prince of shepherds, who gave his life for his sheep."[84]

Here, an ontological understanding of ordained ministry is assumed in explaining the concrete hierarchical structure of the ecclesial community. The context of the statement is service to the Spirit in building up the body. In this way an effort is made to avoid a pejorative understanding of hierarchy as remote or authoritarian. This servant context is often repeated in admonitions to bishops and priests alike. Perhaps most interesting are the words directed to those responsible for seminary formation: "Students must clearly understand that it is not their lot in life to lord it over others and enjoy honors, but to devote themselves completely to the service of God and the pastoral ministry . . . to living in conformity with the crucified Christ and to giving up willingly even those things which are lawful, but not expedient."[85] Conformity to Christ crucified is to be the goal of formation for those who are to be ordained to participation in his servant-headship.

The concrete, tangible witness of priests, as individuals and as a presbyterate, is important in disposing the faithful toward a profitable response to Christ the head whom priests represent. The words and actions of priests and the corporate ministry of the presbyterate are meant to be outward signs of a grace God wills for his church. The ascetical component of presbyteral spirituality revolves around the discipline and transformation needed for priests to be apt visible signs of the invisible grace of Christ the head of the church. The purpose of priestly asceticism is that this distinctive grace would become visible and effective in the ecclesial community.

When ordained ministry is properly understood and well lived, the presbyterate is a sign which enlivens and activates the people of God. The ecclesial dimension of priestly spirituality will be treated more thoroughly in the next chapter.

3.

Members and Representatives
of the Local Church

The Ecclesial Dimension of Priestly Spirituality

Priests are members of the church, having been made such by the sacrament of baptism, which relates them to Christ in a distinctive way as those who belong to his body. Moreover, the gift of faith was given to them through the activity of the ecclesial community, their identity as Christians and ministers was shaped by the witness of the faithful, and the church asked for their ordination to the presbyterate. Thus their vocation, in all its dimensions, is a gift from God which is mediated by an ecclesial experience. By the very nature of things, then, priests are indebted to the church, since the church has given them life, nurtured their growth and called them to ministry. Like all Christians, presbyters are dependent upon the ecclesial community for the word of God, the bread of life, the fellowship of love, and a community of prayer and service.

As those called to public ministry, priests have the care of the ecclesial community as their constant preoccupation and responsibility. This concern fills their day and shapes their personality and vision of life. Since priests represent the church in pastoral service, its life is their daily interest, for they live in the midst of the ecclesial community in a very obvious manner and act in its name.

In the previous chapter presbyters were considered as participants in the headship of Christ. The insistence of the council that the church itself is the primary sacrament of Christ makes it clear that the sacramentality of ordained ministry must be seen as an expression of ecclesial life. Through ordination priests are related distinctively both to Christ and to the church which mediates his presence; thus as public ministers they are to act in the name of Christ and the church in a way which manifests a unified sacramental reality. Ordination, consequently, far from separating priests from the church, or placing them above it, or positioning them over and against the common experience of the faithful, deepens their involvement in the life of the ecclesial community. Through ordination priests are oriented more radically toward that which all are called to be, becoming servants of the mystery of the church in others while seeking to be examples of ecclesial life themselves.

It is sometimes suggested that there is an incongruity between an ontological understanding of the distinctive relationship of priests

51

to Christ in his headship and a more existential approach to priests as members of the church with a special function. Many, in fact, would feel more comfortable with an existential and functional approach to priesthood, since mutual service among equals is a contemporary ideal, if not always an attained reality. It is obvious that Vatican II was sensitive to the cultural preference of today and often expressed its pastoral insights in terms of that aspiration, drawing its understanding from a clearer articulation of the nature of the church. This fact challenges priests to a spirituality which places them in the midst of the church as servants and as fellow pilgrims in one ecclesial community.

The council, then, embraces two philosophical vantage points; it speaks in existential and ecclesiological terms while maintaining the ontological and sacramental affirmations which were delineated in the previous chapter. The apparent incongruity between the ontological and existential affirmations of the council may arise more from the experience of church life than from the teaching itself. The existing tension between the ontological/sacramental and existential/ecclesial aspects of ordained ministry needs to be better understood and more satisfactorily integrated in the spirituality of the ordained before it can be more fittingly resolved in the life of the total church. Recognizing the tension, this chapter considers priests as members and representatives of the local church, articulating those aspects of priestly spirituality which flow from their existential situation as ecclesial persons.

I. Christ as the Life of the Church

The church is both a visible human community and a transcendent spiritual communion. It exists as a concrete historical tradition at the same time that it reaches beyond history to a promised fulfillment. Truly human in its membership, yet the church participates in the saving presence of Jesus Christ; it is the kingdom of Christ already present in mystery and growing tangibly through the power of God in the world.[1] The church is a complex reality, and the council uses a number of images to express its nature. This section will examine the church as sacrament, people of God, body of Christ, Spirit-filled community and spouse.

Vatican II calls the church a sacrament, a sign and instrument of the saving activity of God.[2] As mentioned earlier in treating the hierarchy, the council relates the church to the mystery of the incarnation, seeing a parallel between the humanity of Christ and the human instrumentality of the ecclesial community. In both instances God's activity is manifested through human signs, that is, through the humanity of Christ on one hand, and the human community of the church on the other.[3] The church participates in Christ who is the archetypal sacrament; hence the theological foundation for the seven sacraments is to be found in the sacramentality of Christ himself, and in his continuing presence through a church which is sacrament.[4]

As a sacrament of the saving work of God the ecclesial community makes Christ present in its worship, life and service.[5] Priests are called to share in a sacramental spirituality which challenges the baptized to a personal and communal authenticity revealing their participation in Christ. While presbyters live a sacramental spirituality common to the whole church, it is further specified by the sacrament of orders which empowers and moves them to convincingly manifest Christ, the head of the church.

The people of God is an image of the church which has been closely associated with the council. It underlines the corporate nature of God's saving activity which calls into existence a new people as a visible and historically verifiable communion of believers.[6] As participants in Christ, all members of the people of God have a common dignity, a mutually acknowledged principle of life and a shared goal. Vatican II affirms that this people enjoys the freedom of God's children, being filled with the Spirit and called to live the commandment of love; thus the common destiny of the whole people is the kingdom of God, begun on earth and to be completed when Christ comes again, when all will share in his glory.[7]

Since membership in the people of God has an ontological foundation in the sacrament of baptism,[8] the activities of this graced people express a true consecration and thereby proclaim the glory of the God who called them out of darkness into his light.[9] *Lumen Gentium* moves quite deliberately from a consideration of the church as sacrament into an explanation of it as the people of God; an obvious effort is to keep attention focused on the church itself as participant in Christ.

In using the image of the people of God, the council paints a picture of a pilgrim people gathered together by the power of God and gathering in all peoples.[10] It is a largely undifferentiated image of a total people journeying together under divine guidance, fellow travelers, brothers and sisters, equals and helpmates in an arduous pilgrimage. In a pivotal statement the council affirms that "everything that has been said of the people of God is addressed equally to laity, religious and clergy."[11] Accordingly it uses the phrase "the faithful" in a way which includes the ordained,[12] affirming the unity of all members of the church as participants in Christ, and therefore in spirituality and mission at the most basic level of Christian existence, the sacraments of initiation.[13]

The faithful are incorporated into Christ and the church by baptism and so appointed to Christian religious worship. They are bound more perfectly to the church by confirmation and given a special gift of the Spirit. Not only do all have a part in the liturgy,[14] but they share in Christ's prophetic office. The charism of infallibility resides in the agreement of the whole church, as well as in conciliar and papal definitions of dogma. The people of God is clearly the context in which the council places priests: they are "those among the faithful who have received holy orders."[15]

This understanding is reflected in the church's liturgy, where the preface for the chrism mass, often used at ordinations, prays: "By your Holy Spirit you anointed your only Son high priest of the new and eternal covenant. . . . Christ gives the dignity of a royal priesthood to the people he has made his own. From these, with a brother's love, he chooses men to share his sacred ministry by the laying on of hands."[16] Each statement in the prayer is important. There is but one priesthood, Christ's. He gives the dignity of this royal priesthood to his people. Those who are to share in the ministerial priesthood by the laying on of hands are chosen from within this priestly people. This liturgical text flowing from the council clearly enunciates the theology of Vatican II.

What does this mean for the spirituality of priests? First, it indicates that their spirituality is the same as that of the church. Although shaped and formed by a distinctive role among the people of God, at its most basic level presbyteral spirituality is ecclesial.[17] The priority given to the image of the people of God in *Lumen Gentium* affirms the ecclesial spirituality common to all, making ministerial priests more like the people they serve than different from them.

Secondly, this common heritage sets up a relationship of mutuality between priests and people. Formed by the same word, nourished by the same eucharist, called to the same quest for holiness and justice, priests and people are able to serve one another. Thus spiritual growth in the life of priests, because it is nourished and expressed in the common legacy of the people of God, becomes a resource for ministry as well. That which priests learn in their own spiritual journey has application, at least in general outline, to the community they are called to lead, and vice versa. The common experience of the faithful is a rich spiritual resource for the growth of priests, since the spirituality of the church is one, and priests and people grow through a common, yet distinctive, participation in Christ.

Vatican II also uses the body of Christ as an image of the church. This image is, in a way, more traditional and better known. It is employed by the council in conjunction with the other images, although not with the same prominence as sacrament or people of God. It affirms the unity and common life of the church, while giving fuller expression to the diversity of its various parts: "As all the members of the human body, though they are many, form one body, so also are the faithful in Christ. Also, in the building up of Christ's body there is engaged a diversity of members and functions."[18]

The Spirit of Jesus gives diverse gifts and ministries so that all may grow in Christ.[19] Since by its very nature the Christian vocation is a participation in Christ, all of those who share in the life of his body share in His activity as well; thus the church seeks to fulfill its mission through the involvement of all its members. All who participate in Christ are responsible for the growth of the body.[20]

In this way the council paints another picture: a Christian community of many parts, called in diverse ways to participation in Christ and involvement in activities which build up the body, yet united in one communion of life in him. In this way Vatican II asserts that all the members of the church are by nature active, and the whole ecclesial community is ministerial. This perspective is maintained in the opening paragraphs of *Presbyterorum Ordinis:* "The Lord Jesus . . . makes his whole mystical body sharer in the anointing of the Spirit wherewith he has been anointed; for in that body all the faithful are made a holy and kingly priesthood. . . . Therefore there is no such thing as a member that has not a share in the mission of the whole body."[21]

The image of the body allows the council to distinguish roles among the members of the church, and to recognize the relationship of various ministries to the good of the whole. Consequently, Vatican II states that among the gifts given to the body the primacy belongs to the grace of the apostles, since the function of the apostolic ministry is leadership and discernment.[22] It is a service to the community which sees to it that the diversity of the body truly serves the common mission of the church.[23] The council affirms that priests share in this apostolic ministry through union with the episcopal college.[24]

The image of the church as the body of Christ presents a number of challenges to an authentic ecclesial spirituality. First of all, members of the church are collaborators with no one ministry or role as the sole source of activity in the ecclesial community. When the relationship among members is envisioned in this way, a trinitarian model of spirituality is once again seen to be appropriate. Thus that which was said about a Trinity of equal persons sharing a common life and participating in diverse ways in the one mission of salvation applies to the graced assembly of the whole church as well as to the community arising from the sacrament of orders. Theological affirmations about the Trinity which at the outset seem puzzling become, in an analogous way, the lived experience in a ministerial church, since shared ministry within the body of Christ transforms abstract theological speculation into a graced way of life, an authentic and life-giving spirituality.

This ecclesial spirituality is particularly significant for priests, since Vatican II calls them to authoritative leadership, as well as to receptivity and sharing. Presbyters are challenged to discern both what is appropriate in their own ministry and what is for the common good of the community within which they preside. The listening heart asked for by King Solomon is the operational foundation for this ministry inasmuch as it is essential in fulfilling the special role assigned to priests in the body of Christ.[25] The contemplative life of priests is directly related to the spiritual vision of the community, and is therefore essential to their effective involvement in a church enriched by many gifts.

In a somewhat embryonic way, the council documents point to an image of the church based on universal empowerment by the Holy Spirit. In doing so, Vatican II acknowledges both the insights of the oriental church and the contemporary experience of pastoral ministry. Just as "people of God" opens new possibilities for a common identity as equal participants in church life, so, too, the council's insistence on the universal empowerment of the baptized by the Spirit opens new prospects for a vital Catholic laity. The gifts and acts of service which enrich the community are not limited to the seven sacraments and the officially sanctioned ministries, since the Holy Spirit is the source of a multiplicity of charismatic favors: "Allotting his gifts according as he wills, he also distributes special graces among the faithful of every rank."[26] The Spirit responds to needs in the church with gifts that are so creative, particular or varied that they challenge definition, yet these too flow from the mission of Christ and must interact with other roles and graces in the ecclesial community. Very significantly, the ordained are admonished to recognize, respect and cherish the work of the Spirit in the laity.[27] Priests are challenged to effect unity in a diverse community of many gifts, bringing all together in one church and one saving mission. In this context, the ordained begin to emerge, not only as a sacrament of Christ, the head of the body, but also as a sign of the Spirit who is the unifying force in the church.

The image of "Spirit filled people" is woven throughout the council documents, giving depth to the other images, and providing needed contrast to the tendency of the western church to focus on structure and predictability. It offers subtle insight into the nature of the presbyteral mission which could easily be missed in a cursory reading of the documents.

Spouse of Christ is the last image of the church used by the council which will be considered here. It is an image which portrays Christ's loving union with the church and its passionate longing for completion and transformation in him. *Lumen Gentium* says that "it is she (the Church) whom he unites to himself by an unbreakable alliance and whom he constantly 'nourishes and cherishes.' It is she whom, once purified, he willed to be joined to himself, subject in love and fidelity, and whom, finally, he filled with heavenly gifts for all eternity. . . ."[28] Therefore the church is concerned about those things which are above, where Christ is seated at the right hand of God, while her life is hidden with Christ in God until she appears in glory with her spouse. Vatican II comes back to this image in many contexts and through it depicts the ecclesial community in a way which is powerfully dynamic and easily assessable to human experience.

The importance of the image of the spouse is hinted at in the final chapter of *Lumen Gentium:* ". . . the church reverently penetrates more deeply into the great mystery of the incarnation and becomes more and more like her spouse."[29] Since the goal of the ecclesial community is conformity to Christ, members not only act like Christ or for Christ, but are transformed and sanctified in his image. The council affirms that Christian holiness is more than how God looks at the Christian or on how the Christian acts; it involves actual configuration to Christ, that is, true participation in him. Hence the being of the Christian is truly sanctified and transformed.

The image of the spouse is associated with the activity of the Spirit who dwells in the church, guiding it and enabling it to keep the freshness of youth, while constantly purifying it and leading it to perfect union with Christ. The Spirit and the bride together say to Jesus, "Come."[30] "Christ loves the church as his bride, having been established as the model of a man loving his wife as his own body; the church, in her turn, is subject to her head."[31] Thus Christ, in whom the fullness of the Godhead dwells bodily, fills his church, which is his fullness, with divine gifts so that it might grow into the very fullness of God. Since the church is a graced participation in the reality of Jesus Christ, it is his fullness precisely because it shares in his Spirit; thus Christ and the church are two in one Spirit.[32] The Spirit of the Lord, which is poured out upon it, leads the church toward perfect fidelity.[33]

The liturgy most clearly manifests the spousal relationship between Christ and the church, since there Christ associates the assembled community with himself in his work of salvation. Through the mediation of the church God is glorified and humanity is sanctified. Not only does the God who spoke in the past through the scriptures continue to converse with the spouse of his beloved Son,[34] but the council also declares that the church is the beloved bride who calls to her Lord, and through him offers worship to the eternal Father.[35] In the eucharistic liturgy the spousal imagery and interaction are most profound; thus Vatican II asserts: ". . . the sharing in the body and blood of Christ has no other effect than to accomplish our transformation into that which we receive."[36] Eucharistic communion ultimately means participation in the identity of the divine spouse.

The image of spouse is interpersonal and intimate, self-liberating and transforming, passionate and profound. It demands commitment and a total response in the gift of self, and it impels the church forward to a marriage feast which is yet to come. The council applies this image of the church to the sacrament of matrimony,[37] to religious life,[38] and to priestly celibacy. It sees the ministry of the priest as "espousing the faithful to one husband" and clerical celibacy as a sign of "that mystical marriage, established by God and destined to be fully revealed in the future, by which the church holds Christ as her only spouse."[39] Hence Vatican II portrays the consecrated celibate life of the priest as a public witness to the nature of the church.

The development of a spirituality of celibacy depends on this image of the church as one of its sources. This is especially significant in the light of contemporary insights into the psycho-sexual dynamic in human life. And yet this spirituality is not meant to be individualistic or private, since it is an expression of the longing of the church. As such, Christian celibacy grows from the same root and expresses the same reality as the sacrament of matrimony and has much in common with it. This aspect of presbyteral spirituality, then, is a distinctive expression of a Christian community seeking fulfillment in Christ.

The fact that priests participate in Christ as members of the church is a significant and recurring conciliar theme. Among the many images of the church utilized by the council, the five considered here have special importance for an authentic priestly spirituality. It is precisely because priests share in the life of the church that their spirituality is shaped by the way in which the ecclesial community understands itself.

II. Priests as Members of the Church and Examples of Its Life

The church, as a visible and historical community, is localized in time, culture and place. The universal church is a communion of local churches under the leadership of the successor of Peter. Each local church is gathered around its bishop who for that church is the visible source and foundation of unity. The council declares that "it is in these (local churches) and formed out of them that the one unique Catholic Church exists."[40] The college of bishops, being composed of many members, comes from and represents the variety and the universality of the people of God.[41] Thus local churches express themselves in a particular place and through a distinctive culture, and they find unity in the college of bishops, thereby forming together the one church of Christ.

Christ the shepherd fashioned his church in a manner which guarantees that the people of God will have their own priests; by the very way in which the church is constituted, those who lead it come from the ecclesial community.[42] Consequently presbyters not only represent Christ, but they also epitomize the races, cultures, nations and localities in which they serve. By reason of their origin the ordained are truly members of the ecclesial community.[43]

In other words, priests lead a people who are truly their own.[44] They are not outsiders imposed upon the people of God, but members who have been nurtured within a diocesan, regional or cultural community, sharing with it bonds of affection, esteem and understanding.[45] Priests approach the church, then, with the allegiance of brothers, seeking to be supported by fellow members of the ecclesial community, brothers and sisters sharing a common origin and a common destiny.

It follows from the way the church is fashioned that an authentic

spirituality is indigenous, since it belongs to the local church. Not
only are priests to engender the life of the universal church in a local
situation, but they are also to express the faith within a cultural
heritage and in an idiom which they hold in common with the people
they serve. Accordingly, an appropriate presbyteral spirituality
shares in the heritage of the universal church while maintaining its
relationship to the local community. In this way it links the universal
and the particular, binding the local community to the total church.

Since the church of Christ is truly present in legitimately organized local communities of the faithful united to their pastors, these
congregations are in fact the new people of God.[46] In this way,
priests, in union with their bishop, "render the universal church
visible in their locality."[47] The parish community, constituted in a
particular place, shares in the reality of the whole Church.[48]

Because the Church exists in human history, it expresses itself
through each culture into which it has been sent.[49] Indeed, Vatican
II sees this kind of adaptation in the proclamation of the revealed
word as the unchanging principle of all evangelization. Thus the
teachings of the council seek to foster vital contacts with a diversity
of cultures in expressing the message of Christ, challenging pastors
and theologians to listen to the signs of the times in the midst of their
own cultural setting, so that the truth of the gospel might be better
understood and more suitably presented.

This inculturation is an extension of the mystery of the incarnation which the council links to the paradigm of revelation itself: "In
his self-revelation to his people culminating in the fullness of manifestation in his incarnate Son, God spoke according to the culture
proper to each age."[50] Thus Jesus used the most ordinary social
events and the imagery of everyday life to explain his teaching. He
sanctified human relationships, observed the laws of his own land,
and led the life of a carpenter.[51] In the same fashion, the church has
continued to utilize the resources of different cultures in preaching
and explaining the message of Christ.

The council charges bishops with the responsibility of presenting Christian doctrine in a manner suited to the needs of the times so
that it might be relevant to the troubling questions of those they
serve. From this injunction an aspect of the spirituality of ordained
ministry begins to emerge which has profound pastoral significance:
"Since it is the mission of the church to maintain close relations with
the society in which she lives the bishops should make it their special
care to approach men and to initiate and promote dialogue with
them."[52] It is apparent, then, that the local church is meant to be the

expression of the truth of the gospel in terms of the culture and challenges of a particular ecclesial community. In order to foster effectiveness, priestly spirituality must advance authentic dialogue with the cultural milieu and cannot be abstract or pre-packaged since it must be a response to its human environment.

It is not surprising, then, that Vatican II tells priests that they are both to live in the midst of the community they aspire to serve and to seek to understand it, for "they would be powerless to serve men if they remained aloof from their life and circumstances."[53] While they are not to be conformed to the world, presbyters are required to live in the human community and to know those whom they serve. They are reminded of their special obligation to be present to those who are outside the ecclesial community, being challenged to extend themselves beyond a narrowly conceived ecclesial environment.

There are several implications here for priestly spirituality. First of all presbyters must understand their pastoral setting and, by a reverent sensitivity to their environment, come to appreciate the assets and the problems of the community. This demands the asceticism of presence and interaction, as well as the contemplative skills which allow them to understand, in mind and heart, the events unfolding around them. Consequently, prayerfulness must empower priests to hear the voice of God and the voices of the human community, not as separate or conflicting realities, but as a common utterance joined by an inner grace which seeks to bring them together. The prayer of priests as ecclesial leaders is practical inasmuch as it seeks to hear the invitation of God in the midst of the human community. This form of prayer is an expression of ecclesial sensitivity, combining attentiveness to the prompting of grace with a compassionate understanding of a portion of the human family.

While effective presence in a local community is essential, it may not be forced; priests must be freely welcomed into the lives of those they serve. Growth in virtue has a pastoral impact in this regard, facilitating pastoral relationships by giving priests a popular appeal and witnessing to the authenticity of their lives, thereby opening the way to dialogue. The fostering of virtue, then, is an important aspect of a truly pastoral spirituality.[54] Since there is a correlation between the authentic humanity of priests and their pastoral effectiveness in the local church,[55] they are expected not only to be ministers of the gospel, but also examples of the Christian life.

This emphasis on Christian authenticity in presbyteral life is characteristic of the teaching of the council. Because priests are truly members of the church, that which their ministry enables in others is a gift they themselves have also received and must continue to develop. Accordingly, when the council refers to priests it often begins by reminding them of their origin among the people of God, locating the roots of their ministry in the sacraments of initiation.[56] Even though presbyters have a special role, they are followers of the Lord along with all the faithful and have been made partakers of the same grace and called to the same kingdom. "Priests, in common with all who have been reborn in the font of baptism, are brothers among brothers as members of the same body of Christ which all are commanded to build up."[57]

And so an authentic spirituality directs presbyters to the places of nourishment common to all the faithful, especially the double table of the scriptures and the eucharist.[58] With all Christians they are reminded that although the modes and tasks of life are many, there is but one holiness, obeying the Father's voice, by the power of the Holy Spirit, and adoring him in spirit and in truth as disciples of Jesus crucified.[59] Because of this, Vatican II situates the foundation of priestly spirituality both in the grace of ordination and in the consecration of baptism. This perspective is the basis of a more ecclesial articulation of priestly spirituality grounded on a correlation between the emphasis on baptism in the documents of Vatican II and the preference of the council for the image of the church as the people of God.

Consequently, priests administer baptism as those who also seek salvation within the community of the church. As they preach, priests are also hearers of the word.[60] At the altar they too are given merciful communion, since they reconcile as those who know the burden of sinfulness, and invite to unity as those who experience brokenness. In view of the fact that priests represent the people of God from a position which is genuinely ecclesial, they are challenged to take a stance which enables them to identify with the community in its highest aspirations as well as in its sin and weakness. An authentic priestly spirituality, then, enables priests to minister from an experienced solidarity with the people of God.

Furthermore, the ordained must seek ministry from other representatives of the church since they are as much in need of the grace of God as any other member of the faithful. An authentic spirituality puts them solidly within the fellowship of the poor who make up the body of the church and are therefore open to the kingdom of God. This dependence upon the ministry of others affirms that ordination is not an elevation beyond church membership, but an intensification of it, and a new incentive to ecclesial life and holiness.[61]

The council sees this common membership in the local church as the basis for interaction between clergy and laity. "Although by Christ's will some are established as teachers, dispensers of the mysteries and pastors for the others, there remains, nevertheless, a true equality between all with regard to the dignity and to the activity which is common to all the faithful in the building up of the body of Christ."[62] *Lumen Gentium* states quite simply that those in ordained ministry are brothers to the laity after the model of Christ, who came to serve and not to be served.

In living among the laity as brothers, then, priests are given as their model not only the Lord himself, who dwelt in the midst of the human family and became like it in all things but sin, but also the apostle Paul, who sought to be a Jew for the Jews and a Greek for the Greeks, indeed all things to all.[63] In pointing to a lifestyle which is rooted in the mystery of the incarnation and the early experience of apostolic ministry, and which has often been obscured by the abuse of clericalism, *Presbyterorum Ordinis* refers to the letter to the Hebrews: "Therefore he had to be made like his brethren in every respect, so that he might become a merciful and faithful high priest. . . ."[64] In encouraging familial relationships between priests and those they seek to serve, Vatican II is underlining the significance of ecclesial membership for a sound presbyteral spirituality.

III. Priests as Representatives of the Local Church

Priests are ministers of the ecclesial community, acting in its behalf in fostering the growth of the local church, and giving it voice in its relationship with God. Consequently, presbyters function not only as servants of Christ the head, but also as representatives of the ecclesial body. This gives ordained ministry both christological and ecclesial dimensions which are mutually interrelated, since the ecclesial community truly participates in Christ its head, and Christ shares in the life of the church which is his fullness.

Because presbyters are members of the church who truly represent it, they are set apart "in a certain way" in the midst of the people of God, "but this is not in order that they should be separated from that people or from any man, but that they should be completely consecrated to the task for which God chooses them."[65] It is immediately evident that this "separation" is, in the mind of the council, a consecration for a pastoral task in behalf of the church. Therefore, far from removing priests from the lives of people, it focuses and dedicates their presence in the human community, giving them a mission and making them an expression of the venturesome love of the good shepherd.

It is important to make a distinction between separation from the world and separation from worldliness, as Vatican II recognizes. In defining presbyteral ministry, it puts priests in the midst of the human community, in the world and for the salvation of the world, while emphasizing the need to avoid worldliness. Although the presence of priests in the world has a different focus than that of the laity, they are no less urged to be present to all, to preach to all, and to seek out what is lost.

An appropriate priestly spirituality has two tasks in facilitating and maintaining this consecration for ministry. The first is to strengthen priestly identity, and the second is to instill zeal in fulfilling the presbyteral mission. The first task, then, is to keep priests focused in their identity as ministers of the gospel. Worldliness militates against this sense of identity, since the spirit of the world often presents itself in a blurred vision and ambiguous decisions which lead to inner confusion. This may result in a fixation on false gods or inappropriate values, or, perhaps, in the lack of any focus at all.

An authentic spirituality is a way of life which allows priests to be in the world while not being confused by it. As such, it is a mode of ecclesial existence which renews and strengthens an ontological reality, the consecration of baptism and holy orders. In prayer, in friendship and community, and in the experience of ministry itself, an inner focus is maintained and deepened which supports priestly identity. This ministerial identity, which may be reinforced by appropriate ecclesial structures, remains primarily an interior realization which is sustained and fostered within the life of the local church.[66] Priestly consecration is not, then, a separation from the world, but a deepening sense of ecclesial and presbyteral identity in the midst of the world, having continual inner conversion to the truth about oneself as its central concern.

Missionary zeal, the second task of presbyteral spirituality, is rooted in a compassionate understanding of the community and an ardent desire to be present to it as a herald of salvation. The source of the penetrating love and abiding courage which must impel priests to go into the midst of the community and even to its furthest reaches as ministers of the gospel is a distinctive participation in the pastoral zeal of the good shepherd. This dynamic sharing in the mission of Christ is raised to consciousness in prayer, but is fully acquired only when expressed through ministry, an ecclesial expression of pastoral concern. As stated earlier, Vatican II never tires of reminding priests that ministry itself clarifies and deepens their participation in Christ. Consequently, in the exercise of priestly ministry the ontological and the existential work together in creating a living whole. Growth in pastoral charity is a result of the interaction between contemplation and action, the recognition of one's special mission and the actual experience of it. Prayer and ministry together are the source of this particular kind of missionary zeal.

An authentic presbyteral identity, cultivated within the local church, enables priests to facilitate a growing sense of identity in the lay community as well. Vatican II reminds priests that "very little good will be achieved by ceremonies however beautiful, or societies however flourishing, if they are not directed toward educating people to reach Christian maturity."[67] Seeing life and solving its problems in light of the will of God and the universal demands of charity are at the heart of this maturity. As leaders of the ecclesial community priests are to seek the full development of each member of the local church.[68] The council underlines the need to focus the identity and spirituality of the laity on the renewal of the temporal order in Christ.[69] The goal is conversion to Christ, to the life of the church, and to social responsibility. Fostering maturity in the lay community requires that the ordained recognize the right and responsibility of all the faithful to participate fully in the apostolate of the church. It also presumes the mutuality of adult relationships.[70] Since the faithful have a right to receive in abundance from the spiritual goods of the church through the ministry of their pastors, an active laity influences the priorities of the ordained.[71] This orientation toward service to the laity clarifies ministerial values and shapes presbyteral activity.

In no way does this alignment of presbyteral ministry with service to the laity deny that the only adequate goal for priestly activity is the glory of God. In fact, Vatican II defines God's glory in terms of the spiritual development of the ecclesial community: "That glory consists in men's conscious, free, and grateful acceptance of God's plan as completed in Christ and their manifestation of it in their whole life."[72] Presbyteral spirituality must be guided by the conciliar understanding that the community of the church is the place where God dwells and manifests his greatness. Priestly ministry gives praise to God precisely through the building up of the church.

Priests are placed in the midst of the local church to lead the

people of God to the unity of charity. Their task is to bring about
agreement among the various viewpoints and the many gifts and
tasks which enrich and test the local church.[73] Priests, then, are to be
agents of mutual care, shared activity, communal discernment and
ecclesial harmony. As representatives of the ecclesial community
they facilitate those relationships among members of church which
allow it to manifest its sacramental identity as sign and instrument of
communion.

As a prerequisite, a life of communion must be characteristic of
priests themselves, since their actions are an enduring sign and invitation to those whom they serve. Priests must deal with their own
unitive energy, seeking to possess an adequate sense of themselves
and yet an ability to transcend themselves. As servants of the common life of the community they are challenged to give and receive in
relationships which are both mutual and intimate. This summons
priests to a healthy integration of sexuality, a capacity for sharing
work, and a potential for deep friendship.

Relationships with the laity test the affective maturity of priests.
Vatican II insists that the laity are to be respected, listened to, given
brotherly consideration and recognized as competent in many fields.
Priests are to promote the dignity of the laity and recognize the
liberty which belongs to all in civil society. Moreover, they are to
willingly unite their efforts with those of lay people and to be present
to them as their servants.[74]

Since through the ministry of priests the local community is
called into being, develops an ecclesial identity and grows in maturity, Vatican II offers a number of insights into the intimate relationship between the presbyteral role and ecclesial life. First of all,
the faithful are formed into one by the word of the living God;[75] thus
there is a correlation between the preached word, the response of
faith, and the existence of the local church. In preaching priests are
to call the community together and prepare it for worship and service. Their proclamation of the gospel, which is a constitutive element of ecclesial life, both gives birth to the local church and renews
it in faith. Having been told by the council that they are to preach "in
such a way that the light of the gospel will shine on all the activities of
the faithful,"[76] the ordained must apply the scriptures to the concrete circumstances of the local church, since it is an ecclesial word
which they speak, with a concomitant ecclesial effect. Preaching,
then, establishes the local community, enlightens it and challenges it
to action.

Respect for the ecclesial dimension of preaching is to move

priests to prayer, careful study, and responsible preparation for this ministry. Concrete experience of the relationship between the word and the life of the church establishes the scriptures as a central feature of priestly spirituality. Furthermore, responsibility for the ecclesial ministry of preaching focuses attention on the community itself as the context for prayerful pondering of the word.

The sacramental ministry of priests flows from the proclamation of the word and completes it. Because the sacraments are expressions of the life of the church incorporating those who participate in them more deeply into the ecclesial community, in celebrating them presbyters act, not only in the person of Christ, but also in the name of the church. Accordingly, through baptism priests admit members to the people of God; in the sacrament of penance they reconcile people with the community of the church; and in the eucharist the faithful are fully incorporated into the body of Christ since "the eucharistic celebration is the center of the assembly of the faithful over which the priest presides."[77] In this gathering presbyteral ministry brings together the spiritual sacrifices of the faithful and the one sacrifice of Christ; here, too, priests act in the name of the church and on its behalf.[78] They pray in the name of all present,[79] and as representatives of the community bring the local church to ever deeper communion with Christ. In this way their ministry manifests the unity which exists between Christ and the church, that is, between action in the person of Christ on one hand, and action in the name of the church, on the other.

Vatican II sees the responsibility of priests to pray for the church as an expression of ecclesial solidarity; thus in the Liturgy of the Hours they are to pray for the people committed to their care.[80] As an ecclesial prayer, the office best manifests its true nature when prayed with other members of the local community. It is clear, though, that in whatever form it is prayed, the council envisions priests as representatives of the church in the fulfillment of this responsibility.[81] It challenges them to regard the Liturgy of the Hours as an ecclesial activity, not as an imposed discipline separate from ministerial responsibility, since this official prayer is meant to be an expression of dependence on God, an ongoing demonstration of pastoral love, and a source of nourishment. It is apportioned among the major divisions of the day so that ministry may be joined to a regular rhythm of ecclesial prayer. Because its purpose is to sanctify the day, the council invites priests both to pray the Liturgy of the Hours at the appropriate times, to the extent that this is possible,[82] and to share it as a communal prayer among presbyters sharing a common ministry or residence.[83] Active priests, then, are encouraged to see this prayer as an integral part of ecclesial life, being neither monastic nor private, but set within the rhythm of the day and shared with the broader community of the local church whenever feasible.

It is clear that an authentic priestly spirituality can not be articulated apart from its ecclesial context, since the priesthood exists for service to the ecclesial community, sharing in its essential structure and being shaped by its self-understanding. Inasmuch as priests are both members of the church and ministerial representatives of the local community, their spirituality is existentially specified by these two ecclesiological relationships. That which priests are ontologically, then, must be understood and expressed in terms of ecclesial service. The way in which this service relates priests to the social order will be further clarified in the next chapter.

4.

Servants of the Poor in Society

The Social Dimension of Priestly Spirituality

T he church exists within society; its members are influenced by the cultural context, and, in turn, seek to foster gospel values in the broader community. While Vatican II recognizes the true autonomy of the human community in pursuing social and scientific growth, this right to self-determination cannot be divorced from moral and transcendent values. All of creation is dependent upon God, speaks of God and leads to him.[1]

Political communities and the church exist independently of one another, although they often share a common membership and devotion to the same values.[2] Although political communities arise to serve the common good within the limits of the moral order, the concrete forms of public authority vary according to the character and historical development of various peoples. The purpose of civil authority is the formation of a human person who is cultured, peace-loving and well disposed toward others with a view to the welfare of the whole human race.[3]

By the very nature of its mission the church is universal, and is not tied, therefore, to a particular culture or political, economic or social system. The ecclesial community is free to associate with a wide variety of ideological understandings in witnessing to their unity within a global human family.[4] Because of the specific role and competence arising from its mission, the church is not bound to any particular political community, but exists within all of them, and in the human family as a whole, as a witness to the transcendent value of the human person.[5]

The church is present in society in two ways: it influences the social environment through men and women formed by gospel values, acting alone or in groups specifically as citizens of the political community, and it addresses the civic community through people working and speaking explicitly as representatives of the church.[6] The distinction between these two forms of ecclesial presence is of great importance. Accordingly, Christian citizens, especially the laity, are impelled by the very nature of their baptismal vocation to participate in the political process.[7] Through responsible involvement in politics, lay members of the church apply the values of the gospel to concrete issues in society. On the other hand, the church, as an

71

institution, witnesses to moral values while avoiding identification with a particular political system or activity which is explicitly partisan. Both of these forms of ecclesial activity are directed toward the healthy development of the human community.[8]

In response both to the pragmatism of contemporary social thought and to the challenge of Marxism, accusing Christians not only of doing nothing for those in need, but also of anesthetizing them into a state of non-involvement in their own struggle for advancement, Vatican II draws attention to two elements in the social mission of the church: the discernment of moral principles and their application to the social order, and advocacy for the poor.

This chapter is directed to an analysis of the teachings of Vatican II on the role of priests in the total social mission of the church.

I. The Mission of Jesus to the Poor

Jesus was in fact poor; through the incarnation he entered into the human condition with its limitations, weaknesses and sufferings, sharing human nature in every way except for sin. Possessing the unlimited perfection of God, he became human with all the imperfection which that entails, taking upon himself the frailty which belongs to the created world by definition. This radical identification with humanity is the beginning of his saving work.[9] Vatican II often repeats the phrase: "Though rich, he was made poor for our sake, that by his poverty we might become rich."[10] The identity of Jesus is tied to freely chosen poverty for the sake of the work of salvation.

Yet, the poverty of Jesus is the result not only of his entry into the human condition, but also of his status within society where he shared the lot of the poor. Accordingly, at his birth his mother made the offering specified for the needy in presenting him in the temple.[11] Throughout his days he continually sought fellowship with the poor, choosing for himself a life among them.[12] Poverty, for Jesus, was much more than a tolerated condition; it was a freely chosen way of life.

Although the ministry of Christ was often directed to care for the poor, they were more than the favored group among those to whom he addressed the gospel; Jesus was born among them and lived out his days in their company. As one dispossessed of all things he established the new covenant through the poverty of the cross. There is, then, a correlation between the poor, on one hand, and the identity of Jesus, his messianic mission, and the fulfillment of his saving work, on the other.

The fact that Jesus chose the status of the poor as a significant aspect of his own identity must be taken seriously in an appropriate spirituality. At the most basic level of human experience, the lifestyle of Jesus witnesses to total dependence upon God. He was poor not only because it served his mission, but also because it clarified and supported his relationship to the Father. Human beings are to live by every word that comes from the mouth of God; the many hungers of poverty accentuate this state of dependence.

Because the poverty of Christ is a freely chosen aspect of an identity which he sought and deepened throughout his days, simplicity of life is more than a pragmatic concern for those who follow him. The recognition and acceptance of limits, brokenness and material neediness challenges all members of the church to move beyond themselves, opening the way to a healthy dependence on God. Poverty is more than a discipline or a ministerial expedient; it is an avenue for spiritual growth. Seeing poverty as a value does not idealize human destitution; it affirms the paradoxical emptiness which accompanies that fullness of life which is a gift from God. Consequently, it is an essential value in appropriating the paschal mystery.

Celibacy, with its loneliness, its more nebulous relationships and its lack of family stability, also invites reflection on the human condition. Humanity is radically dependent upon God, and celibacy is a summons to accept this truth about human life. This form of poverty invites some disciples to a distinctive kind of dependence on God, engendering a special rapport with him by placing them in the company of the outcasts, the unfulfilled and the hungry whose hearts are open to the kingdom of God.

The council associates poverty with celibacy in two places. It points to Mary as the virgin who will bear a son, saying that she stands out among the poor and humble of the Lord, confidently hoping to receive salvation from him.[13] In the same vein, Vatican II draws attention to those among the faithful who are called "to that kind of poor and virginal life which Christ the Lord chose for himself and which his Virgin Mother embraced also."[14] In the mind of the council there is a correlation between celibacy and poverty in expressing dependence on God. These two traits were joined together in the human journey of Jesus, placing him among the needy in Jewish society.

Human cravings, arising from a desire for convenience or from an enslavement to addiction, easily become the foundation of life. This inclination toward subjection to the material world is the background against which Christians are challenged to consider the example of Jesus who freely chose to be poor. Possessions are not what is in question, but the deeper and more illusive foundational principle of human existence.[15] The function of an authentic spirituality is to guarantee that God continues to be the groundwork of reality. In pursuing this end, the witness of Jesus is a very strong recommendation for simplicity of life.

The poverty of Jesus finds its fullest expression in his death on the cross. The conclusion to his human journey is an amplification of what went before, not a departure from it; stripped and nailed, Jesus brings to full view the need to turn to God for life and salvation. His incarnation, human journey and death are diverse and consistent expressions of one reality, his choice of poverty so that humanity might be enriched.[16]

A consistent manner of life which truly mirrors the pattern manifested in Christ must form the core of an authentic Christian spirituality. The cross is sincerely embraced only when disciples are willing to embrace the frailty of their own humanity, thereby finding their place among the poor. The poverty of Christ summons them to embrace the vicissitudes of human existence on a journey with fellow pilgrims, ultimately to death itself. Hence, poverty and dependence are to be espoused not only at the final moments of life, but also in a sustained and many-faceted lifestyle. All three aspects of the poverty of Jesus are important: the vulnerability of human life is to be embraced, an unencumbered journey sustained, and a humble death entered into.

Not only did Jesus come from among the poor and witness to the value of a simple way of life, but he also directed his message of salvation to those who were vulnerable enough to receive it. Making the proclamation of the gospel to the poor a sign of his messianic mission,[17] Jesus went through towns and villages healing every sickness and infirmity. The servant stance which he took in the midst of humanity modeled the active charity which was to characterize his followers.

As was indicated in speaking of Christ's headship, the council declares that the servant love of Christ most clearly reveals the kingdom of God. After affirming that the words, miracles and works of Jesus inaugurate the kingdom, the council chooses Christ the servant as its primary focus: "But principally the kingdom is revealed in the person of Christ himself, Son of God and Son of Man, who came to serve and to give his life as a ransom for many."[18]

As the source of its teaching, *Lumen Gentium* cites the instruction of Jesus occasioned by the request of James and John for seats on his right and left in the glory of the kingdom. Looking at the context of this citation is helpful, for Jesus explains that among the Gentiles rulers make their authority felt. He commands that this must never be so among his followers, saying: "Whoever would be great among you must be your servant, and whoever would be first among you must be slave of all. For the Son of Man also came not to be served but to serve, and to give his life as a ransom for many."[19] In the course of a few lines, Jesus moves his disciples from reflection on thrones to reflection on the cross. The latter is the image of Jesus which the council proposes as the pattern for those called to participate in his messianic mission.

The servant love of Jesus flows from his messianic identity. Emptying himself, he took on the nature of a slave. Emptying himself still more, he accepted public disgrace and painful execution for the sake of the human race. Distancing himself from what was his right as God, Jesus embraced, purchased and purified the church on the cross.[20] His followers sing of the love of such a head in the midst of the central liturgy of the year: "Father, how wonderful your care for us! How boundless your merciful love! To ransom a slave you gave away your Son."[21] The image of God emptying himself to kneel in service to humanity is the key to salvation history and the central insight of the gospel.[22]

The fact that Jesus as servant is a pivotal image of the council is very significant for Christian spirituality, since the way in which Christ is perceived and understood has a great impact on the identity of his disciples. The ongoing foundation of a healthy spirituality is clear insight into the messianic identity of Jesus as crucified servant. Deeper penetration into the meaning of his servant-mission flows from prayer, from models of service in the ecclesial community and from the experience of ministry itself. Each of these elements strengthens the interaction between the messianic identity of Jesus and the self-understanding of those who seek to follow him. An accurate appraisal of the identity of Jesus and inner transformation in light of it are the roots from which authentic Christianity grows.

In developing the theme of Christian service, Vatican II is very sensitive to the fact that the poor wear many faces. Hence, the poverty which Christ was sent to alleviate is a multi-faceted reality, all aspects of which are included in his messianic mission. The council makes the inaugural address of Jesus its own, as he proclaims the meaning of his ministry: to bring good news to the poor, to heal the broken-hearted, to proclaim release to captives, and to give sight to the blind.[23] Because the physically poor and oppressed are an obvious segment of society, the council often defines poverty in terms of concrete social realities.[24] Any attempt to dispose of the poor by relegating them to the realm of abstract ideals championed by Jesus is thwarted by the concrete concerns mentioned in *Gaudium et Spes.* There, the love of Christ for the poor is spoken about in terms of the "immensity of hardships which still afflict a large section of humanity."[25] Jesus touched the blind, the lame, the outcast and those suffering material want, and made their lot his personal concern.

Even though the mission of Christ addresses more than material poverty, his earthly ministry was always marked by special compassion for the outcast, the sick and the suffering. An authentic spirituality must empower disciples to be physically present to suffering humanity as a source of comfort, healing and reconciliation for them. As Jesus lived among the poor and lovingly touched them, so those who participate in his mission must embrace the most marginated in society.

The mission of Christ to the poor is broader than care for those beset by material need or physical oppression; it extends to enlightening human understanding, healing a sinful people, and giving hope to a race doomed to death. Since the most pitiable form of human poverty is alienation from God, Christ overcomes sin and gives new life, which will flower on the final day of resurrection, by the power of the Holy Spirit.[26] In Christ, humanity is reconciled to God, freed from the bondage of sin, and healed of personal and communal brokenness.

The lack of answers to the meaning of human existence is also a perplexing impoverishment. Hopelessness, emptiness and lack of direction create a great void at the core of individual existence, cultural self-understanding and national life. Vatican II declares that it is "through Christ, and in Christ, that light is thrown on the riddle of suffering and death which, apart from his gospel, overwhelms us."[27] Christ is sent into the midst of the human dilemma as light in the midst of darkness.

The servant-mission of Christ, then, is directed to three forms of poverty: material and social deprivation, alienation from God and neighbor, and lack of meaning. These three are related to one another and compound one another, forming a web of poverty which oppresses the human race. An appropriately balanced spirituality must stress that Christ himself is good news to the poor, sight to the blind and release to captives, for he is "the goal of human history, the focal point of the desires of history and civilization, the center of mankind, the joy of all hearts, and the fulfillment of all aspirations."[28] To be without Christ and the new order which his presence establishes is to be truly poor.

Vatican II clearly teaches that material poverty is related to a social order alienated from God. The sin of the world, alienation from the divine source of order, expresses itself in lack of integrity within the human person and in disordered relationships within the community.[29] The council declares that "the dignity of man rests above all on the fact that he is called to communion with God."[30] It is this communion which Jesus came to reestablish and strengthen. Lack of union with the purpose and meaning of life is true poverty, even for the materially rich. Furthermore, the absence of integrity and interior harmony in some members of society leads to a denial of rights and resources to others. Jesus addressed poverty, then, from a broader perspective than the obvious examples of material destitution. For him, all of life was subsumed into a vital and self-transcending relationship with God.

An appropriate spirituality, which sees the poverty of the rich as also worthy of service, refuses to reduce the mission of Jesus to an exclusive focus on the materially poor; rather, it views sin, lack of meaning and disordered relationships within the total society as basic problems which he came to address. The mission of Jesus is fully realized only in a spirituality of communion with God which involves all the members of society in a new community of justice and love. To be authentic, this new community must participate in Christ's preferential care for the most obviously poor, bringing together service to those in need and communion with God. As a way of life, Christian discipleship is neither simplistic about the mission of Jesus nor narrowly focused upon a particular group. At the same time, it is concrete, courageous and active in serving the ills of humanity.

II. The Mission of the Church to the Poor

The ecclesial community participates in Jesus' identification with the poor and gives expression to his care for them. Vatican II affirms that "the church, urged on by the Spirit of Christ, must walk the road Christ himself walked, a way of poverty and obedience, of service and self-sacrifice even to death. . . ."[31] From the very beginning, the church has regarded its sharing in the suffering and oppression of the poor as a participation in the humiliation of Christ. This configuration to the poverty of Jesus is no accident of historical circumstances, but is, as the council asserts, a significant feature of ecclesial life.

There is, then, but one path for the church; as Jesus carried out the work of salvation in poverty and oppression, so the church is called to follow this same path in participating in his saving mission. The Christ who emptied himself is the model for the Christian community.[32] He who went from being rich to being poor by his own choice invites the church to embrace this same option.

The identification of the church with the poverty of Christ involves more than the witness of vowed religious within the ecclesial community; it belongs to the Christian life itself.[33] Consequently, Vatican II proclaims a lofty ideal for the laity: "Following Jesus in his poverty, they feel no depression in want, no pride in plenty; imitating the humble Christ, they are not greedy for vain show . . . always ready to abandon everything for Christ and to endure persecution in the cause of right. . . ."[34] All Christians are to order their lives according to the beatitudes, and "in particular by the spirit of poverty."[35] Because association with the poor and crucified Christ flows from the necessity of taking up the cross in order to be his disciple, the church sees all expressions of baptismal life as a participation in the simple, poor and suffering lifestyle of Jesus.[36]

To fulfill its mission within the historical process the church needs material resources. Yet, the ecclesial community uses material possessions without identifying its mission with them; in fact, it witnesses to a paradoxical set of values manifested in the poverty and humility embraced by Christ.[37] The tension between having and not having, possessing things and yet not being possessed by them, is an important dynamic in the spiritual life. Since justice, charity and the glory of God are the proper objectives of disciples, the acquisition of material goods is not an adequate goal, in itself, for the Christian. This radical reordering of values challenges economic systems, ecclesial decisions, and individual priorities.

The difficulty which the church experiences in adhering to the values of Christ testifies to its own poverty, weakness and sinfulness, and to its constant need for penance, purification and renewal.[38] Even though it participates in the holiness of Christ, the ecclesial community is still an assembly of sinners which both collectively and individually makes choices that are at variance with the gospel. In all honesty, Vatican II admits that the sinfulness and weakness of members of the church may be a source of the distortions in society.[39] The church shares not only in the limitations of the human condition, but also in the poverty of sin. Because it is a weak instrument, the ecclesial community has a vivid experience of its poverty and a concrete awareness of its involvement in a sinful world.

Furthermore, the church must confront the poverty of incomplete understanding by seeking the growth and development of its members. Every generation must stand humbly before the truth of revelation, waiting for the Spirit to unfold new riches. "Thus, as the centuries go by, the church is always advancing toward the plenitude of divine truth, until eventually the words of God are fulfilled in her."[40] While the church is gifted with truth, it is also plagued by limited understanding and tried by mistaken judgments. In the daily life of the community, there are times of tension between abstract infallible teaching and the practical judgments of a pilgrim journey, as the ecclesial community enjoys enlightenment at the same time that it endures the poverty of darkness.

Physical and material need, sin, and limited understanding are aspects of ecclesial life inviting Christians to humility and conversion. In all of these areas disciples experience poverty in themselves, finding, thereby, a common identity with the poor. This experience of need on the part of the church and its members is essential to an appreciation of salvation as an unmerited gift, and conducive to a freely undertaken mission to the poor. Accordingly, the church, which is at the same time holy and in need of purification, embraces sinners; it welcomes those afflicted by human misery, recognizing itself in them. Clinging to the poor and the suffering, the church sees in them the image of its poor and suffering founder. In ministering to the poor, the ecclesial community serves Christ and continues to be a sign of his messianic mission.[41]

The correlation between the messianic identity of Jesus and the mission of the church is clearly articulated by Vatican II: "The joy and hope, the grief and anguish of the men of our time, especially of those who are poor and afflicted in any way, are the joy and hope, the grief and anguish of the followers of Christ as well."[42] The urgency of this servant-mission is even more evident because of the poverty of so many in the contemporary world. The church is confronted with the contrast between the developed world, much of which claims to be Christian, and a vast array of peoples suffering starvation, ignorance and disease, most of whom are not Christian. The abundant resources of predominantly Christian countries is a source of scandal in the face of so much human misery. Vatican II forcefully pictures Christ himself crying out for the charity of his disciples through the mouths of the poor.[43]

More than ordinary generosity is required to remedy the situation. The council teaches that the whole people of God has a duty to alleviate the hardships of the needy, giving not merely out of what is superfluous, but also out of what seems indispensable. Vatican II challenges the ecclesial community to an heroic conversion to the service of the poor.[44] Because care for the poor is an integral part of living the gospel, and not an optional devotional practice, it is a responsibility for which every Christian will be held accountable on the day of judgment. Assistance given to the poor is a response to the will of God, which, to be effective, must involve both words and deeds. Vatican II proclaims quite bluntly that only those who "manfully put their hands to the work" can hope to enter the kingdom of heaven.[45]

By its very nature, the Christian community is bound to works of charity. Assistance to the poor, to the sick, and to a wide variety of human needs has always been held in great esteem in the church, and works of this kind have often been organized under ecclesiastical auspices. While all Christian efforts are to be rooted in love, "certain works are of their nature a most eloquent expression of this charity; and Christ has willed that these should be signs of his messianic mission."[46] In the evident care which the ecclesial community offers to the poor, the messianic identity of Christ continues to be revealed.

Personal and corporate charity are the responsibility of each Christian and of the ecclesial community as a whole. The seriousness of this duty is revealed in a quotation from the fathers, which Vatican II states as axiomatic: "Feed the man dying of hunger, because if you do not feed him you are killing him."[47] *Gaudium et Spes* expands the concept of Christian service, extending it to that form of charity which empowers the poor to help themselves.[48]

Yet works of charity do not exhaust the responsibility of Christians toward the poor; the mission of the church also embraces the perfection of the whole temporal order in the spirit of the gospel.[49] Vatican II teaches that it is imperative for Christians to involve themselves in promoting the common good of society, cooperating with others in the proper ordering of social and economic affairs.[50] While the renewal of society is the work of the entire church,[51] it is a duty which rests principally on the laity.[52]

Accordingly, the institutions and processes of society are the proper objects of Christian concern, since the goal is to conform the total social environment to the norms of justice, thereby bringing about a situation which favors the practice of virtue. The involvement of Christians in the political and economic spheres is meant to permeate the entire culture with moral values. Besides advancing the common good, the active presence of members of the ecclesial community in the total social milieu prepares the way for the proclamation of the gospel.[53]

The vision embodied in an authentic Christian spirituality must be enlarged to include the mission of the church to the social order. Although presbyters are not ordinarily the primary agents of political and economic change, they are ordained to assemble and lead an ecclesial community which sees itself as sent beyond the boundaries of ecclesiastical institutions into the total social environment and the processes and structures of society.[54] Ordained to serve the total mission of the church, and to support the full implementation of the apostolate of the laity, priests must know the social, political and economic realities which surround them, thereby ordering their own spirituality to the effective development of the lay community.

All members of the church are to be formed by the gospel in the light of existing conditions in the social order. Isolation from society or naiveté about the cultural environment is an obstacle to the fulfillment of the church's mission. Although the ordained are usually not called to direct action in the political arena, they have an essential role in an authentic ecclesial spirituality, having been commissioned to be prophet, shepherd and priest for those who must exercise political responsibility.

Sensitivity to issues of justice and charity within the ecclesial community itself is a proper concern flowing from the principles enunciated by the council. In challenging public and private organizations to be at the service of the dignity and destiny of the human person, the church calls itself to accountability as well.[55] Thus, a convincing spirituality begins at home.

III. The Mission of Priests to the Poor

The continuing service which Christ renders to his church through ordained ministry is an extension of the incarnation, with the limitation and frailty which bodily existence implies. Priests participate in the mission of Christ through their identification with his humanity. In calling attention to the fact that presbyters are conformed to the image of Christ, the supreme and eternal priest, through the sacrament of orders, the council cites the letter to the Hebrews, affirming that as high priest Christ is not only a heavenly being enduring forever, but an earthly one as well: "In the days of his flesh, Jesus offered up prayers and supplications, with loud cries and tears, to him who was able to save him from death . . . he learned obedience through what he suffered, and being made perfect he became the source of eternal salvation to all who obey him. . . ."[56]

Presbyters participate in Christ, then, not only as sharers in his headship and as members of his body, but also as partakers in the same humanity. Through humanity itself, priests are associated with Christ in a way which makes human nature a pivotal aspect of their spiritual identity. Since the human family was created in the image of God and renewed in the image of Christ, Vatican II says: "By his incarnation, he, the Son of God, has in a certain way united himself with each man."[57] Because Christ shares human nature, the entire race is related to God in a way which transcends the boundaries of the visible church and the structures of ecclesial office. In enabling priests to be more deeply conformed to Christ, an authentic spirituality also relates them to the condition, struggle and destiny of the entire human race.

In embracing the whole human family, priests are challenged to bridge division and dissension in every form, so that the human race may be led to the unity of the one family of God.[58] They are to transcend a narrowly conceived ecclesiastical view of reality and reach out to all, in response to the theology of the council. *Gaudium et Spes* states that since "all men are in fact called to one and the same destiny, which is divine . . . the Holy Spirit offers to all the possibility of being made partners, in a way known to God, in the paschal mystery."[59] Presbyteral spirituality must free priests to embrace humanity with its light and darkness, on the familiar terrain of the ecclesial community and in the unfamiliar forms of the world beyond. Moving outside of the comfort and security of one's environment and culture is a distinctive way of participating in the self-emptying love of the incarnate Christ.

An authentic priestly identity willingly embraces bodily existence by involvement in the concrete circumstances of the historical situation, and by acceptance of the limitations of human nature. Presbyteral spirituality invites priests to a deeper appreciation of the human condition with its tears and joys, defeats and victories. The very existence of ordained ministers is an affirmation of the fact that the human family was saved through the instrumentality of human nature, and it is through the poverty of the flesh that people continue to come to salvation. "Advancing through trials and tribulations, the church is strengthened . . . by the action of the Holy Spirit . . . until through the cross, she may attain to that light which knows no setting."[60] To deny the significance of the body and the reality of the human struggle would be to repudiate the way in which the Holy Spirit works in the church.

A spirituality adopted in imitation of Christ challenges priests to become ministers of salvation who enter into life and share human vulnerability in the midst of the community. It rejects a way of life which keeps itself safe from human experience by beckoning to people from afar. Not only do the ordained discover who they are through the earthly journey they share with Christ and the human race, but they are chosen from the human community as those subject to weakness, and thus able to be compassionate with the ignorant and the erring.[61]

Priests are encouraged to be even more radical in their identification with the poor, imitating Christ by embracing voluntary poverty. The two aspects of this freely chosen poverty which are emphasized by the council are community of goods and simplicity of life. Consequently, priests are invited to consider ways of sharing their possessions in imitation of the community life extolled in the Acts of the Apostles. While no concrete suggestions are offered, strong endorsement is given to this kind of sharing as providing an excellent opening for pastoral charity.[62] Likewise, proper provision is to be made for the health care and retirement needs of priests, so that, free from anxiety about future needs, they can more easily appreciate and practice the gospel invitation to poverty and simplicity of life.

In stating an ideal which it recommends as appropriate for all priests, not only for religious, the council also enunciates a mandatory minimum: "Priests and bishops alike are to avoid everything that might in any way antagonize the poor."[63] Even more than the rest of the disciples of Christ, those who lead the church are to put aside vanity in their surroundings. Their houses are to be arranged in such a way that they are approachable even for the humblest, since the poor must not be intimidated by the possessions of the ordained. Yet, presbyters are not to be without resources. They are to be given sufficient compensation so that they are capable of "personally assisting in some way those who are in need."[64] Vatican II sees generosity to the poor as a venerable tradition in the church, and a practice to be expected from priests.

Most importantly, the relationship of priests to the poor is a privileged one. The council states that those who take on the likeness of Christ in the sacrament of orders are to seek him in the people to whom they are sent, "especially the poor, little children, the weak,

sinners and unbelievers.''[65] This admonition, given in the document
on priestly formation, makes it clear that Vatican II defines poverty
in terms of a wide variety of human needs which demand the special
attention of ordained ministers.

This broad spectrum of pastoral responsibilities is repeatedly
highlighted. Bishops are told that they are to be especially solicitous
for the poor and the weak,[66] and priests are to show paternal charity
toward the poor and the sick.[67] Attention is drawn to the lot of
women in society and to the inequality of educational and cultural
benefits available to them.[68] The pastoral activity of bishops is to be
weighted in favor of the poor, the suffering, and those undergoing
persecution for the sake of justice.[69] This concrete option for the
poor is most clearly articulated by the council in relationship to the
messianic identity of Jesus: "Although priests owe service to everybody, the poor and the weaker ones have been committed to their
care in a special way. It was with these that the Lord himself associated, and the preaching of the gospel to them is given as a sign of
his messianic mission.''[70] A spirituality focused on service to those in
need marks priests as disciples of Jesus and distinctive participants in
his saving work.

Leadership in the image of Jesus begins with the willingness of
priests to associate with the poor and the outcast. This personal
identification with the needy is a concrete expression of love for
them and a witness to gospel values. The friendship which the leaders
of the ecclesial community extend to the most neglected in society
elevates the poor to a place in the public consciousness which they
would not have otherwise. By inviting the poor into their homes and
into their circle of influence the ordained gather them into the heart
of the community.[71] Identification with the poor both in friendship
and in a simple way of life is a true service to them.

Not only do priests serve the poor by their personal generosity
to them, but as leaders of the community they thereby give an example which encourages the local church to fulfill the messianic option
for the poor to which it is committed as an assembly of believers.
Since the ordained are public persons who make concrete in their
own lives the ideals for which the ecclesial community strives, it is
appropriate that they be a leaven within the church, calling it to
extraordinary charity to the poor.

Those who preach and teach within the ecclesial community
have exceptional importance and influence. Vatican II makes it clear
that this responsibility rests in a special way upon the ordained.[72]
Since their office requires them constantly to articulate the teaching

of the church on charity and justice, presbyteral spirituality must empower priests to proclaim the truth with courage and patience. Instruction begins with the most basic moral concepts; the council gives a poignant example: "Every man has the right to possess a sufficient amount of the earth's goods for himself and his family. . . . When a person is in extreme necessity he has the right to supply himself with what he needs out of the riches of others."[73] Fundamental principles will continue to seem scandalous to the majority of Christians unless the community is properly initiated into the teaching of the church. Because this teaching continues to develop as the community and its leaders ponder the implications of discipleship, priests have a decisive role in bringing this reflection to bear on the life of the local church.

Teaching the gospel with the poor in mind demands insight and boldness flowing from a spirituality which combines knowledge, reflection, and concrete experience of human need. Since the entire human family is the object of the mission of the church, presbyters should have more than an ordinary understanding of the global community as ecclesial leaders. They must be particularly attentive to the admonition of the council in this regard: "The grace of renewal cannot grow in communities unless each of them expands the range of its charity to the ends of the earth, and has the same concern for those who are far away as it has for its own members."[74] In fulfilling their servant-ministry priests are often the mouthpiece for the poor, especially for those who are farthest removed from the experience of the local church.

Since their work among the poor is not a private matter, but flows from their ecclesial mission, priests teach the local church by personally serving those in need. It is not surprising, then, that Vatican II exhorts bishops to aid the poor by their example as well as by their instruction.[75] Even though presbyters influence the social order in a different way from that of the laity, they are in no way exempt from direct action in behalf of those in need. The distinction between that which is properly "spiritual" and that which is political must never be reduced to a preference for words over actions, since priests, too, are to lead and teach by what they do. In other words, pastoral leadership cannot be limited to the sanctuary, or be envisioned in terms of preaching and prayer alone. Although the sphere of their activity may differ from that of the laity, the results are to be no less tangible.

The challenge to an appropriate priestly spirituality is to carefully distinguish between that which is fitting for the ordained, and that which is proper to other members of the church. When priests support, encourage and teach the laity, they must have clarity of vision, exercise self-restraint and show a great commitment to the mission of lay people as members of the church with their own dignity, life and autonomy within the social order. The laity and clergy work together in society, but with a diversity of functions which manifests their interdependence in fulfilling the one social mission of the church. The ministry which the ordained offer must seek to empower the laity in serving those in need. Priestly spirituality is complex in this regard, since presbyters must fulfill their own distinctive role in the renewal of the social order, while enabling other members of the ecclesial community to do so as well.

It would be naive to underestimate the influence of sin in distorting social relationships. In addition to helping mobilize the community on behalf of the poor, priests seek to eradicate the source of poverty as it arises from personal and communal sinfulness, giving birth to deprivation and isolation in society. Because human beings are sinners, the entire life of the human family, both individual and social, is a dramatic struggle between good and evil, between light and darkness.[76] Society and the individuals who compose it are called to more than new insights about the poor; they are summoned to true conversion of heart which shows itself in a new way of life. Repentance, conversion and reconciliation are aspects of presbyteral ministry which liberate from sin and reorient the community to the values of the gospel. The evil lying within the human person and at the heart of society has a power that must be overcome if people are to be free and the poor are to be served.

An authentic spirituality challenges priests and laity alike to conversion and renewal through the sacrament of reconciliation. In this context presbyters represent both Christ and the church so that the faithful "may be daily more and more converted to the Lord, remembering his words: 'Repent, for the kingdom of heaven is at hand.' "[77] Since the coming of the kingdom is manifested in a special way in care for the poor, true conversion always orients Christians to this concern of Christ.

Appropriately enough, the eucharist is central to a spirituality which directs attention to the poor, since it brings the people of God together and unites all in the sacrifice and communion of the poor Christ offered for the whole human family. Vatican II proclaims: "Really sharing in the body of the Lord in the breaking of the eucharistic bread, we are taken up into communion with him and with one another."[78] Accordingly, all the good works, charity and ministries of the church are bound up with the eucharist.[79] In the eucharistic assembly priests not only gather needy and rich alike in the love of the good shepherd, but they clearly announce his messianic message about the poor. In summary of everything that the church stands for, priests invite all to communion, equally and without distinction. In doing so they summon the faithful not only to the common table of the community, but also to those concrete expressions of mutual love which manifest the one whose presence they celebrate.

An effective presbyteral spirituality must enliven the traditional ministries of preaching, reconciliation and communion, since these activities remain central to the service that priests offer to the ecclesial community. A proper understanding of priestly spirituality places the proclamation of the word and the celebration of the sacraments of penance and eucharist against the background of the messianic mission of Jesus and the church, for these ministries serve those in need by challenging the ecclesial community to live its deepest values. Far from diverting attention from the needy, these activities constantly lead back to them, giving birth to a spiritual dynamic which challenges and empowers the ecclesial community in the implementation of its messianic option for the poor. The next chapter will consider the eschatological dimension of priestly spirituality.

5.

Witnesses to the Kingdom in the World

The Eschatological Dimension of Priestly Spirituality

The church exists in the world, yet claims, as integral to its mission, an ultimate goal lying beyond the sphere of historical growth and human evolution. It participates in the human enterprise and contributes to the well-being of society while seeking completion in a realm which surpasses human creativity. The ecclesial community witnesses to human values at the same time that it locates the foundation of these values in a God who transcends history and material reality.

The church is by definition a pilgrim, for its source of life and its goal transcend visible reality. Linked to the material world by human nature and by the very words and signs which mediate its life, the church seeks its true home in a kingdom which is yet to come. Although its members see temporal words and actions as important factors in attaining future beatitude, they do not propose themselves and their activity as the primary determinants of the kingdom nor earthly happiness as the fulfillment of human life.

The church cannot be understood in terms of visible reality and human history alone, for while embracing temporal existence and all that it implies, the ecclesial community explains its being and mission by reaching beyond the material to the saving activity of God. The council proclaims that the church journeys on earth like an exile in a foreign land: "She seeks and is concerned about those things which are above, where Christ is seated at the right hand of God, where the life of the church is hidden with Christ in God until she appears in glory with her spouse."[1]

The pilgrim nature of the earthly church transforms the way in which the ecclesial community views history, the value of the human person, and the destiny of the human race. The Christian community maintains that beneath the changes of life there is much that is unchanging because it has its ultimate foundation in Christ "who is the same yesterday, and today, and forever."[2] From this transcendent perspective the human person is seen as having more than temporal value. Accordingly, Vatican II maintains that human beings are not deceived when they see themselves as superior to the material world, and more important than a fleeting phenomenon in the ebb and flow of history.[3] Because human beings possess an immortal soul with a destiny which is truly spiritual and transcendent, they are able to meet the divine in the depth of their hearts.

Vatican II declares that the human person has a dignity and freedom rooted both in human consciousness and in the authority of conscience: "For man has in his heart a law inscribed by God. His dignity lies in observing this law, and by it he will be judged."[4] Human beings, then, are empowered to seek the creator and attain the fullness of perfection by faithfulness to God.[5]

The dignity, freedom and responsibility of the person point to a transcendent dimension in human existence. The constant testimony of history indicates that human beings will never be totally indifferent to religion, since they will always be anxious to know, if even only in a vague way, the meaning of life, activity, and death itself. It is to this inner need that the Spirit speaks.[6] Although death puts an end to the earthly mode of being, the mission of the church challenges this temporal finality and moves beyond it. The council declares that humanity was created in view of a destiny which lies outside the limits of the present mode of human life.[7] God has promised the human family a share in a life, then, which is divine and free from decay. Even in this life the church witnesses to communion with those who have already died as an affirmation of a human destiny beyond the grave.

It is precisely as the one who has risen from the dead that Christ works in the hearts of all people by the power of his Spirit. Not only does he "arouse in them a desire for the world to come, but he quickens, purifies, and strengthens the generous aspirations of mankind to make life more humane and conquer the earth for this purpose."[8] While the church claims the eschatological as its principal concern, this spiritual mission does not lessen accountability for the present age, but gives it meaning, direction and an ultimate destiny. It is in light of the transcendent and by its power that the church ministers to temporal realities. Eschatological and transcendent affirmations are not an opiate for the people, as asserted by some contemporary political ideologies, but a force promoting human dignity and responsibility.[9] Furthermore, Vatican II endorses the prevailing concern about the shape of the future, focusing attention on the present activity of God which is, even now, leading humanity to final perfection. This chapter explores, then, the eschatological dimension of presbyteral spirituality.

I. Jesus as Eschatological Witness

Although all the words and deeds of the earthly ministry of Jesus witness to an origin and goal beyond temporal reality, it is to the paschal mystery that the council returns over and over again in explaining the transcendent nature of his person.[10] It was in his passage through the cross to resurrection that Jesus destroyed death and enlightened the mystery of human dissolution and suffering.[11] Consequently, the risen Christ is the goal of history, "the alpha and omega, the first and the last, the beginning and the end."[12] Because he triumphed over death, he is constituted both Lord and second Adam; thus he is the new model of the human race.

Accordingly, the risen and glorified Christ gives a new definition to human existence; he is the origin of and pattern for not only the earthly renewal, but also the eschatological fulfillment of the human race. The resurrection and ascension of Christ establish him, then, as the new human one and the only way to the full realization of humanity's potential, since it is in him that the perfection of human existence is found. As the new foundation of the race, Christ's risen body reveals the true greatness of the human calling.[13] In his journey through death into the life of the resurrection Jesus brings eschatological reality to full light. His passage from ordinary temporal existence through the paschal mystery is seen by the council as a birth into a new mode of life.

Christians are challenged, then, to find in Christ the perfect model of the human race. In a milieu which looks to the human sciences and psychological processes for insights into authentic development, the council is clear in its insistence that Christ most perfectly captures the nature and potential of humanity. Thus, he is not just another example of the race to be studied, but the only true measure of its reality; Christ alone reveals what human beings are called to be. This does not subvert the importance of unimpeded scientific investigations; rather, it puts them into context and sees them as aids to a human family seeking to come to the fullness revealed in the risen Christ. The Christian community better understands the human nature of Christ through philosophical, psychological and other scientific and ordered forms of investigation.

Although the sciences have a necessary autonomy,[14] nonetheless they serve a theological and spiritual function when focused on Christ. Welcoming assistance from the broader community in penetrating more deeply into the mystery of Christ is essential to an authentic spirituality today. True discipleship is challenged to use the tools of philosophy, psychology, sociology and the other human sciences in a way which does not make them into a quasi-spirituality, but enables them to point the way to Christ, since knowing him and entering into his way of life are the proper objectives of Christian spirituality. As a living person Jesus defines the truth about human nature, its goal, and its way to perfection; Vatican II declares: "Whoever follows Christ the perfect man becomes himself more a man."[15]

From his place at the right hand of the Father, Christ invites all to participate in the mystery of his passover. Whether the way is clearly understood by believers or only dimly perceived by those who have not yet heard the gospel, the whole human race is invited to participate in this paschal journey.[16] Bound by nature to the experience of death, humanity is summoned by Christ to its ultimate transformation beyond the grave; thus, the mystery of human dissolution becomes the path to a new mode of life. Since Christ in glory is the goal and perfection of humanity, human fulfillment is by definition eschatological inasmuch as the destiny of the race is summed up in his person.

Christ shares his paschal victory with the human family in two stages of human existence.[17] The earthly church experiences the effects of the resurrection during its temporal pilgrimage in a period of realized eschatology. The heavenly church rests now in a state of fulfillment as it awaits the renewal of the human race in the second coming of Christ and the resurrection of the body.

The dominion of Christ, then, is already partially realized in the earthly church, for it is truly experienced through participation in the communion of love and worship by those born to eternal life in baptism. In other words, the life of the church is a foretaste of the perfect glory yet to come. Although the two stages of the paschal journey are distinct and separated by death and judgment, they share in and express the same eschatological reality; the future will bring the present to full flower.[18]

The risen and ascended Christ is truly the first-born of many brothers and sisters.[19] His kingdom, which is at the same time present and yet to come, is foreshadowed in a new human community which participates in his eschatological life.[20] The tangible communion of the church is the kingdom of Christ already present in mystery and growing visibly by the power of God in the world.[21] Through the church the eschatological reign of Christ has an observable presence and impact within the historical process.

Christ constitutes and strengthens his eschatological kingdom and brings it to fulfillment by working in the midst of temporal reality through the power of the Holy Spirit.[22] Sent by the risen Jesus, the Spirit is active in the foundation and continuing growth of the ecclesial community, the raising up of witnesses to the kingdom, and the celebration of the sacraments. It is in the eucharist, especially, that a foretaste of the eschatological banquet is given to those still living in the midst of the temporal sphere. Through the eucharist Christ nourishes the ecclesial community with his glorified body and blood, thereby giving it both a promise of eschatological fulfillment and food for its pilgrim journey.

Since the ecclesial community itself is the primary consequence of the eucharist, it is, as such, a promise of the perfect heavenly communion yet to come.[23] Through the eucharist the Spirit empowers members of the church to witness to the kingdom by the way in which they live in the human community; thus the entire life of the church bears an eschatological imprint. As a result, the foreshadowing of the future kingdom is seen most clearly in the rhythm of worship and charity which are the primary activities of the ecclesial community, and, therefore, constitutive elements of Christian spirituality.

Since the glorified Jesus continues to exercise his earthly ministry through the Holy Spirit, the eucharist, effected by the Spirit, makes the person and sacrifice of Christ present in the pilgrim community in a way which allows the earthly church to already participate in the glorious fulfillment of the cross. The Holy Spirit and the eucharist form a bridge between the temporal and the heavenly church; thus, it is precisely because humanity is nourished on the glorified Christ in the eucharist that the power of the kingdom breaks into the earthly realm, transforming the human family in his image.[24] Through the liturgy the spirit of Christ joins the pilgrim church to the heavenly community, associating it with the worship and fellowship of the eschatological kingdom and configuring it to its way of life.[25]

This correlation between Christ in glory, on one hand, and the activity of the Spirit, the eucharist, and the church, on the other, is very important for Christian spirituality, since through the latter Christ is present in the world, preparing it for its consummation at his second coming. All are called, then, to participate in Christ who is active as the definitive human fulfillment through these realities which join earthly existence and eschatological perfection. The Holy Spirit, the eucharist, and the church are, therefore, the basic dynamic elements of the spiritual life.

Inasmuch as the final age has begun and the renewal of the world is already underway, the new heaven and the new earth are in a real sense anticipated in the earthly church which, as the body of Christ, is endowed with his sanctity, even if in an imperfect way.[26] Because Christian spirituality points to those things which are above, where Christ is seated at the right hand of God, it brings eschatological realities to bear on temporal existence.[27] Thus participation in Christ gives transcendent value to every aspect of earthly life. An authentic spirituality rightly involves disciples in everyday events, since they live in the world, use material things, and benefit from scientific and cultural insights and advancements; yet, it challenges them to live in light of their faith that the kingdom is already achieved, although hidden in Christ. Hence Christians are to draw meaning, energy and direction from this kingdom, witnessing to its existence and moving by its power.

All aspects of the Christian life, then, are to testify that Christ reigns even now, and that his sovereignty will be solemnly manifested at his second coming when "death will be no more and all things will be subjected to him."[28] In the final state of the human family all creation will be ordered to Christ, for when he comes again he will assert his lordship by judging the living and the dead, renewing all things in the likeness of his resurrection, and presenting a universal kingdom to the Father.[29] Hence, the glorified Christ is not only the measure of human perfection, but also the judge of good and evil. He will apportion reward or punishment to each person according to what he or she has done during the earthly journey, as he divides the human race between those called to the resurrection of life and those condemned to the resurrection of judgment.[30] Then, the service which Jesus gave through suffering and death during his earthly life will become the ministry of judgment and authority in the time of consummation. These two dimensions of his saving work have a single purpose, bringing the church to the fullness of life.

The eschatological reign of Christ brings distinctive values into focus and challenges discipleship in a new way. Thus the forgiving Christ is also the just judge. The gentle servant also subjects all things to his authority. Jesus who died to give light and life also permits eternal darkness and death. Although temporal and eschatological existence follow one another in the life of Jesus and lend a particular character to each stage of his mission, the values of each stage co-exist and interact throughout the whole of his ministry. Therefore, the spirituality of those who seek to imitate Christ and to share his values must enable them to choose appropriately between forgiveness and judgment, gentleness and authority in the quandary of daily life.

Since the eschatological permeates the temporal, these two ways of serving can never be simplistically separated from one another; the authority and judgment of the kingdom influences earthly life, just as mercy and gentleness are eschatological values as well. Inasmuch as a balanced spirituality demands that Christians pattern themselves on Jesus both as suffering servant and as authoritative Lord, the dynamic interaction between the two gives strength to gentleness and sensitivity to authority.

Because human history will reach its zenith at the moment of the second coming of Jesus, Vatican II pictures all of creation as groaning and watching for this time of eschatological fulfillment; then the world itself, which is so intimately related to the human race, will also be perfected in Christ.[31] Not only is the present age with the distortions of sin passing away, but material creation itself is awaiting transformation, impatient to be set free from bondage to decay when Christ returns. Then death and weakness will be destroyed as God establishes a new earthly dwelling place exceeding all human desires.

Significantly enough, love will continue as the life of the kingdom.[32] Because there is no absolute separation between the temporal and the eschatological, the accomplishments of humanity during its earthly sojourn will continue into the time of fulfillment, but they will be cleansed from sin and transfigured as the offering Christ makes to his Father. Finally, that which began as promise, foretaste and expectation will come to perfection in the saints gathered by the Spirit around the Father and Christ the Lamb in adoration and love.[33]

Christian discipleship is by its very nature focused on this future moment, cherishing and pursuing a perfection which transcends earthly existence. Thus, both a contemplative attitude fixed on Christ in glory and a sense of discernment which evaluates the temporal in light of the life to come are essential features of the spiritual life. Neither the way of life nor the specific choices of the followers of Jesus can be judged by temporal criteria alone, for, in fact, these flow from a vision of reality which is more than earthly. Conversely, outside of an eschatological perspective gospel values are difficult to justify and burdensome to maintain, since they are a response to the risen Christ and participate in the vision, energy and goal of the new people established in him.

II. The Church as Eschatological Witness

The church is a visible organization that "in its sacraments and institutions, which belong to this present age, carries the mark of this world which will pass"; thus, as a spiritual community, it takes its place "among the creatures which groan and travail yet and await the revelation of the sons of God."[34] While the ecclesial community contains both divine and human elements, those which are visible and those which are invisible, it is present in the world in a way which directs the human to the divine, the visible to the invisible, activity to contemplation, and life in the present world to an anticipated joy in that which is yet to come.[35] Hence, the ecclesial community has an eschatological purpose which can be fully attained only in the next life.[36]

As stated earlier, the earthly church shares the historical journey of the human race inasmuch as its members truly belong to the temporal city. Yet, it transcends the limitations of earthly existence and acts as an instrument of the risen Christ; thus, the ecclesial community has as its mission the proclamation and establishment of the kingdom until it is perfected in a glory which is beyond temporal existence.[37]

As a pilgrim people the church uses earthly signs to manifest divine realities, for in tangible actions the ecclesial community is nourished, worship is given to God, and grace is received.[38] The earthly and the heavenly city penetrate one another, then, in a mysterious way which will be revealed only at the end of the current age. In the meantime, the church exists as an eschatological witness in the midst of earthly realities and employs the temporal to serve the human race and to challenge it to prefigure its fulfillment in a world yet to come.

Vatican II makes it clear that the church has a strictly religious purpose, revealing the mystery of the Lord in the world until he is manifested in full light at his final coming. Consequently the very mission of the church is eschatological inasmuch as it does not have an institutional goal in the political, economic or social order, as such.[39] Nevertheless, there are close links between the things of earth and those aspects of the human condition which transcend the present world. Therefore, the church uses temporal realities to advance its eschatological mission, while at the same time rousing the human community to the renewal of civic life.[40] Yet, its presence and activity in society have only one purpose: "that the kingdom of God may come and the salvation of the human race may be accomplished."[41]

Every benefit offered by the church to society is rooted in its identity as the sacrament of salvation which manifests and demonstrates the love of God for all.

Thus, the eschatological mission of the church challenges its members to see themselves as people with definite obligations within the social order, but always in a context which invites them beyond present occupations and concerns to a fulfillment which is religious, transcendent, and yet to come. Such a sound spirituality preserves a religious focus and a transcendent goal, while freeing Christians to work with the temporal realities which mediate present participation in the kingdom of God. This spirituality does not invite them to accentuate the next world and abandon the present one, but constantly to seek the eschatological through the mediation of daily life.

Furthermore, the church's identity as the eschatological community is witnessed to by the universality of its membership. As one people it unites men and women of every race, culture and nation, making of them a community which transcends human divisions. Since a worldwide communion created by the Holy Spirit is itself a present manifestation of the promised kingdom,[42] appreciation of legitimate diversity, involvement in ecumenism, and dialogue with non-Christians are important aspects of an ecclesial spirituality.[43]

Since the earthly church exists in the present world like a stranger in a foreign land,[44] Vatican II offers a number of signs which identify pilgrim members of the eschatological community. They are free from slavery to riches because they are in search of goods which will last. Exerting their energies in extending the kingdom, they bring a Christian spirit to the revitalization of society.[45] Thus, they struggle with evil, suffering and death, yet go forward in hope as participants in the paschal mystery.[46] Inasmuch as they witness to the future kingdom both by explicit proclamation and by service to society,[47] eschatological faith binds them to earthly responsibilities; hence, social and professional life are seen as means of expressing future hope.[48] Putting self-love aside, they use temporal resources to serve human life so that one day the human family itself may be an acceptable offering to God.[49]

Vatican II affirms that there are many diverse ways in which eschatological realities are made present in the world through the life of the pilgrim church. It finds vivid and explicit testimony to future hope in religious life, Christian celibacy, and contemplative prayer. Accordingly, religious life witnesses to the fact that "the people of God has here no lasting city but seeks the city which is to come. . . ."[50] In greater freedom from the concerns of temporal life, religious more clearly reveal the eschatological realities which are already a part of the present age. They give visible expression to the new way of life made possible now by the redemptive work of Christ, and capable of reaching perfection in the glory of the heavenly kingdom.

Religious life witnesses to the transcendence of the kingdom of God and the precedence which it takes over all temporal realities, since those committed to the consecrated life focus attention, in a distinctive way, on the charity, communion and worship which are its present manifestations.[51] Participating in the vitality of the kingdom, the characteristic charisms of religious impart greater effectiveness to their apostolic endeavors.[52] Furthermore, celibacy for the sake of the kingdom recalls the wonderful marriage between God and humanity to be fully manifested in the future age.[53] It offers evidence of the power of Christ active here and now through the Holy Spirit for the salvation of all.

Religious priests offer a special witness to the kingdom through the lifestyle and gifts of their religious institute. For this reason the council asserts that the common foundations of the Christian life, the special characteristics of vowed religious, and the spiritual charisms proper to each institute are to be treasured, deepened and made constitutive elements of the distinctive expression of the ministerial priesthood embraced by them.[54] They are called to religious life so that they may have "a special gift of grace in the life of the church and may contribute, each in his own way, to the saving mission of the church."[55] Because holiness and effectiveness flow from one's total being and lifestyle, the gifts of religious life are an important aspect of the identity of many priests; as such they contribute to their credibility and forcefulness as witnesses to the kingdom.

Service rendered to others also witnesses to the coming of the kingdom and prepares for the eschatological perfection of the human race. The age to come is, therefore, foreshadowed in a new human family, already present and growing in the world. This is evident in its pursuit of human dignity, fraternal communion, and true freedom. Although it is necessary to carefully distinguish between earthly progress and the increase of the kingdom of God, nevertheless the former is important to the latter in that it builds a better ordered society and already expresses the work of grace.[56]

The visible church is bound to a larger assembly of believers by the Spirit in a communion of love which transcends the temporal order. As already indicated, the one church of Christ presently embraces several modes of ecclesial existence. The council says that some of the followers of Christ are pilgrims on earth; others have died and are being purified. Discipleship's goal is already achieved in still others who are in glory, contemplating "in full light, God himself triune and one, exactly as he is."[57] All stages of ecclesial existence share in the same charity toward God and neighbor, and all participate in the same divine worship; thus the entire church is united in adoration, love and witness.

Since the ecclesial relationships which began in the proclaimed word and the sacraments of baptism and eucharist continue beyond the boundaries of temporal existence, ecclesial ministry serves a communion of charity which is broader than the visible church. Christian spirituality extends charity past the limits of the earthly sphere, and places the solicitude of the pilgrim church at the disposal of those who lie outside of the visible community, yet truly belong to its fullness. In serving the needs of deceased members of the church who are undergoing purification, Christians manifest the work of the Spirit who unites the total church in communion and in works of ministry.[58] Accordingly, this apostolate of solidarity and prayer is an expression of ecclesial faithfulness and eschatological faith.

The saints in glory, who constitute the ultimate mode of ecclesial existence, are those who gave testimony to the kingdom in their earthly lives and now rest secure in its realization. In remembering their temporal journey the church has evidence of the work of the Spirit in people presently living in various states and conditions of life. In celebrating their triumph the ecclesial community recognizes the diversity of human endeavors which lead to full union with Christ, who is "the crown of all the saints."[59]

The vast community of saints is both a sign of the kingdom already present, and a promise of its future coming.[60] In its devotional life the ecclesial community recognizes the powerful ways in which the kingdom has penetrated temporal existence in every time and place, and finds examples for its own pilgrim journey. Therefore, it sees the saints as members of the church who understood the eschatological significance of earthly life and enjoy its promised fulfillment in a more complete way.

Furthermore, through the prayers of the saints the pilgrim church is both sustained and enhanced; thus, the heavenly assembly, in union with the glorified Christ, exercises a true ministry to the earthly community.[61] Vatican II affirms that just as Christ's priesthood is shared in various ways by his ministers and the faithful, and the goodness of God is radiated in different ways by his creatures, "so also the unique mediation of the redeemer does not exclude but rather gives rise to a manifold cooperation which is but a sharing in this one source."[62] These words, applied to Mary in a special way, also appertain to all the members of the heavenly church; and so the pilgrim community cherishes and is enriched by the intercession of the saints.

The council proposes Mary as "the type of the church in the order of faith, charity, and perfect union with Christ."[63] Therefore, as virgin and mother she is what the ecclesial community seeks to be—espoused to Christ and fruitful in grace. The role of Mary, as image of the church come to full eschatological perfection, gives a broader ecclesial vision to Christian spirituality and strikes a powerful blow at the distortions of clericalism.[64] Since "Mary has by grace been exalted above all angels and men to a place second only to her Son"[65] without participating in the hierarchical structure of the church, she clearly witnesses to the primacy of holiness, that is, "perfect union with Christ,"[66] as the goal of the Christian community. It is significant that the mother of Jesus is offered to all, clergy and laity alike, as the model of the ecclesial community come to full stature. Because the church strives to be like Mary in her union with Christ, pastoral ministry and priestly spirituality must be ordered to the attainment of this goal.

Animated and drawn together by the Spirit of Jesus, members of the pilgrim Church press forward to the consummation of history in the final coming of Christ.[67] Then heaven and earth will be united in him, and the ecclesial community will be perfected when Christ, as Lord of all, will change the earthly bodies of his members to be like his in glory. Then those who as earthly pilgrims possessed the Spirit as guarantee of a heavenly inheritance will become like God, seeing him as he is. Thus, having brought the church which is his fullness to perfection,[68] Christ will be glorified and marveled at in his saints.[69] The goal having been attained, the church of the saints will adore God and the Lamb in the supreme happiness of charity.[70]

III. Priests as Witnesses to the Kingdom

Since the ordained are conformed to Christ both as members of the church and as sharers in the apostolic ministry, they participate in his eschatological mission and in the transcendent orientation of the entire community. As members and ministers of a church which longs for future fulfillment, priests share attitudes which challenge them to treat temporal realities in a distinctive way, since they serve a kingdom which is mysteriously, yet really, present now, while entering into its perfection only when the Lord comes again.[71] Therefore, the values by which they live are often counter-cultural or paradoxical. As a result, an authentic presbyteral spirituality challenges priests to identify with eschatological values by trusting in the hidden power of God and by accepting their own weakness as instruments of the gospel.[72]

Rather than being discouraged by the difficulties they encounter, priests are to be continually nourished by contemplation, and thereby brought to greater holiness.[73] They are to grasp with mind and heart the concealed meaning of what they are about. Because this regular interaction both with the person of the risen Christ and with the concerns and values of the kingdom must manifest itself in the way priests live, Vatican II proposes two areas for their consideration: power and relationships.

The council says quite bluntly that the task to which priests have been called is beyond human power, since the proclamation and establishment of the kingdom is made effective by the might of God alone.[74] Moreover, God chooses the weak to draw attention to the primacy of his own power and activity. Thus, as members of the church, and still more as its public ministers, priests are to pattern their lives on the will of God and to seek to fulfill it with the help of the Holy Spirit. The immensity of the task constantly challenges them to admit their weakness and to live and work in the strength which the Spirit provides. As those who are sacramentally conformed to Christ, they have already received the first fruits of the Spirit which make it possible to fulfill the new law of love; yet, the Spirit and the charity which the Spirit effects are given as a promise of an inheritance which will be fully realized only in the time of resurrection.[75]

Consequently, the paschal mystery is the fundamental pattern for the initiation of the reign of God in the world,[76] since the relationship between human weakness, suffering and death, and total trust in the power of God, on one hand, and the gift of resurrection and the newness of life, on the other, lies at the heart of the Christian faith.[77] An accurate assessment of the human situation as understood by the gospel leads to an appreciation of the eschatological nature of the task and a recognition of the impotence of unaided humanity in its fulfillment. The wisdom flowing from this insight makes it imperative that priests avoid the heresy of activism by opening themselves to the activity of the Spirit in the midst of the concerns of ministry. An attitude of receptivity to a ministerial competence which only God can impart is essential to priestly spirituality.

Relationships, too, are to be oriented to the kingdom and to

draw their strength from it. Because celibacy freely embraced for the
sake of the kingdom allows disciples to hold fast to the Lord with an
undivided love, the council proposes it as "profoundly in harmony
with the new covenant."[78] It recommends celibacy, then, as a witness
to the future resurrection and as a means to the pastoral charity
demanded in the present for effective ministry. Vatican II sees this
radical reorientation of the most basic human capacity for affective
relationships toward eschatological realities, which an authentic
commitment to celibacy involves, as a manifestation of the kingdom
in the temporal sphere. Hence celibacy is a way of being in the world
which mediates, here and now, a tangible experience of the future
kingdom. Since it is a temporal reality which mediates grace, dedicated celibacy partakes of the sacramental nature of the church in a
way which is analogous to Christian marriage.

As a sign of the reality of eschatological joy, celibacy announces
the mystical marriage between Christ and the church, thereby witnessing to the state of the ecclesial community at the time of its
fulfillment. Since celibates seek to participate in that relationship by
which "the church holds Christ as her only spouse,"[79] they enter
more deeply into the vision, orientation and dynamic of ecclesial life.
Celibacy is not meant, then, to separate priests from the baptized,
but to bring them into their midst in a dedicated way. The assurance
that celibacy is truly an ecclesial reality is confirmed by the insistence
of the council that it produces pastoral charity.[80]

Both a receptive humility and a singlehearted celibacy testify to
the way in which power and relationships must be transformed by an
effective spirituality if priests are to serve the future orientated life of
the church. Since Vatican II describes priests as those who "assemble
the family of God as a brotherhood fired with a single ideal, and
through Christ in the Spirit . . . lead to God the Father,"[81] this
transformation is essential. While the exercise of priestly ministry is
present and temporal, its objective is transcendent and eschatological. Therefore, the goal which lies behind every pastoral activity must
be the completion of the journey of the baptized through Christ in
the Spirit to the Father.

This eschatological orientation of presbyteral spirituality does
not detract from the importance of temporal endeavors, but it always
sees behind them a significance which transcends earthly existence.
Consequently, it is because of the eschatological mission of the
church and in the implementation of it that priests contribute to the
welfare of the human family. Their ministry fosters the mission of the

church which, in pursuing a salvific and trans-historical goal, heals individuals, elevates the dignity of the person, unifies society, and endows human activity with a deeper sense of purpose.[82]

The influence of the eschatological orientation of priestly spirituality on the present age is seen most clearly in the eucharist, since it is to this sacramental moment that all the activities of presbyteral ministry are directed.[83] Here, a ministry which begins in the proclamation of the gospel is consummated in the eucharistic sacrifice. It is important to remember than an appropriate spirituality leads not only to participation in the death of the Lord in the eucharist, but also partakes of his resurrection and the new life of the Spirit. The gathering of the community in worship of the Father through the efficacy of the paschal mystery is a foretaste of the eschatological banquet and a promise of its fulfillment.[84]

The eucharistic assembly both manifests the kingdom and participates in it, since in this celebration the whole church is gathered, pilgrim community and heavenly multitude. Here, Christ exercises his headship, leading his people in worship of the Father through their participation in the mystery of his dying and rising.[85] Through the ministry of presbyters the heavenly banquet is anticipated and its effects are made visible in the temporal sphere.[86] By means of sacramental signs the Holy Spirit acts in the eucharistic assembly, joining all those redeemed by the blood of Christ in the common song of rejoicing and praise offered the divine majesty by the one church.[87] In this way the pilgrim church prefigures eschatological realities, is invigorated and transformed by them, and lives the present moment in light of a future it has already experienced through the eucharist.

Solidarity in the communion of faith and love which derives from the eucharist and manifests itself in mutual service must increase until it is brought to fulfillment in the heavenly kingdom.[88] The eucharist is central to the life of the church and pivotal for the spirituality of priests because it is that food for the Christian journey which already contains the heavenly banquet that it promises.[89]

It is clear, then, that the eschatological dimension of the eucharistic assembly has immense importance for priestly spirituality. While it is true that the words and signs of liturgical celebration are rooted in the temporal and must have significance and effectiveness there, the liturgy is in no sense pedestrian, since in it the Christian community articulates its deepest meaning and experiences its ultimate mode of existence. An approach to the eucharist which seeks simply to enlighten and intensify life within the temporal sphere does not move deeply enough, no matter how humanly enriching it may be. It is crucial that priests understand what they are celebrating and invite others to the fullest possible participation in the fraternal and transcendent dimensions of the eucharist.

Thus, the responsibility for leading the eucharistic assembly is a complex one. As those who preside in the person of Christ, presbyters must foster both the communal or ecclesial dimension of Christian worship and its messianic thrust toward service of the poor, while at the same time encouraging an awareness of the eschatological promise which makes such community and service possible. The prominence which Vatican II gives to the eucharist underscores the fact that earthly service and community flow from the participation of the pilgrim church in the heavenly assembly. In a like manner, community and service, rooted in the eucharist, lead to the heavenly assembly and contribute to its ultimate perfection. This understanding of the eschatological significance of the eucharist and its relationship to the earthly mission of the church is essential to a healthy eucharistic piety among priests and people alike.

As teachers, priests are to articulate the relationship between the temporal and the eschatological, presenting them as modes of existence which must be embraced simultaneously by Christians, inasmuch as the earthly mediates the heavenly, and in turn the future exerts its power within the temporal sphere. The tendency of some to choose an overly transcendent and disembodied spirituality, and the preference of others for an excessively utilitarian and materialistic approach, must be balanced by the incarnational vision which lies at the heart of an appropriate priestly spirituality. Because the temporal and the eschatological are intimately linked in the vision of Vatican II, the heavenly kingdom is not an excuse for abandoning the world, but an invitation to a paschal journey which leads through earthly life to the perfect realization of humanity in the reign of God which lies beyond it.

Pastoral activity, then, is to be shaped by the paschal mystery in seeking to penetrate every aspect of human life with the power and vision of the journey of Jesus. Accordingly, priestly ministry itself will find completion only in the glorious coming of the Lord.[90] Then what was begun in the temporal sphere for the glory of God and the benefit of humanity will find its fullest expression in the company of the saints in glory. The ultimate goal of presbyteral spirituality is that Jesus return in glory and his people realize their potential to become saints.

The eschatological significance of earthly life is verified by the insistence of the council that mutual love and communal worship are the most noble activities of the church and together constitute a foretaste of the heavenly liturgy; it is this love and worship which the Lord will bring to perfection at his coming.[91] By the spirituality pervading their leadership and teaching, priests offer the people of God intimate fellowship with the Christ who is already present in these realities, and yet to come.

Priestly spirituality, then, has a twofold goal. While it seeks the effective establishment of the kingdom now, it looks beyond present successes and failures to a future resurrection and a share in the reign of God. Since the present and the future interact with one another and are complementary, it is sometimes necessary to choose between immediate success and ultimate victory. Commitment to the values of the kingdom is tested in making judgments about the relationship between present accomplishments and eschatological fulfillment. The limited success or apparent failure of Jesus in his own ministry highlights an apparent dilemma, underscoring the fact that pastoral leadership stands or falls by the standards of the paschal mystery.[92]

The final state to which the priestly activity of the baptized is directed is variously described as the marriage feast of the Lamb, the heavenly banquet, the final gathering of all under the headship of Christ, and the perfect revelation of the beloved family of God.[93] Vatican II sees the task entrusted to ordained priests as "espousing the faithful to one husband and presenting them as a chaste virgin to Christ."[94] Presbyteral spirituality is centered on bringing the community to full union with the Lord. Since Christ is always the sole mediator, in the heavenly city he alone is the light, the priest and the sacrifice. Because the sacraments and institutions of the church belong to the present time,[95] when Christ returns, sacramental presence and priesthood will find completion in him. After the purpose of pastoral service has been fulfilled, charity and its consequences will remain, and all creation will be renewed, elevated and made perfect in Christ.[96]

The very existence of the ordained among the baptized affirms that the church in its preaching, sacraments, and activities is necessary for the salvation of those engaged in the earthly pilgrimage.[97] Yet in the midst of these temporal necessities a mature spirituality is focused on those things which endure—union of the community with Christ and a love which subjects all things to the Father. Not being misled or unduly impressed by the structures of the present age, priests are to recognize that an authentic spirituality consists in the communion of truth and love.

These reflections complete the survey of the teaching of the Second Vatican Council on the ministerial priesthood. Each element considered in the last four chapters has a role to play in explaining the complex spirituality of ordained ministry, and each was meant to enhance and balance the others. Taken together they offer the theological background for a consideration of the teaching of the bishops of the United States which implements the vision of the council on presbyteral spirituality.

6.

Members of the Church
and Sacraments
of Christ's Servant–Headship

The Bond Between Membership and Leadership
in Priestly Spirituality

T ension can be either positive, revealing diverse and complementary aspects of a complex reality, or negative, provoking the disintegration of the entity undergoing stress. The council documents on priestly ministry lay bare two tensions which it proposes as healthy and positive, for they derive from a necessary complexity in articulating a spirituality of ordained ministry which is authentic in itself and credible to others.

The tension between priests seen as members of the church and society, on one hand, and as leaders of these same communities, on the other, is the subject of this chapter. The tension between priestly ministry as a service to temporal realities, and the same ministry as a service to a future kingdom, will be treated in the next chapter. In providing teaching, example and strategy to help resolve the contemporary quandary regarding priestly identity, the bishops of the United States offer an important service to the ecclesial community.

I. Christ as Member and Leader of the Human Community

The complexity of the ecclesial community, and of the role of the ordained within it, has its origin in the belief of the Christian community about the identity of Christ. The American bishops, in offering guidance to priests, stress the significance of the fact that Christ shares fully not only in the nature of God, but also in humanity. This affirmation creates tension within the life of the entire church, and especially in the lives of priests, since the ecclesial community and its ministers also share in both the divine and the human nature of Christ. In a true yet analogous way, Christians participate in both the life of God and the condition of humanity.[1]

The uniqueness of Jesus both in his role and in the origin of his authority is a constant focus in the teaching of the American bishops. "There is only one priesthood, the priesthood of Jesus Christ. Jesus is the sole mediator between the human family and God."[2] These words of Cardinal Joseph Bernardin, the archbishop of Chicago, are often echoed in the statements of the bishops. Thus, there is but one ministry and service which God lavishes on creation, that which he

111

gives through his Son in the power of the Holy Spirit.[3] The risen Jesus is the only priest and the unique mediator between God and his people.[4] He alone is the priest of his own sacrifice; hence, Jesus is the unceasing source of the priesthood in the Church.[5] The Christian community depends on the ministry of Jesus alone for initial formation and continual preservation.[6] All other ministry is a participation in his.[7]

Both the role of Jesus and his authority flow from his unconditional attachment to the will of the Father. No other love or interest can compete with that relationship.[8] Moreover, since Jesus came as a spokesman for God, he stood not only within the human community but also against it. As prophet, his primary function was to uncover the presence of the divine by being sensitive to God in the midst of contemporary issues.[9] He served the human community by pointing to the consequences of the divine presence.

Jesus announced his unique identity within the context of his mission as the agent of God's saving love. The fact that he was a man of God made him also a man for others. He applied to himself the title "Son of Man" in order to avoid mistaken political interpretations of his mission.[10] First and foremost he was the servant of the God of Israel.

The American bishops underscore the fact that Jesus entered fully into the condition of the human family in order to accomplish a saving mission having its origins in God. It is precisely because he totally accepted human nature that Jesus has this saving ministry.[11] The bishops' document *As One Who Serves* sees this as one of the great paradoxes of Christ's life: "a leader, exercising authority by seeing himself as friend to those over whom he exercises authority and his subjects responding with their friendship."[12] At the heart of this paradox is the unique mission and divine authority of Jesus expressed as service from the humble vantage point of true solidarity with the human family. The result of the concurrence of the divine and the human in Jesus, that is, an origin from above and from below, is profound friendship and reconciliation.

The reconciliation of the divine and the human expresses itself most radically in the paschal mystery. This divine-human friendship is not an easily achieved reality, since Jesus must die as the servant of reconciliation if he is to show the way to true life. As the one anointed by the Holy Spirit for service, the true nature of his ministry is made unmistakably clear by his death and resurrection.[13] Enigmatically, in reconciling the divine and the human Jesus makes death the path to life. This creative tension gives birth to the church and its ministers; thus, Christian asceticism must focus on the reconciliation of the divine and the human by living the paschal mystery if it is to be faithful to the example of Jesus.

Jesus claimed to be the very compassion of God,[14] since in becoming a servant, in entering into the human condition, he revealed the depth of God's love for the human family.[15] Therefore, when the early church reflected upon the ministry of Jesus, it saw him as the divine Son who gives God's life and, at the same time, as the brother who was taken from among the human family and made its representative before God.[16] The unique identity of Jesus as the Son of God and the bearer of divine prerogatives is not compromised by his position as member and representative of the human family. In fact, it is only because he is both Son of God and son of Mary that he can fulfill his salvific role. In him the movement of God toward humanity and the movement of humanity toward God converge. An undue emphasis on either his divine or his human origin tends toward the destruction of his role of mediation and reconciliation.

Similarly, since all Christians by definition participate in both aspects of the reality of Christ, they are simultaneously creatures sought and found by God, and the graced instruments of his quest for the human family.[17] For those among the faithful who share a distinctive identity as ordained ministers within the Son's unique priesthood, the life pattern of Jesus as sanctifier, servant and leader has special importance.[18] Taking him as model, then, it is apparent that the tension between leadership in the name of Christ and membership in the church, far from rending ordained ministry, is indispensable to its mission. It is only by sharing in both that priests effectively participate in the mystery of Christ and the church and thereby play their unique role as ministers and mediators of that mystery. The integration of leadership and membership is a positive and essential aspect of the spirituality articulated by the American bishops.

On the one hand the identity of Jesus is rooted in the transcendent in a way that gives him an authority and a lifestyle which has its origin in God; thus, he is able to confront the community as well as represent it. Although Jesus is completely human, he is not simply a member of the race; for he claims for himself a personal participation in the divine nature through which the community is enriched, and by which it is led and judged. On the other hand, as a true son of Adam, Jesus shares in the joys and sorrows of humanity, and as a member of the race he is its representative before God. It is this complexity which gives Jesus authority in the relationship between the human and the divine.

The ecclesial community is thoroughly human, yet mysteriously more; although it shares the condition of the human family, it also makes present the authority and saving power of God. Ordained ministry echoes the pattern revealed in this understanding of Christ and the church. Presbyters are sharers in humanity and members of the church in the fullest meaning of these terms. Yet, they are not simply members of the church, since they participate in the mission of Christ in a distinctive way as servant-leaders who come in the name and power of the Lord. They act *in persona Christi* specifically as participants in the divine prerogatives of his servant-leadership, as well as *in persona ecclesiae* as members and representatives of the community of the baptized.

An authentic presbyteral spirituality must be rooted in both realities if priests are to take their proper place within the pattern revealed by the incarnation. Just as humanity and divinity are one in Christ, and the human and divine are joined in the church's self-understanding, so, too, the roles of Christ as leader and of Christ as member are united in the identity of the ordained. This christological principle influences all aspects of priestly spirituality, underscoring the fact that participation in the divine and human realities being served is the pattern of ministry revealed in Christ. Hence, an effective presbyteral spirituality must unite the human and divine in a way which mediates unity and peace. Just as Christ is in the church and the church is in Christ, so also are priests participants in both, ordained specifically to serve their relationship to one another.

The church of Christ is a living body composed of limited yet graced creatures, each making visible some aspect of his work of salvation.[19] Participation in Christ involves the baptized in a diversity of roles within his ecclesial body. As a community of many gifts, the church is built up by the dynamic tension between leadership and membership within individuals and among them. There is, then, an inner complexity to the Christian community. It is the effective living out of the dynamic of ecclesial relationships which allows the church to be the sacrament of Christ. In his pastoral letter on collaborative ministry, the archbishop of Baltimore, William Borders, says: "Much of the misunderstanding and conflict that often mar the life of local church communities today serve to underscore our need for a renewed sense of a common baptismal purpose and mission, and of the right and need of all the baptized to find a way to participate actively in that mission and ministry."[20] The vision of the church affirmed by the bishops of the United States insists on a multiplicity of roles within the common status belonging to all the baptized. This assertion invites priests to a spirituality which is baptismal as well as presbyteral, received from the people of God and lived among them at the same time that it ministers to them.

Turning to the second theme, it is evident that since the whole church is the sacrament of Christ, the prayers and actions of the ecclesial community and its members are Christ praying and acting.[21] Precisely because it is a sign of Christ, the church is a complex reality, its structure or concrete hierarchical constitution being a part of its sacramentality. Cardinal John O'Connor, the archbishop of New York, quotes Karl Rahner who said: "We must recognize a really christological reason for the teaching authority of the church and formulate it. . . . Now the church of Christ is the ongoing presence and the historical tangibility of this ultimate and victorious word of God in Christ Jesus. . . ."[22] Archbishop Borders reminds us of the teaching of St. Augustine: "a sacrament of a reality is that reality."[23] The ordained have a special identity, then, because of the distinctive way in which they share in the sacramentality of the church which is "a living, effective sign of Christ really present."[24]

In response to a leveling tendency in the American culture which is inclined toward blurring differences in the name of equality, James Malone, the bishop of Youngstown Ohio, and then president of the National Conference of Bishops, reported to the Secretariat of the 1985 Synod that the dichotomy between the church as communion and the church as hierarchical structure would be set in a healthier context by a renewed emphasis on the ecclesial community as Christ's mystical body.[25] Thus, while the entire church is the presence of Christ in the world, and Jesus expresses his saving action through all,[26] attention would be called to the fact that the members of the church have diverse roles and responsibilities in the community. Hierarchy and communion, leadership and membership, are necessarily related in an authentic expression of an ecclesial spirituality.

As a people redeemed and united in Christ, the church is an instrument of reconciliation. Its mission is to exist for others, not for itself.[27] The various institutions, structures, and processes of ecclesial life have validity to the extent that they enable the church to be an effective sign of Christ. Since Jesus taught that his followers were to be present to others as those who serve,[28] the ecclesial community and those who exercise authority within it are oriented, by definition, toward ministry to the human family and away from self-centered concerns about personal powers and prerogatives.[29] Moreover, that which is distinctive and specialized within the community is focused on the accomplishment of the common task; thus, the community as a whole has a mission which is furthered by the diversity of its members. The example of Jesus in combining a unique identity with a shared mission is the paradigm meant to shape an ecclesial spirituality in his image.

Accordingly, while a diaconal mission is shared by the entire people of God, a distinctive identity as servant-leader within the context of the ecclesial community is the special call of the ordained.[30] The bishops challenge seminaries to form pastors of the people of God after the model of Christ, teacher, priest and shepherd.[31] All presbyteral formation is to emulate Christ's own focus in fashioning disciples, especially his concern that the twelve be intimately related to him. Hence, from the beginning of his ministry Jesus called others to be with him in the proclamation of the kingdom, molding them through personal fellowship and demanding of them total attention and full surrender in faith and love. Their development was rooted more in an intimate relationship with him than it was in his teaching; they were transformed by his example and conformed to his person.[32] Since servant-leader is both who Jesus was and what he taught, servant-leadership is a key distinguishing characteristic which underlies the spirituality of ordained ministry.[33]

In summary, the spirituality of the ordained must be presented in a way which recognizes complexity and tension as necessary and, when lived in a faith context, also beneficial. The American bishops enunciate an understanding of Christ and the church which bonds the human and the divine, on the one hand, and church leadership and ecclesial membership, on the other, into a creative and life-giving whole. It is the creative tension between these complementary aspects of church life, understood as paschal mystery, which is the source and pattern of an ecclesial spirituality. The task of the ordained is to enter into this tension, often initially perceived as rending and death-dealing, in a way which bridges opposing shores, thereby wedding both the human and the divine, and the head and the members.[34] The spirituality of ordained ministry places priests at those points in the real world where the values of God and those of humanity contend, there to act in a distinctive way as servant-leaders of reconciliation and witnesses to the power of resurrection.

II. Members of the Church and Leaders in the Person of Christ

While affirming the Second Vatican Council as "the greatest gift of the Holy Spirit to the church in this century,"[35] Howard Hubbard, the bishop of Albany, New York, enumerates a number of problems in the post-conciliar church. Among them is a lack of clarity about the distinctive roles of the ordained and those who are not. The emergence of lay ministry, while universally acclaimed a blessing and a necessary consequence of the council, is also seen as a cause for some distortions in church life, and as a challenge to articulate a more adequate ecclesiology.[36] At the same time that more of the laity have claimed the prerogatives of their baptismal consecration, the once clear lines between the lay and priestly vocations have become blurred, leaving the church without the familiar landmarks of the past.[37] Thomas Murphy, the bishop of Great Falls and Billings, Montana, sums up this confusion: "Despite the strong teaching of Vatican II and the repeated statements of the Holy Father, there is an attitude among some of almost an egalitarian approach to understanding and appreciation of ordained ministry and all other ministries in the church today."[38]

In addressing the situation, Cardinal Bernardin proposes that the proper context for understanding the ministerial priesthood is the mission of the laity to the world, lay ecclesiastical ministry, and the distinctive ministry of the ordained—all three taken together. He underlines the paramount importance of using precise language in speaking about these realities.[39] This is necessary to avoid "a blurring of roles, a tendency to telescope everything into a kind of common ministry."[40] While rightly emphasizing the vocation of all Christians which is rooted in baptism and confirmation, some have overlooked the essential difference between ordained and non-ordained ministry, thereby creating the impression that all ministry is the same.[41] In his role as president of the National Conference, Bishop Malone summarized the sentiments of many bishops in his 1985 pre-Synod Report by saying: "The distinctiveness of the priestly role stands in urgent need of clarification and celebration; the radical difference between ordained and non-ordained ministry must be repeatedly emphasized."[42] The importance of this challenge to the bishops will be returned to as part of the evaluatory comments in Chapter 8.

Present indications are that the ministerial priesthood remains in a state of transition from one self-understanding to another, and that older and younger priests in the United States continue to live in different worlds.[43] The net result is tension within priests, between them, and between them and the representatives of the newly emerging ministries in the church. Cardinal Bernardin spoke to the American bishops at their 1986 Collegeville Assembly, challenging them to bring into clear focus their identity as priests.[44] He went on to say that the American church needs a theology of priesthood which is profound, understandable, and convincing. Because this theological understanding must be faithful to the council's articulation of the mystery of Christ and the church, it is necessary to see priests as members of the church who participate in Christ through the ecclesial community, on the one hand, and as distinctive ministers through whom the church encounters Christ on the other. This reciprocity lies at the heart of the spirituality articulated by the American bishops.

The starting point for this spirituality is the church itself, the community of believers. The inner principle of ecclesial unity is the common faith shared through the action of the Holy Spirit; its visible unity is found in the presence and ministry of the bishop.[45] The ecclesial community is first and foremost the gathering of those who have been called into a covenant relationship with the Lord through faith and baptism. Offices and ministries are necessary for the service of this covenanted community, but they are secondary. The primary reality is the presence of Christ in the assembly, the people of God.[46] Because images are important, *The Priest and Sacred Scripture* suggests that "family of God" is more characteristic of the New Testament than "people of God," inasmuch as it better reflects the true nature of ecclesial friendship and communion in Christ.[47]

As members of an ecclesial family, then, the leaders of the church do not stand apart as those who are the sole possessors of the truth or as those who rule from the heights. Since the ordained are members of the ecclesial body with specific and essential tasks to perform in maintaining its organic unity, they may never position themselves apart from or above the community they serve.[48] The relationship between lay people and their pastors should be characterized by a collaborative spirit rooted in the fact that all the members of the church are fellow-servants.[49] Through baptism, which is the source of the Christian vocation, every member of the church is called to share in its life and mission.[50] The document *As One Who Serves* quotes Walter Kasper as saying: "The brotherhood and equality of all members takes precedence over all later distinctions and persists in them."[51] Since the entire church is seen as the primary recipient of Christ's mission, a properly nuanced spirituality challenges priests to act as a part of the whole, and indeed as an expression of it.[52]

Because of their incorporation into the body of Christ through the sacraments of initiation, all members of the church possess a common power and dignity as "a holy nation, a royal priesthood, and a people set apart."[53] It is on this foundation that the Lord provides further gifts of ministry or service for the church. This understanding of the common roots of the diverse ecclesial ministries does not lessen the importance of the ministerial priesthood. On the contrary, it highlights the significance of priestly ministry by bringing its distinctive relationship to Christ into clearer focus.

The profound influence of ecclesial membership on priestly spirituality is made clear in a comment by Rembert Weakland, the archbishop of Milwaukee, at a pastoral conference for priests: "The spirituality that we have is really the *Christian* spirituality; and to talk about the five percent that might be specific to us I think would be to miss the whole force of what baptism is all about."[54] He goes on to develop his thoughts around a shared baptismal spirituality, returning later to the specific characteristics of presbyteral life. His emphasis on the call to discipleship, the paschal mystery, the sacraments, and the faith community clarifies the essential relationship which presbyteral spirituality has to the spiritual lives of the people priests are called to serve.

This is also the message offered in *The Continuing Formation of Priests:* "The priest stands under the Word he proclaims, the Word which interprets and judges his own life and the life of his people. In other words, he is challenged to the same faith, the same conversion, the same love and thanksgiving to which he calls his people. He immerses himself in the same mystery taking place and involves himself in the action he performs, becoming thereby a transparent witness in his own person to what he expresses in sacred word and symbols."[55] Because participation in the life of Christ through the action of the Holy Spirit is the source, driving force and goal of ordained ministry, priests cannot be true leaders in the church unless they are ever more profoundly imbued with the grace which animates it. In other words, the Spirit which fills the church is the principle of the spirituality they seek to live and impart.[56]

Accordingly, priests themselves must grow in the life they endeavor to foster in others. Inasmuch as human beings mature by participating in life, not simply by observing or directing it, personal relationships are particularly important for spiritual growth. These offer the ordained a nurturing environment of care and concern, and a challenging milieu of trust and acceptance. The most formative influence in a priest's life is his surroundings, especially the circle created by his friends.[57] An important aspect of this social environment is the fellowship shared among priests, once a given in the American church, but now often replaced by a new loneliness stemming from an overemphasis on work or a fear of clericalism. John Sullivan, the bishop of Kansas City–St. Joseph, Missouri, says: "Nothing causes greater concern than the thought of a priest who no longer has the desire to form personal relationships with his fellow priests. . . . If priests lose the ability to reflect with one another on the importance, the challenges, and the demands of their faith, it is difficult to imagine they will be able to reflect with their parishioners."[58] His apprehension is obviously a pastoral one, based on a desire that priests be able to relate warmly to those they serve.

Concern about the disengagement of priests from the normal process of human development is echoed in statements of the Bishops' Committee on Priestly Life and Ministry. *The Spiritual Renewal of the American Priesthood* calls attention to the 1971 NCCB psychological study on American priests which reports that a large proportion of them are psychologically underdeveloped, since they do not relate deeply or closely to other people.[59] The implications are both that their faith is not well integrated into life and that their Christian maturity is limited by an inability to embrace the pain of human growth. In 1984, *The Continuing Formation of Priests* repeats this concern.[60] This insight has led to a reformulation of the central thrust of programs aimed at growth among priests, resulting in more group interaction and individual guidance. Similarly, spiritual direction and group discernment have become common aspects of presbyteral spirituality.

While the spiritual life cannot be reduced to psychological development, both emotional and spiritual growth usually occur best in an atmosphere of community marked by warm human relationships, since love of God and love of neighbor are related aspects of the Christian life. *The Spiritual Renewal of the American Priesthood* emphasizes this theme: ". . . no priest can claim that he has no need for interpersonal relationships in his life. Human loves mediate Christ's presence and action in our lives."[61] Priests are on a lifelong journey with a pilgrim people. Those who choose to enter into the relational life of the community open themselves to the possibility of a freer, richer life. Not only do they thereby enhance their personal well-being, but, more importantly, they increase their ability to minister to others with renewed vision and imagination.[62]

Involvement in the life of the community, then, lies at the heart of an appropriate priestly spirituality. Pastoral service entails searching with the people of God and sharing with them the fruits of the quest. It means giving and receiving, laughing and crying, remaining silent when there is nothing to say and speaking in spite of one's fears. In sharing the human condition of those they serve, priests remind them of God's love for them in Christ.[63]

While a fuller treatment of presbyteral celibacy is found in the next chapter, it is important to pause here to draw attention to the way the bishops relate it to the involvement of priests in the life of the community.[64] In their 1969 statement on celibacy the National Conference declares: "Celibacy does not separate the priest from the Christian community; indeed it is the instrument of his full and rich relationship to it. As a husband pledges his life in faith to his wife, so the priest pledges his life to the Christian people."[65] Thus, celibacy is proposed to priests as a special way of following Christ by entering into relationship with the people they are sent to serve.[66] When the celibate lifestyle is seen as a distinctive approach to being human, Christian, and priestly—and therefore, a way of living, hoping and believing—it doesn't lessen the priest's capacity for love, but enlarges it.[67]

Similarly, the bishops present celibacy as an opportunity for wholehearted service to the people of God. Daniel Pilarczyk, the archbishop of Cincinnati, observes that celibacy "is a gift from the candidate to the church . . . a pledge of a lifetime of full and individual ministerial witness and service to God's people."[68] It is pastoral, not only because it frees priests for greater service, but also because it symbolizes the gift of the heart of their identity to the ministry of the Lord in saving his people. *The Program of Priestly Formation* maintains that by celibacy "priests commit themselves to their people without reservation and seek to be for them signs of hope and witnesses to the coming of the kingdom of God, not only in the future but in the life of today."[69] It is clear, therefore, that priests do not give up human affection, for the "emptiness" of mature celibates is to be filled not only with love of God, but also with love of the people they serve.[70] Archbishop Pilarczyk observes that priests should be able to say that they love their people, and not anyone else as much. They should make this affirmation in the same straightforward manner as married men would about their wife and children.[71] Celibacy, then, is meant to relate priests to the baptized so that they can be more completely one with them and hence better leaders and representatives.

Far from exempting priests from the need for community, celibacy highlights the ecclesial relationships which nourish Christian spirituality. Not only does the community require the ministry of priests, but priests need the care of the people of the church; they must find support within the ecclesial community.[72] At the center of the summons to ordained ministry is the invitation to friendship, calling priests to intimacy with both the Lord and the people they serve.[73] Thus celibacy is meant to introduce a distinctive spiritual dynamic into presbyteral ministry, resulting in special bonds of ecclesial friendship.

Because celibacy is closely related to community, *The Spiritual Renewal of the American Priesthood* places it in a relational context: "The priest wishes to be brother to everyone and spouse to no one. . . . The sign that one has the charism of celibacy is precisely this: the celibate is able to love more genuinely, more profoundly and joyfully by having the freedom of the celibate state."[74] On one hand, celibacy qualifies all the relationships of priests and promotes a radical interpersonal way of life based on the universal character of Christian charity; on the other, it is founded on concrete relationships through which priests come to know themselves and experience growth as celibates.[75]

Moreover, personal relationships form an important part of the context for this way of life in the teaching of the American bishops, since for many priests the obstacle to serenity is not celibacy as much as finding a joyful and effective way of living and working. Because priests remain fully human, a fruitful response to the gift of celibacy must also be a valid realization of their humanity.[76] The cultivation of healthy relationships which put joy and peace into life demands leisure in various forms. The correlation between friends and others willing to listen, on one hand, and spiritual progress, on the other, cannot be overestimated; thus, leisure and friendship are significant aspects of presbyteral spirituality.[77]

In seeking a better understanding of the role of human sexuality, the bishops open a new area of discussion in their relationship with priests. It is an important one, for the candid way in which sexual matters are dealt with in the United States has both distressed and challenged priests. The ordained have certainly benefited from a better appreciation of the importance of sound psycho-sexual development for healthy relationships. It is not surprising, then, that the bishops' document *Human Sexuality and the Ordained Priesthood* describes sexuality as "a dynamic quality of the gift of human person-hood springing from the marvelous goodness of God."[78] Since every human being is by nature also a sexual person, priests retain their male sexual identity and masculinity; thus their individual sexual development must continue as long as they live.[79]

Human sexuality is an aspect of the God-given capacity for re-lating to people in a loving, caring way. It gives a quality of sensitivity, warmth, openness and mutual respect to interpersonal relationships. Cardinal Bernardin comments that, since priests choose to forego genital activity, there is also a tendency for them to ignore or deny their sexuality. The result is that many do not understand its power for good, even, and perhaps especially, in a celibate.[80]

A capacity for sensitivity and warmth is an important dimension of presbyteral spirituality, since priests are leaders of an ecclesial community which fulfills its mission of communicating the incarnate love of God to all by engaging in dialogue with the human family. Therefore, priests must be open to everyone, ready to listen not only to their words but also to their hearts, trying thereby to welcome and respect all by discovering truth in the beliefs, experiences and lives of others.[81] Sylvester Treinen, the retired bishop of Boise, Idaho, says that Vatican II is a challenge to the church, and especially to priests, to "grow, be meaningful to the world, observe the signs of the times, or be passed up and left in the dust, a disappointment to your divine founder."[82]

The American setting offers a distinctive challenge in that the ordained must open themselves to the qualities and values found in the many cultural and racial groups which seek to take their rightful place in both the ecclesial and the civic communities in the United States.[83] By creating these diverse cultures God shows forth his greatness and his love for humanity.[84] Because individuals are con-ditioned by the environment in which they live, the church seeks to evangelize cultures, not only individuals, for in doing so the total person is reached.[85] Joseph Francis, an auxiliary bishop of Newark and a member of the black community, cites attention to culture as a top priority in the Afro-American segment of society. Not to worship in the idiom of the people is to make the religious gathering mini-mally effective.[86]

The conclusion of the bishops is that since the ordained must be cognizant of their own milieu, and also of the differing cultures of those they serve, they must be willing to learn from the people.[87] The special gifts of each cultural heritage are placed at the service of the community through its openness to the ethnic and racial legacy of diverse segments of society. Priests, in particular, are invited to a trans-cultural vision of life.[88]

On the other hand, the ordained can not afford to be naive about the negative influences of culture. American society puts pressure on the spirituality of priests in the areas of affluence, authority and sexuality.[89] An increasing stress on individuality, growing materialism, secularism, and uncritical acceptance of the media also has an adverse effect on priests and their ministry.[90] In this milieu the ordained are summoned to affirm counter-cultural values; among them are poverty, obedience, chastity, community, and the ordering of the material world to the transcendent. An appropriate spirituality, then, challenges the ordained both to appreciate and learn from their culture, and to evaluate and take a prophetic stand in regard to it.

The diocesan church is given special attention because it is rooted in a particular place and setting. The clergy of the diocese have a special responsibility to esteem the local culture while seeking to evangelize it more thoroughly. Accordingly, they must know the people well, understanding their history, diversity, burdens, and hopes, as well as the demons which beset them.[91] It is only by helping priests permeate the life of the society they seek to serve that presbyteral spirituality can fulfill its purpose.

In their interaction with society, presbyters seek to foster a spiritual maturity which more perfectly reflects the life of Christ, since this is the groundwork underlying all their activity.[92] Within the ecclesial community itself, priests are to give special attention to adults, as emphasized in *Called and Gifted: The American Catholic Laity:* "The adult character of the people of God flows from baptism and confirmation which are the foundation of the Christian life and ministry."[93] Since adulthood connotes freedom, responsibility, and mutuality in relationships, as baptized Christians priests are themselves called to this maturity, and as leaders they are to promote the same full development of those they serve. The ability of the ordained to enter into relationships, community and culture is an important aspect of spiritual maturity; when these are immersed in Christ through baptism and orders, presbyteral ministry is empowered to fulfill its distinctive potential in extending the incarnation in church and society. Thus, the reasoning of the bishops becomes clear: profound sensitivity to the human condition and involvement in both the life of the ecclesial community and in society as a whole are essential components of the spirituality of ordained ministry, since without membership there can be no true leadership. The insistence of the council that priests are participants in church and society is mirrored in the teaching of the American bishops, making the stance of dynamic member a constitutive element of an authentic priestly spirituality.

Building upon this principle, and never apart from it, priests are empowered to be members in a distinctive way—as leaders who act *in persona Christi.*[94] *Sharing the Light of Faith,* the National Catechetical Directory for the United States, says: "All the faithful are participants in this mystery of redemption as they share in Christ's work. Yet ordained priesthood confers the power to act in the person of Christ and in his name and with his power to renew these mysteries, especially the mystery of the eucharistic sacrifice."[95] Although the entire church is the great sacrament of Christ,[96] the priest is a specific sacrament, sealed by the Spirit and empowered by ordination to participate in the headship of Christ in his servant-leadership of the church.[97] Since through the laying on of hands they are conformed to Christ as priest and head for the benefit of the church,[98] priests are not delegates of the people, but their servants as his representatives.

In an ordination homily, Archbishop Pilarczyk declared that for those who do not accept orders as a sacrament, ministers are chosen by the people and are deputed by them to be their representatives. For those who do believe that orders is a sacrament, the people have a role in the identification and the preparation of candidates, but it is the Lord who deputes for ministry; and it is the Lord whom ordained ministers represent.[99] Although priests are called and ordained through the instrumentality of the community, they are, at the same time, qualified and empowered for ministry by the Holy Spirit.

Because presbyters are empowered by the Spirit to be effective signs of Christ in the ecclesial community, they are a distinctive reflection of its self-understanding, being both "person-symbol" of its members, and enduring pledge of its faith in the saving presence of Christ.[100] In insisting that orders, like all sacraments, is ecclesial, the bishops maintain that ordained ministry captures a particular and essential aspect of the way in which the church participates in Christ. Even though everyone in the church is called to be another Christ, priests are called to be such as those who lead and serve the Christian community.[101] Since leadership and service together lie at the heart of the distinctive charism of ordained ministry, this is specifically what priests are empowered to be, servant-leaders in the image of Christ the head of the church.[102] Whereas other sacraments express other aspects of the church's participation in Christ, orders mediates his servant-headship.

As anointed servants, then, priests exercise a distinctive ministry because of the special election of God expressed in ordination. Their words and actions have a different, indeed special, meaning and authority since they stand in the community as those identified and anointed for the service of leadership.[103] The ministerial priesthood is more than a specialized function; it is a distinctive, permanent participation in the mediatory existence of Christ as head of the church. Archbishop Borders tells us that "ordained priesthood is not an essentially greater share in the common priesthood of all the baptized, for to view it as such would be to imply that the ordained minister enjoys a greater participation in the life of Christ. . . ."[104] Rather, it is an essentially different way of sharing in the Christian vocation which finds its purpose in actualizing the ministerial potential of the whole people of God. In his address to the 1986 Collegeville Assembly of the National Conference of Bishops, Archbishop Pilarczyk stated: ". . . the priest is simply not 'just like everybody else.' In fact, it is a matter of faith that he is different from everybody else. He is an unchangeable sign or sacrament of the love of Christ the head for his church."[105]

The phrase *in persona Christi* is used often by the American bishops to describe the distinctive character of the ministerial priesthood. In an ordination homily James Hickey, the archbishop of Washington, D.C., says that priests are changed, sealed and made uniquely to resemble Christ, so that "in his very person," and configured to him, they teach, offer, celebrate and lead God's people.[106] Victor Balke, the bishop of Crookston, Minnesota, states that priests are patterned after Christ so deeply and indelibly in their being that they are empowered to act "in the person of Christ as head of the church."[107] Cardinal Bernardin describes the ordained as "instruments who minister 'in the person of Christ.' "[108] John Whealon, the archbishop of Hartford, Connecticut, tells candidates for ordination that "You will be ordained to act, to work, *in persona Christi*."[109] Cardinal O'Connor says that priests act as ministers in Christ's place, that is, in the person of Christ.[110] The archbishop of Denver, J. Francis Stafford, says that *in persona Christi* signifies more than "in the name of Christ"; it means "in specific sacramental identification with 'the eternal high priest.' "[111] Some use different language to convey a similar understanding of the ontological significance of ordained ministry. Cardinal John Dearden, the former archbishop of

Detroit, uses the term *alter Christus,* another Christ, as a way of describing the distinctive identity of priests.[112] The same usage is followed by Cardinal John Krol, the retired archbishop of Philadelphia,[113] and Archbishop Whealon.[114]

Others insist on the essential distinction between the common and ministerial modes of priesthood by referring to the teaching of *Lumen Gentium* 10. Thus James Niedergeses, the bishop of Nashville, Tennessee, says that it is the constant and universal tradition of the church, confirmed by the council, that the ministerial priesthood differs from the priesthood of all the faithful not only in degree, but in its very essence.[115] Repeating the distinction between the priesthood of the ordained and that of all the baptized, Raymond Hunthausen, the archbishop of Seattle, Washington, calls the ministerial priesthood "Christ's precious, unique gift to his church."[116] Citing the same differentiation from the universal priesthood, John Quinn, the archbishop of San Francisco, says that "the priesthood is irreplaceable and of central importance to the life, the existence and the mission of the church."[117] In the words of Archbishop Weakland: "The ordained ministry was established by Christ for a sacramental presence that goes in its essence beyond the powers conferred on each Christian at baptism."[118]

A helpful suggestion for a contemporary articulation of the distinctive identity of the ordained is offered by Roger Mahony, the archbishop of Los Angeles. He proposes that older theological expressions may have relied too much on the concept of ontological change in explaining the ministerial priesthood. While true enough, they did not give sufficient importance to the talents and dispositions required for effective ministry. In reaction a so-called functionalist theology has arisen which focuses on the skills priests must develop to be effective. The weakness of this approach is in its inability to account for factors usually associated with the priesthood—for example, lifelong commitment, celibate lifestyle, holiness, and a simple way of life; thus, the tendency is for priesthood to become more a job than a special call. He therefore proposes redrawing the contemporary understanding of the priesthood within the context of a more symbolic or sacramental theology, thereby describing the priest as a kind of sacrament or sign. The question then would not be what priests can do and others cannot, but who priests are for church, and consequently what role flows from this sacramental identity. This emphasis would both retain the very real change insisted upon by ontological theology and also make clear the need for developed pastoral skills.[119]

The bishops agree that it is not a matter of ordained priests having "more" of the same modality of priesthood as all the faithful; they participate in a different, yet correlated, mode of priesthood. The source of the priesthood of all the faithful is the action of Christ as the model of sanctity for every human being in the sacrament of baptism. The source of the ordained priesthood is the action of Christ as head of the church in the sacrament of orders.[120]

Inasmuch as the essential equality among all human beings is a foundational principle of the American culture, an affirmation of ontological distinctions among people can be easily misunderstood. In order to clarify the matter Archbishop Pilarczyk asks himself if priests are somehow better than everyone else because the ministerial priesthood is essentially different from that of the baptized. He responds: "I do not think so."[121] What is being affirmed by the bishops is a distinctive way of being in the ecclesial community which has profound implications for the growth of the church in holiness. Ordination does not guarantee that priests are holy, but it does impart an objective holiness in that it brings a sanctifying ministry to the Christian community. The realization that someone exercising a baptismal ministry may be a better person, in talent or holiness, than a priest does not minimize the fact that the Lord chooses to act in a special way through the ordained.[122] The special identity of priests neither makes them better than others, nor entitles them to singular privileges. It does indicate who they are, whom they represent, the nature of their mission, and the demands made on them for spiritual growth and commitment to Christ through service to others, all crucial aspects of their spirituality.[123]

Even though the sacred character of ordination affects priests at so deep a level that their whole being and all their actions are directed to a priestly purpose,[124] yet they must constantly seek to grow in what they were ordained to be.[125] It is by offering the eucharist, leading God's people, preaching the gospel and celebrating the other sacraments that they become priests ever more deeply.[126] Thus, the ordained are called upon to be totally engaged in what they do, to be identified with Christ not only in their actions, but in their very persons. This means, among other things, that they can never be dispassionate dispensers of truth or sacraments, since love must be the force behind all their actions.[127] Priests are to be conformed to Christ and so captivated by him that in radiating his presence they may in fact be called "another Christ."[128] Accordingly, they are to put to daily use the sacramental grace which empowers and sustains their distinctive ministry.[129]

The bishops recognize the distinctiveness of ordained ministry as a foundation for their spirituality. By their initial identification with Christ as head of the church at ordination, and by their continual assimilation into his servant-leadership throughout life, priests grow as effective instruments of his presence. In acting like him they become experientially the image of Christ the head who has identified himself with them.[130] The ordained, then, are to be possessed by the gospel; that is, they are to be sacraments of Christ, not merely to preach him.[131] They are to let themselves be so fully formed in the person of Christ that in the totality of their being they are faithful and fruitful extensions of his servant-leadership of the people of God.[132] Hence priests become instruments who truly mediate Christ's love and mercy by totally abandoning themselves to him and placing themselves in his hands.[133] The gift given at the beginning of their ministry is to expand to fill their whole mind, heart and life, so that all that they have and are is transformed by this great grace.[134]

Moreover, since it is for the benefit of the laity, and thereby for the salvation of the world, that the church primarily exists, the ordained priesthood makes sense only in the context of service to the ecclesial community.[135] Bishop Thomas Murphy, while chairman of the Bishops' Committee on Priestly Formation, drew attention to the fact that there is an ordered relationship between the ministry of priests and that of the laity.[136] Each has a special way of sharing in the single priesthood of Christ; thus, the ordained are oriented not only toward Christ, but also through him toward the baptized. This orientation to the church and its mission sets the context for presbyteral spirituality.

Because the ordained are ordered by definition to the laity, it is impossible to understand the ministerial priesthood without reference to them.[137] The dignity of the baptized is so great that Christ, acting through the church, chooses some from among them as presbyters for their service and salvation.[138] To insure that the people of God may be the priestly people they are called to be, Christ gives certain members of the community the power to sanctify, to make his redemptive sacrifice present, and to mediate divine life to them. It is as mediators of this life that priests are known as "father." Bishop Hubbard says: "To speak of the priest's actions as fatherly is not simply metaphorical because the priest truly gives to those whom he serves that life which comes from God the Father. . . ."[139] Presbyters have a nurturing role in the church; thus, the ordained priesthood is not an end in itself, and the priesthood of the baptized does not exist fundamentally to sustain the ministerial priesthood.

Since through the sacrament of orders presbyters are charged with pastoral responsibility,[140] all priests by reason of ordination are in some sense pastors.[141] Above all, their ministry looks toward effecting unity by opening people's hearts to the cooperative effort which the Spirit of God inspires.[142] Because they minister to the common task of the church, *The Program of Priestly Formation* states that priests are "to serve the holy people as they grow in likeness to the Lord and share more deeply in his redeeming mission."[143]

Because of the interrelatedness of the church, the eucharist and the priesthood, presbyters have a unique role in the ecclesial community. Accordingly, the eucharistic assembly both lies at the heart of the ecclesial community and occupies a central position in the identity of the ministerial priesthood.[144] Far from diminishing the primacy of preaching the gospel in presbyteral ministry, focus on the eucharist serves to reinforce it.[145] Following the insight of Vatican II, Archbishop Pilarczyk sees the eucharist as the source and apex of this proclamation, the basis of Christian community, and the entire spiritual wealth of the church.[146] Through the eucharist priests proclaim the pastoral love which is the center and root of their spirituality.[147]

Although historical developments have tended toward a cultic emphasis in the theology and spirituality of the priesthood, there are many other aspects of the ministry of Jesus which must be considered if priests are to grow to full stature.[148] Since the Lord uses the mediation of ordained ministry to touch people's lives, priests must be present to them in many ways and many places. Thus, presbyters must move beyond the celebration of the sacraments,[149] as Peter Gerety, the retired archbishop of Newark, says quite bluntly: "No room for sacristy priests here."[150] The ordained are to be personally present to those they serve and well versed in every aspect of their lives.

One of the most consistent insights in the post-conciliar church in the United States is that ministry to the laity does not mean service in place of them. Lay people are co-workers in witnessing to Christ. Priests have the privilege of helping their brothers and sisters assume their God-given role in the church and the world.[151] The participation of the laity in the mission of the church has a sound foundation in sacramental theology and ecclesiology. They have the right and the responsibility, then, to share in more than token ways in all aspects of the life of the church, including the decision-making process. The leadership which the church needs today demands that priests share responsibility with parish staffs and parishioners.[152]

Just as through ordination priests have been given authority to serve the people of God, so through the consecration of baptism and confirmation lay men and women have been given a responsible share in the mission of the church.[153] The ordained or hierarchical ministry is to be exercised in a way which creates opportunities for various members of the church to be involved in policies, decisions and apostolates in accordance with their talents and charisms.[154] Bishop Sullivan remarks: "The priest or parish administrator who reserves all major decisions to himself, who fails to tap the hundreds of resources in his parish, bluntly, is not practicing pastoral leadership."[155]

Priests are to work in a collaborative manner with the entire community, as well as with their peers. This means they are to take seriously the role of the laity and religious women and men in the life of the church.[156] In speaking to the 1986 Collegeville Assembly, Bishop Francis emphasized that religious want to be collaborators in the mission of the church. Mutual respect, cooperation and interdependence are attitudes which those in religious life would like to see in their relationship with the ordained.[157] Since contemporary society has brought about a greater awareness of the significant role of women in the community,[158] priests are expected to interact with them in relationships which are mature, honest, responsible and appreciative.[159] Moreover, they are to exercise real responsibility in the complex question of the developing role of women in the mission and ministry of the ecclesial community.[160]

Cardinal Bernardin brings leadership and membership together in suggesting a vision which is helpful to a further articulation of a spirituality of ordained ministry. On one hand, he calls attention to the church as a community in which all have a common goal, the emergence of the kingdom of God. It is, thus, a community with a common life and mission which all share because of a basic equality flowing from baptism and confirmation. On the other hand, the church is a community of ministers, ordained and lay, who understand and accept uniquely different but necessarily complementary roles, thereby working together for the common good.[161] Distinctions among ministries are gifts which enrich the church. This diversity makes sense only as a part of a greater whole and in service to the common life and mission of the community.

Thus, the teaching of the American bishops integrates two aspects of the life of priests, binds them together, and seeks to define presbyteral spirituality in terms of both. The bishops address the apparent tension between the membership of priests in the church and their special identity as leaders of the community by articulating more clearly the relationship between these two truths. This does not eliminate the practical tensions involved in the complexities of ecclesial life, but it does provide a meaningful vision in which the tensions can be handled. Not only does this clearer perspective reduce stress, it also opens up a broader repertoire of experiences and resources indispensable for the development of an authentic priestly spirituality. At the same time, it reminds priests that the pain experienced in entering into the tension between membership and leadership, when it is properly understood, is an aspect of the paschal mystery and a source of life.

In summary, then, the relationship between two major dimensions of presbyteral spirituality has been clarified. First, in accord with the incarnation and the subsequent ministry of Jesus, leadership demands involvement in the life of the church. Those who are ordained to lead must enter ever more deeply into the condition of those they serve, since the first service which Jesus gave was becoming one of those he came to save. This, indeed, must be the primal impulse of those who seek to lead in his name. A constantly intensified involvement in the life of the church and an ever deepening solidarity with the human family is a prerequisite for all that follows.

Second, an authentic priestly spirituality flows from a proper understanding of presbyteral identity within the ecclesial community. Priests participate in Christ not only as the life and holiness of the church, but also as its servant-leader and head. Their identity is essentially different from that of the baptized, although it is oriented toward the upbuilding of all and has no meaning apart from this task. Because Christ the servant-head of the church is the model for ecclesial leadership, those who participate in his headship are constituted servants to the community. In other words, the special office that could set priests apart from the community radically orients them to it. This well-defined sense of identity as servant-leaders in the person of Christ is a second essential dimension of priestly spirituality.

These two dimensions come together in Christ himself. In imitation of him, an appropriate spirituality enables presbyters to bring the community to full stature so that God might be glorified in the lives of all. In this way, the bond between leadership and membership is deepened, since the goal of priestly ministry lies outside of itself and in the enrichment of the people of God. Hence priestly spirituality is self-giving and other-empowering by definition.

III. Delegates of the Bishop and Representatives of the Community

A more detailed consideration of the ecclesial context of the ministerial priesthood, in faithfulness to the teaching of the council, further defines the nature both of presbyteral service and of priestly spirituality. As servant-leaders in the person of Christ, presbyters exercise this ecclesial service in the context of a community of ordained ministers led by the bishop. Furthermore, as specially delegated members of the church, priests are involved in its life in a distinctive way as representatives of the community.

The teaching of the American hierarchy underscores the distinctive role of the bishop as Christ ministering in word and sacrament in the midst of the local church.[162] Since the bishop is the primary leader of the community in the task of building the church, presbyters are called as his brothers and helpers, sharing his role of leadership.[163] Accordingly, the presbyters of the diocese receive ordination and the capacity to serve through their relationship with him.[164] The most fundamental ministry within a diocese, then, is that of the bishop. Priests are sent by the bishop, are accountable to him for their ministry, and are an extension of his presence throughout the local church.[165]

Priests are not only partakers in the ministry of the bishop, but also key recipients of his pastoral care. Cardinal Edward Szoka, the archbishop of Detroit, notes that his episcopal ministry is directed first of all to the presbyters of the diocese in that bishops and priests share one priesthood, enjoy a special unity in the charism of ordination and undertake a unified ministry to God's people.[166] In serving the presbyterate the bishop is, in fact, ministering through them to the total community committed to his care.

Archbishop Pilarczyk finds a clear delineation of the pivotal role of the bishop in the teaching of Vatican II. Because on its most basic level the ministry of presbyters is meant to extend the work of the bishop to a part of the diocese, he says that the priest is "the *alter ego*" of the bishop. The archbishop attaches special importance to this concept, the significance of which will be weighed in Chapter 8. All priests, then, diocesan and religious alike, are collaborators with the bishop in his pastoral office.[167] Consequently, he proposes the episcopate as the primary analogue for presbyteral ministry. Although priests are not mere stand-ins for the bishop, the significance of the service they offer can be properly understood only as a participation in his pastoral ministry.[168] In fulfilling their own role in the local community, presbyters also make the bishop present as "chief pastor."[169]

The ordained ministry of a diocese is ordered to and flows from the eucharistic assembly. Just as the eucharist is central to the identity of the ministerial priesthood, so too each mass reveals the foundational role of the bishop in the local church, for it is always offered explicitly in union with him. The unity of both the community and its ministry is sustained and nourished by the eucharist which always relates those who share in it to the distinctive ministry of the bishop.[170] Therefore priests are not ordained to a solitary ministry, but to one in solidarity with the bishop and within the context of a diocesan church.[171]

Since the bishop and presbyters together form one priesthood in a diocese, they are co-workers and friends. Their relationship to one another is a "sacramental" one, according to Archbishop Stafford: "It should be 'sacramentalized' over and over again through friendship, mutual concern for the order of the local church and cooperation."[172] This rapport, therefore, is of an order different from that between president and senators in a civil government. Since the ministry of priests, in a certain sense, derives from that of the bishop, they form one sacramental body with him. Thus, a juridical relationship between bishop and priests is secondary to this sacramental bond. The difficulty of existing in a sacramental fellowship is embodied in the daily struggle of the ordained to live out a sacrificial love.

As an expression of his sacramental bond with his priests, Bishop Treinen opens a letter to them with the greeting: ". . . to the priestly men for whom I exist and without whom I can accomplish little."[173] On the night before his ordination, Robert Brom, the bishop of Duluth, Minnesota, told his priests that "in the providence of God, we will soon constitute together a unique sacerdotal college or presbytery dedicated to the service of the people of God who comprise the church of the diocese of Duluth."[174] Following from this sacramental rapport is a need for dialogue and an impetus to shared ministry. Bishop Brom continues: "I look to you to make up in your own personal attributes and pastoral expertise for what you will discover as my deficiencies."[175] Archbishop John Quinn highlights this same sacramental reality, calling priests his closest co-workers in the diocese as those who share with him the apostolic office in the church through the bond of the sacrament of orders.[176]

The document *As One Who Serves* points out that the council takes two approaches to the relationship between a bishop and his priests. The first is a hierarchical stance in which priests are dependent upon the bishop, exercise the priestly office in a limited degree, act in the bishop's name, and make him present. The other is more communal, seeing priests as co-workers, friends, sharers in one priesthood and in a collaborative service in a diocese.[177] The tension between these two understandings comes to the surface in the affirmation of Archbishop Pilarczyk that priests, on one hand, make the bishop present in the local congregation and extend his work to a portion of the diocese,[178] and, on the other, that priests have their own proper role in pastoral leadership.[179]

This tension is addressed by drawing attention to the unity which is to permeate the ordained community. Bishop Niedergeses speaks of the *"presbyterium unum,"* the communion which exists between bishops and priests in both the local and the universal church, as a foundational condition for unity among the people of God.[180] Thus, ministries are not to be ranked in a way which separates them, but as diverse gifts given to one body.[181] No bishop or priest can accomplish the mission of the local church in isolation. It is together, as participants in the one priestly ministry of Christ, that they are called to be a sacramental expression to the world of the salvific life of the church. Therefore, the fellowship of those sharing the sacrament of orders is more than communion of mind and heart; it is a sacramental reality, a common mediation of Christ's servant role as leader of the church.[182] Since the task committed to bishops and priests can only be accomplished by working together, they are bound to each other in the one ministerial body by which the church is served and led; it is only together that they reflect the richness of the sacrament of orders.[183]

Acting in union with the bishop, then, presbyters serve the local community. While each priest has a role to play, he does not serve any person or group as an individual, but only as a member of a ministerial community.[184] Since priests draw the vision for their mission from a pastoral charge which surpasses a particular ministerial appointment, each member of the presbyterate is bound to the others by a spirit of collaboration in the common diocesan mission.[185] Even though the parish is the basic unit of the diocesan community in which the faith, life and mission of the local church resides, yet it is not the church in miniature. The parish and its ministers are related by definition to the entire local church which is guided by the bishop and his presbyterate.[186]

A practical expression of the relationship which exists between bishop and priests is found in the way in which authority is exercised and responsibility shared. This is a particularly sensitive question in the American context, and one that has special importance for priests. Since the council, priests have been encouraged to pursue that mature freedom by which they take on responsibility for their life and ministry. Thus, dialogue with diocesan authorities and among their peers has greater significance for them in exercising this freedom. One of the difficulties in ministry in the current situation in the United States is that for some priests the legitimate exercise of authority has become a disproportionate issue, while for others the abuse of authority causes conflict and internal dissatisfaction.[187] The continuing existence of extreme positions points out the need both for a clearer understanding of the relationship between bishop and priests, and for growth in the maturity of all ordained ministers.

The tension which priests experience between membership and leadership cuts a new direction here, for priests are servant-leaders both as members of a presbyterate and as incumbents in a particular pastoral assignment. Their spirituality must empower them to partake in a ministerial community with a vision and a mission which is broader than a given assignment, while enabling them to be true leaders in their own right within a specific pastoral context.

Even though, in practice, presbyteral ministry usually relates priests to a parish community, an appropriate priestly spirituality must be based on a vision and oriented to a mission which are wider than the parish. In fact, even diocesan boundaries must be transcended, since the presbyterate is ordered to the universal mission of the church.[188] Thus, priestly spirituality focuses on a ministry which is particular, concrete and often parochial in scope, while it is by definition diocesan and universal in its vision and mission.

The corporate aspect of priestly ministry is expressed in many ways. The first is in the relationship among presbyters, especially in the spirit of fraternity and co-responsibility which should characterize all facets of their common ministry. A second is seen in the presbyteral council which not only assists the bishop in his ministry to the entire body of the faithful, but also promotes the personal, spiritual and ministerial welfare of the ordained community.[189]

The ministry which priests offer one another is an important witness to the unity of the ecclesial community and a source of new ministerial energy and effectiveness. Archbishop Quinn observes that the mutual charity to which priests are called is the "type and model of the charity for all the believers according to the word of Christ."[190] Accordingly, priestly relationships should not be characterized by antiseptic professional courtesy, but must indeed be an expression of true friendship. Philip Hannan, the former archbishop of New Orleans, tells his fellow priests that "we are ordained to serve in Christ, and therefore our first duty is to serve each other."[191] He sees this service as a way both of strengthening priests, and also of strengthening the people by contributing to the welfare of the church. Bishop Niedergeses posits a connection between the unity of the presbytery and the effectiveness of the eucharist. He states that unless priests learn to wash one another's feet, and even consider it a privilege to do so, the meaning of the eucharist will not be readily discernible to the people because of the lack of identity with Christ on the part of their ministers.[192]

The corporate life of the presbyterate, then, is important to its effectiveness. The document *As One Who Serves* reminds priests that they are to befriend the bishop as one to whom they are deeply united in faith, fellowship and common responsibility.[193] Although the ministries of religious priests may differ from those of the diocesan clergy, the difference does not flow from the priesthood as such.[194] Since the presence of religious in a presbyterate is a source of enrichment, they are to be welcomed as those who share an increasingly pluriform but common priesthood.

Careful initiation into the presbyteral community is also important to its effectiveness. An internship program can facilitate healthy relationships with new members of the presbyterate and thereby deepen the extant bonds of fellowship.[195] Young priests are much more than ordained helpers for an overburdened pastor; they are colleagues preparing for full pastoral responsibility. This realization should help establish closer, more collaborative ties between pastors and associates.[196] Since the council the "assistant pastor" has moved, at least in theory, from a clearly subordinate position to that of "parochial vicar," a position which more obviously shares in the pastor's responsibility and mission.[197] On the other end of the age spectrum, the role of "senior priest" is being more clearly formalized as a position of wisdom and experience which enriches the common mission of the presbyterate.[198]

The sacramental identity of the total presbyterate, a fitting period of initiation into its life, and an ever more effective participation in its corporate ministry are seen as important issues by the American bishops. The traditional rugged individualism of American priests is challenged by this emphasis on the presbyteral community. Since it is through this community of ordained ministers that servant-leadership is provided for the local church, the bishop must strive to create a bond with the priests who, in a special way, share his ministry. Archbishop Weakland declares that the bishop fosters the holiness of his priests because their ministry is an extension of his own.[199]

The presbyteral council gives candid expression to the common responsibility and ministry shared by the bishop and the priests of a diocese. Archbishop Stafford views the involvement of the bishop in the presbyteral council as "an indication of his respect for his priests, his trust for the gift of holiness they received at ordination and his love for them."[200] He goes on to say that the bishop has the right to expect the respect and love of priests as well; they must also trust in the gift of the Spirit invoked upon him at his ordination. Hence the relationship between bishop and priests is a spiritual one having its source in the Spirit whom they mutually recognize as the origin of their ministry. While the primary thrust of the presbyteral council is toward the total pastoral endeavor of the church, it makes a major contribution to the ecclesial community by promoting spiritual growth among priests, since it is only in the power of the Holy Spirit that they can be authentic servant-leaders of the people of God.[201]

The polarization of the contemporary ecclesial community is a source of stress in the lives of priests and points out the need which they have for psychological maturity as individuals and for communal support as leaders. There must be room in their lives for critical evaluation of ideas and for tranquil dialogue about pastoral issues. This reflection happens best in an atmosphere which is not marked by extreme positions and fragmented by partisan biases. At times priests experience pressure because of tension between church teaching or discipline and the attitudes, circumstances or insights of the people they serve.[202] In a ministerial setting which is complex and sometimes even hostile, the presbyterate as a community of prayer, wisdom, and fraternity is crucial if priests are to minister effectively. The presbyterate recognizes its significance for the development of each of its individual members by actively fostering strategies aimed at support and personal growth.

Properly understood, the leadership community constituted by the sacrament of orders does not separate priests from the people they serve, but unites them all the more to them. The presbyterate has meaning only when it empowers priests to be servants of and collaborators with the laity. Priests, then, are not only members of a presbyterate, but also representatives of a particular ecclesial community. The teaching of the bishops again binds leadership and community together by orienting the relationship among priests arising from ordination to the service of the baptized.

In speaking to his priests, Matthew Clark, the bishop of Rochester, New York, quotes extensively from an address of Pope John Paul II to the bishops of France. He draws attention to the role of the bishop in helping priests better implement collaboration with the laity. The vision of the church, according to Pope John Paul, is "to awaken the laity to the vocation which is properly theirs and give them real responsibilities!"[203] He goes on: "On the practical level, it is also important to bring more imagination and daring to the concept of possible areas of participating by the laity, since these are far from being fully explored."[204] Bishop Clark sees in these words both an invitation to find strength through union with the people, and a challenge to be fully among the people by calling them to deeper and more active responsibility for the life of the church.

As members of the church called to represent the community, priests are truly "sacraments" of ecclesial life. Bishop Balke says that the priest embodies the people: "His very being and the way or style of his being ought to remind them of who they are called to be and ought to call them to be more than what they already are."[205] Since priests exemplify the call and mission of the church, people should be able to look to them and say: "That's what we're supposed to be and do in virtue of our baptism and confirmation and in virtue of our union with the eucharistic Christ."[206] Through ordination priests are not only conformed to Christ as head of the church, but are also more deeply configured to the body of believers in a way which makes them both representatives of and examples to those they serve.[207]

In this way, the American bishops clarify the relationship between presbyteral leadership and ordained membership in the community of the faithful, proposing priests as ministers who truly represent the baptized while they participate in a special way in the unique servant-headship of Christ. Therefore, priests involve the people of God in the mission of the church by personifying the self-understanding and activity of the ecclesial community among them.[208] It is by being what they proclaim that their leadership is made effective. Archbishop Borders sees the ordained priesthood as "the sacramental embodiment of the essence of all ministry" and a catalyst which enables others to take part in the mission of Christ.[209] Accordingly, the pattern revealed in the incarnation is again affirmed. Both participation in the headship of Christ and representative ministry for the community of the faithful are constitutive elements of the total reality attributed to priests.

Since communities usually form around pivotal personalities

with a vision which others find attractive and useful, God has used the charismatic qualities of certain individuals for the benefit of the church. The document *The Priest and Sacred Scripture* says: "An amorphous and faceless community, undistinguished by men of outstanding faith and energy, cannot exist, much less serve as the means for transmitting the experience of God's revelation to succeeding generations."[210] The distinctive gifts and personalities of ordained ministers and the manner in which they embody the aspirations of the people are very significant for their effectiveness.

Kenneth Untener, the bishop of Saginaw, Michigan, sees ecclesial ministers as leaders at the cutting edge of Christianity, who must rid themselves of a caricature of their role as bland, colorless, safe, withdrawn and secure.[211] Priests must have the capacity to learn, grow and adapt, for it is by who they are that they set the tone and energize the spirit of the parish.[212] In affirming the need for a more faith-filled and dynamic presbyteral presence in the community, Roberto Sanchez, the archbishop of Santa Fe, New Mexico, quotes an observation of Pope Paul VI: "In the long run, is there any other way of handing on the gospel than transmitting to another person one's personal experience of faith?"[213] More is being suggested than greater availability, since the transmission of faith is rooted in companionship with those who already share the gift they are trying to impart.

Presbyters are challenged to be more than enactors of prescribed rituals and procedures; they are representatives of the community who themselves share the common struggle to make sense of life.[214] By identifying with the people they serve, priests assist them in interpreting the on-going revelation of God in their midst.[215] Diocesan priests, in particular, are challenged to share a common life with the people of a given place through direct service in a parish community.[216] Parishioners are looking for religious leaders who are loving and forgiving, ministers who will pray with them and remind them that no matter what their difficulties, God is near and will never abandon them. Cardinal Bernardin sees this as the preferred style of spiritual leadership today.[217] Patience, friendliness, faith and the admission of personal struggle are characteristics treasured in priests by those they serve.[218] As a result, priesthood is becoming more a way of living and less a state of life.

Proclamation of the word and celebration of the sacraments must flow from a sensitivity and a creativity that only loving familiarity with a community can impart, if they are to be truly effective.[219] *Fulfilled in Your Hearing* states that unless the preacher knows what the assembly needs, wants, or is able to hear, there is not much possibility that he will address the situation of his listeners. This is not to say that priests should proclaim only that which those present want to hear. It simply affirms that effective preaching is the result of compassionate understanding.[220]

Since the preacher represents the community by giving voice to its concerns, naming its demons, and enabling it to grow in understanding, one of the principal tasks of the homilist is to provide people with words to express both their faith and the human realities to which it responds.[221] Priests serve as mediators within the community by making concrete connections between temporal existence and faith in Jesus Christ; thus, the faith of those who preside is itself crucial. It is not surprising, then, that Archbishop Mahony strongly suggests that which priest celebrates the eucharist makes an important difference for the growth of the people in Christ.[222] The quality of the presider's faith has an inevitable effect on the receptivity of those he leads.[223] The interaction between the disposition of the celebrant and that of the community is summed up in a statement of Aloysius Wycislo, the retired bishop of Green Bay, Wisconsin: "In practical terms, the only priest who will prove necessary to you (the laity) in your parish is the priest who is conscious of the full meaning of your priesthood and his."[224]

Conscious of their representative role, effective preachers strive to identify with the people in speaking. In order to make connections with their lives the homilist must be a listener before he can be a speaker.[225] The task of the preacher is not so much to explain the scriptures as it is to encourage faith by interpreting the human situation through the biblical texts. Consequently, the homily has the character of a personal conversation about a very serious subject, God's active presence in the world.[226] A stance in the midst of the people enables the homilist not only to use the insights of scripture and theology, but also knowledge of the social, political and economic forces active in the community, in proclaiming the kingdom of God. Here again, a prerequisite for effective representative leadership is profound membership.

Cardinal Krol gives strong emphasis to the preeminent position of preaching in a proper understanding of presbyteral ministry: "We have at times developed a false sense of priorities, putting off the work of preparation to the last hour for some of our other valid duties, forgetting the *primary duty* of the priest is to proclaim the gospel to all."[227] The proclamation of the word, which is an indispensable and essential means of generating faith, can bring the homilist satisfaction and enjoyment, on one hand, and stress and disappointment, on the other. Part of the problem is the lack of an appropriate definition of the presbyteral role, and a consequent inability to clearly articulate an authentic spirituality and reasonable priorities. The result is that many priests are victimized by countless demands.[228]

Leadership and membership must come together, then, in the effective homilist. While preaching is certainly an action flowing from the distinctive way in which priests are conformed to Christ and related to the ministry of the bishop, it is also a living word spoken by ministers who are true representatives of the community. Preachers are empowered not only by Christ in whose name they speak, but also by the body of the faithful who recognize themselves in the words of the homily. Cardinal Bernardin says that the authority most needed today, and the kind which is most readily respected and accepted, is the authority of wisdom and compassionate love.[229] The two attributes which people want most in their priests, that they be warm, understanding people, and that they preach well,[230] are intimately related to one another.

As members of the community of the faithful, priests are called upon to orchestrate liturgies which express the needs of the people and are sensitive to the size of the congregation, the age and ethnic background of those involved, and the resources available. As representatives of the eucharistic assembly, it is their role to call forth a wide variety of ministries from within the gathering: readers, musicians, servers, ushers, and ministers of communion among them.[231] In this way, the role of the presbyter as one who presides is seen more clearly as lay people assume their proper liturgical roles. Since the ordained fulfill their responsibility by bringing together the diverse gifts of the community,[232] the priestly role of representing the people is exemplified in leadership which enables active lay participation in the liturgy.

Francis Quinn, the bishop of Sacramento, California, declares: "To conceive of ordained ministry as a service and as a fostering of the unordained ministry, or baptismal ministry, is the only way that we shall preserve unity in the future."[233] Priests live and serve among the people to awaken their gifts. They are ordained to nurture a priestly people, to help this people grow in the gifts of the Spirit, and to guide and inspire, not dominate, them.[234] The point underlined in the teaching of the bishops is that presbyteral ministry to the laity arises from solidarity with them. The ordained identify, coordinate and affirm the diverse gifts bestowed by the Spirit on the lay community because they themselves are members of the same priestly people and representatives of it.[235] In lovingly representing the community they are strengthening the body to which they also belong.

Although ministry was once seen as the domain of priests and religious alone, it is now understood to be the responsibility of the whole ecclesial community.[236] The American bishops recognize the priest as the "director of ministries" within a ministerial church.[237] Accordingly, presbyters are leaders of active Christians, and no longer the only ones expected to take spiritual initiative. Now, priests not only serve, but are also served by the people in a way which complements their own ministry. They stand in the midst of the community gratefully receiving and humbly coordinating the gifts of the Spirit, seeking to bring a particular cell of the body to perfect maturity. *As One Who Serves* compares the task of the parish priest to that of the conductor of an orchestra: "The conductor succeeds when he stimulates the best performance from each player and combines their individual efforts into a pattern of sound, achieving the vision of the composer."[238] Priests achieve the purpose for which they were ordained when all the talents of the community are developed and coordinated in a way which advances the designs of the Lord.

An appreciation of the pastor as one who encourages and enables those he serves has assumed a central place in the American church since the council.[239] In fact, the animation of the community has come to be seen as his pivotal role. This theme is often echoed by individual bishops. Joseph Ferrario, bishop of Honolulu, Hawaii, sees priests as those who identify other leaders in the parish, empower them, give them direction and support, and call them to accountability.[240] Patrick Flores, the archbishop of San Antonio, Texas, says that bishops must be leaders in calling forth the people as co-missioners with the ordained in the leadership of the church. He observes that people are ready and willing; they must be trusted even at the risk of making mistakes.[241] Bishop Hubbard connects the role of priests as enablers and facilitators of ministries to their eucharistic ministry. In the same way that they gather God's people in all their variety at the table of the Lord, they also bring together the talents and charisms bestowed upon them by the Spirit for the building up of the kingdom.[242]

In the interaction between the laity and the ordained the exercise of power sometimes causes concern. Protectiveness of position may well be the result of an improper view of ecclesial relationships.

Movement toward imitation of the servant Christ, by clergy and laity alike, is made difficult by disordered expressions of power often espoused in contemporary society and echoed in the church. By setting aside worldly ambitions for status and power, priests are able to claim the true endowment proper to their servant-ministry: liturgy, preaching, reconciling and healing.[243]

The ministries which priests nurture, affirm and support make possible a community in which many people exercise a representative role, guaranteeing that the ordained are no longer the only official servants of the community.[244] Because parish ministers are not substitutes for the ordained, but servants in their own right, their prominence does not diminish the importance of priests; it enhances it by reorienting presbyteral activity toward fostering a servant-community. Bishop Untener sees this new presbyteral role as analogous to that of the bishop.[245] Since the exercise of authority, in this context, takes on a collaborative character, the diocesan pastoral council, the parish council and the many committees within a parish community assume greater significance.[246] These new structures demand that priests exercise their ministry through meaningful relationships.[247]

Priests are not only representatives of the community and those who foster its life; they are, at the same time, recipients of the love and support which community gives. As priests move more obviously into a representative role within the people of God, they benefit from the relationships which are created among those with whom they minister and with the community at large. Since shared ministry and rapport with the community stimulate and nourish priests in their own distinctive service, the intensification of support for priests within the ecclesial community is a logical consequence of an appropriate spirituality.[248]

The Spiritual Renewal of the American Priesthood states: "The priest is not a pure instrument who effects changes but himself is not changed. He will be sanctified if he allows himself to be affected by what is taking place."[249] As those who preside at the sacramental celebrations of the paschal mystery in the key moments of life, priests are in a privileged position to be deeply touched by the holiness of that which they minister to others.[250] In the eucharist priests find the fullest expression of their identity and ministry, since there they are most clearly recognized as servant-leaders empowered both to involve the assembly in worship, and to call forth ministries for the service of all.[251] Bishop Francis Quinn remarks that people do not seem to be satisfied with a eucharist which is only valid theologically. They want to celebrate a mass in which the priest himself is transformed.[252] Archbishop Mahony makes the same point: "A presider cannot hide his faith, his discipleship—its depth or its shallowness. . . . The very person and spirituality of the priest constitutes the heart of his mission."[253]

Cardinal Bernardin quotes Pope John Paul II in saying that the eucharist brings self-knowledge because it perfects the image of God, which Christians truly bear, within them. It also helps the faithful grow in an awareness of the dignity of others. Because the eucharist is the foundation, dynamic force and goal of priestly ministry,[254] priests both are nourished there on the servant Christ, and offer this same sustenance to others as their greatest service to them. Moreover, inasmuch as all ecclesial service involves participation in the life and mission of Jesus himself,[255] the servant-leadership which is most characteristic of presbyteral ministry is eucharistic both in origin and in expression. The response of the assembly to the priests' eucharistic ministry can be a profound invitation to union with Christ, as the people evoke and affirm the priestly identity of their ministers.[256]

It is clear, then, that presbyteral spirituality finds its primary source of life in ministry itself.[257] The grace of God which is operative in priestly ministry is sanctifying not only for the beneficiaries of that ministry, but for the ministers as well.[258] Thus, the people truly mediate the saving presence of Christ, and God challenges and changes the hearts of the ordained through the experience of ministry in interacting with those they serve.[259]

This chapter, then, has focused on the dynamic relationship between priests as members of the ecclesial community, on one hand, and as its leaders, on the other. Because membership creates and fosters the foundational relationships and activities which lie at the heart of priestly spirituality, before presbyters can effectively minister to the church, they must be perceived as those who belong and truly participate.

An effective priestly spirituality flows from the integration of membership and leadership. The American bishops challenge priests to a spirituality of belonging which complements and enhances their complex leadership role within the community of the baptized. In this way they underline the bond between membership and leadership and summon priests to embrace a more ecclesial view of their spirituality. It is only by embracing both these dimensions of their ecclesial existence that priests can authentically mediate Christ in his servant-ministry as head of the church.

7.

Servants of the Poor and Witnesses to the Kingdom of God

The Bond Between Ministry to Human Need and Testimony to the Kingdom of God in Priestly Spirituality

T he American people have been richly blessed with material prosperity. Abundance has long been a fact of life in the United States, and continuing economic and social progress is an enduring cultural expectation; yet many Americans are in fact poor, and entire cultural groups have been excluded from the American dream.

The importance of American skills, technology, and monetary resources to the global community is universally recognized. Although personal dedication to the welfare of the wider human family is a characteristic respected by the American people, there is resistance to casting this cultural value in moral terms. In recent years the bishops of the United States have exerted a strong influence both in educating Catholics about social morality and in shaping public opinion about human values and economic responsibility. *Economic Justice for All,* the bishops' pastoral on the American economy, clearly states their concern: "Followers of Christ must avoid a tragic separation between faith and everyday life. They can neither shirk their earthly duties nor, as the Second Vatican Council declared, 'immerse [them]selves in earthly activities as if these latter were utterly foreign to religion, and religion were nothing more than the fulfillment of acts of worship and the observance of a few moral obligations.' "[1] As a result, questions often arise over the relationship between this concern for the day to day life of the American people and the proclamation of the kingdom of God.

Americans are a religious people. As was indicated in Chapter 1, recent surveys show that the vast majority believe in God, and most pray with some regularity. Yet they have a tendency both to divorce the concerns of religion from those of their social environment, and to view sexuality as unrelated to religion, or, at best, only minimally integrated into it. This results in a dichotomy between temporal concerns and religion, and in a penchant for shifting from a collectively materialistic interpretation of life into a personally spiritual one with a minimum of reflection—and therefore with little consciousness that the shift has been made. Thus, the American cultural experience offers the bishops a distinct challenge: How are they to advocate a more integrated view of the relationship between religion and daily life?

The widespread dichotomy between personal spirituality and secular activity has shaped the milieu in which Catholicism has taken root in the United States. It is therefore understandable that many of the faithful, including priests, would ask why a church which is committed to the kingdom of heaven would speak so often and so insistently on the economic and social realities of daily life. Divided on the stance they think their church should take, some American Catholics see its teaching on social issues as meddling in politics; others maintain that it is overly concerned about "spiritual" matters and therefore irrelevant to more pressing human concerns.

This chapter addresses the relationship between service to humanity and witness to the kingdom of God in the teaching of the American bishops. Since polarization within American Catholicism has resulted in considerable tension in the ecclesial community, the teaching of the bishops of the United States must address ideological biases within it which exert great centrifugal force, tending toward the rending of the church. As will be shown, the integration of values, often improperly placed in opposition to one another in confrontations between traditionalists and progressives, lies at the heart of an authentic priestly spirituality.

I. Christ as Source of Present Salvation and Future Fulfillment

Because Jesus is the model of the Christian life, Archbishop Sanchez addresses a perennial concern when he asks: "Are we disciples of the carpenter's son, or have we changed our role so as to accommodate worldly expectations?"[2] In affirming that the identity and mission of Jesus is the norm against which Christian authenticity is to be judged, the archbishop quotes the following words of Pope John Paul II to the poor people of a South American barrio: "The Pope loves you because you are God's favorites. In founding his family, the church, God had in mind a poor and needy humanity. To redeem it he sent his Son specifically, who was born and lived among the poor to make us rich with his poverty."[3] Since the first obligation of those who speak in the name of Christ is to be holy in the way that he is holy, the poverty of Christ is a constant challenge to Christian spirituality.[4] Moreover, because Jesus loved everyone, especially the poor, disinherited and outcasts, imitation of this love is the measure of authentic Christian ministry.[5]

Even though the bishops focus attention on the fact that Jesus exercised his ministry by seeking out the despised and rejected, and showing concern for the tired, troubled and unloved,[6] they start with the incarnation in articulating the spirituality of Jesus. In this way, they present his service as more than help generously given to the unfortunate by a privileged outsider. Thomas Grady, the bishop of Orlando, Florida, underlines the significance of the incarnation in explaining the saving work of Christ. He says that in becoming one with humanity Jesus "did not take away the prison of our flesh—the box of our limitations and disappointments. Rather, he entered into our flesh. He did not take away the pain of life. Rather, he shared it with us. He did not take away death. Rather, he died for us and gave us resurrection."[7] Jesus was a servant who experienced the heart-rending limits of human life. Thus he did not heal the sickness or take away the pain of everyone he met, but he did give himself completely to all in a healing touch of reconciliation and peace.[8] The first gift which Jesus offered was the shalom of his friendship; moreover, he left his disciples the example of this saving presence.[9]

The bishops stress that Jesus chose not only to be human, but also to be poor. The posture which he assumed was that of emptying himself and of not clinging to things. According to Archbishop Quinn, Christ moved into the experience of those he served, being drawn into solidarity with them by his ministry. This demanded sensitivity to the poor and vulnerability to them. Thus, Jesus became a poor man because of his desire to be involved in the situation of those he sought to free, thereby joining himself to the sufferings and struggles of humanity by the very style of his life.[10] Consequently, poverty for and as a result of ministry is a profound way of embracing the demands of discipleship, having its roots in the example of Jesus who chose to be poor.[11] Since his body became the very portrait of human neediness, Christian spirituality must pursue a similar identification with the poor as a sign of Jesus' salvific mission.

Insofar as the quest for upward mobility is an obsession in the American social environment, imitating the poverty of Jesus makes strong counter-cultural demands on those who follow him. Bishop Sullivan observes that Jesus is the ultimate symbol of downward mobility, since by the standards of his society he was a nobody.[12] Yet it is this Christ, ultimately executed as a troublemaker and a criminal, whom Christian spirituality emulates.

Nevertheless, the choice of a simple lifestyle did not separate Jesus from the rich, or from any person or human situation, since he clearly came to serve and free all. He shared meals with the whole gamut of his society, from Pharisees to fishermen, from Levites to prostitutes. In fact, he was reproached for being so totally drawn into the human condition. Archbishop Weakland regards this kind of compassion for the plight of humanity as essential to an authentic spirituality. He quotes Anthony Bloom who once said that the holier people get and the more they identify with Christ, the more sensitive they become to those who are hurting.[13] Because true disciples contemplate Christ's way of loving, they begin to take on his attitude toward those they serve.[14] Effective ministry, then, is the result of prayerful reflection on the vulnerability of Christ.

On the other hand, the ministry of Jesus was also explicitly eschatological, since its purpose was to announce the kingdom of God to the people he touched; thus, in revealing his servant-identity, Jesus also made present the reign of the God he familiarly called "Father." Because he stood in the midst of humanity as servant of the transcendent God, he went off in the night to pray by himself in testimony to the fact that his temporal activity was rooted in a personal relationship with the God who offers true liberation.[15] The prayer-life of Jesus, then, is an affirmation of the deepest significance of his servant-ministry as a call to the messianic expectations and actions which should mark the spirituality of his disciples.

Jesus became the suffering-servant in response to the inbreaking kingdom of God, and he demonstrated that the way to God's glory is in the total offering of self, even in pain and death. Consequently, all the elements of Jesus' life—his incarnation, his choice of poverty, his ministry to those in need, and especially his death and resurrection—make it clear that service to humanity and the reign of God are intimately linked.[16]

It is paradoxical, but eminently consistent, then, that when the servant-Christ is totally humiliated on the cross the eschatological age blossoms forth. This climactic event underlines the fact that service to the poor and the coming of the kingdom are explicitly correlated in the mission of Jesus; both proceed from the same source and manifest the same reality: the saving action of God. The gospel of Mark presents the final outburst of Jesus upon the cross as a shout of victory. Matthew sees the death of Jesus as an anticipation of the parousia, since it is accompanied by the resurrection of the dead. The gospel of John relates the dying breath of Jesus to the outpouring of the Spirit of the eschatological age.[17] The bishops drive home the point that when Jesus is most closely identified with the poor as their servant, he is also most powerfully associated with the kingdom of God.

The total ministry of Jesus, then, links service to human need with the coming of the reign of God. His servant-ministry is both the actualization of the full meaning of human existence and the proclamation of the kingdom. The life, death and resurrection of Jesus provide the pattern for the authentic realization of humanity in this life and its fulfillment in the kingdom yet to come.[18] Cardinal Bernard Law, the archbishop of Boston, says quite simply: "Without Christ, we cannot know with certainty and fully what it means to be a human person; we cannot understand fully the human vocation to existence as such."[19] An adequate understanding of human maturity, then, is found only in Christ, since it is precisely by participating in his sacrificial love that the human vocation is perfected.[20] Christian holiness is related, by definition, to loving service.

In the end, the servant-ministry of Jesus is enhanced, not changed, as he enters into eschatological fulfillment, since both the temporal and the heavenly dimensions of his existence are focused on a radically new creation, the realization of the kingdom of God. His earthly solidarity with the poor of Palestine flows from the same mission as his heavenly intercession for the church. Thus, the good shepherd of the historical ministry already embodies the compassionate high priest who as risen Lord continues to exercise a servant role in behalf of humanity.[21] For this reason, all that Jesus is for the poor in his earthly life is already an eschatological manifestation of the saving power of God.[22]

In both his earthly ministry and in his heavenly care for the church Jesus is Lord of history, drawing all things to himself. As a pilgrim who became a sign of contradiction, he taught that the present world is not a lasting city.[23] Yet Jesus also insisted that the God who lies at the end of the journey could already be known and served while on earthly pilgrimage. Now, as heavenly Lord, Jesus empowers the temporal journey of the church by filling it with his wisdom and creative energy.[24]

Accordingly, Jesus continues to minister to the church by making it a participant in his journey to the Father through faith and the sacraments; thus, the pattern initiated in Christ is brought to completion in the church. And so the *Spiritual Renewal of the American Priesthood* says: "Christian spirituality consists in the living out in experience, throughout the whole course of our lives, of the death-resurrection of Christ that we have been caught up into by baptism."[25] Since the glorified Christ continues to influence the earthly activity of the ecclesial community, it is important to understand the dynamic relationship which exists between the salvation which is offered to the church by the risen Lord in the present, and the future fulfillment of this gift in him.[26]

The eucharist is the privileged moment in which the eschatological Christ quickens and guides the pilgrim journey of the church. This celebration nourishes transcendent values, deepens insight into the present identity of the community, and draws attention to its future goal; therefore, it is truly the source of conversion to the life of the kingdom, changing the loves and desires of those who participate in it.[27] There, Jesus himself is offered to the community gathered in worship as a foretaste of the goal of ecclesial existence: perfect communion of life and love in Christ. This dynamic presence of Jesus embodies the grace of his life, death and resurrection, giving power and efficacy to ministry.[28] Since the eucharist renders Jesus present both as crucified servant and as eschatological Lord, it is the source of pastoral charity and the pattern of ministerial spirituality.[29] Because service is the sign of the kingdom and the way which leads to its consummation, the eucharistic Christ unites the present and the future in himself by nourishing the community with his self-giving love as messianic priest.

In summary, it is apparent that service to humanity and zeal for the kingdom are inseparable realities in the life of Jesus. His example, then, lies at the heart of the tension experienced in the ecclesial community between service to the temporal needs of the human family and witness to the reign of God. The church has always struggled with the relationship between these two concerns because Jesus commanded that the poor be cared for at the same time that the heavenly kingdom is sought.

The key to this apparent dilemma lies in the bond which Jesus saw in these two dimensions of his ministry: He always approached ministry to the poor as a proclamation of the kingdom already present and inaugurated. Therefore, since the kingdom is already operative in service rendered to the human community, the present and the future are joined in the servant thrust of the ministry of Jesus, earthly service being true initiation into a kingdom which is yet to be completed. Service to the poor and witness to the kingdom do not stand against one another, but both are animated by the Spirit of Jesus, and both express interrelated aspects of a new way of life which will be fully integrated only when Christ comes again.

It is important, therefore, to underscore the fact that the life and ministry of Jesus are unified by a common thrust which expresses itself, on the one hand, in service to the temporal needs of the human family, and, on the other, in witness to the inbreaking reign of God. These two dimensions of Jesus' ministry spring from the same spiritual dynamic: hunger and thirst for the kingdom of

God. As Jesus lives them they are bound together so tightly that they form but two sides of one salvific mission; thus, Jesus embraces both of them as an expression of the same servant-identity and as directed to the same eschatological goal.

In emulating the example of Jesus, it is clear that the same unity in mission and goal must prevail in Christian spirituality. While the Christian life is concrete, and ordered in a distinctive way to the poor, it must also be empowered by and directed toward the transcendent reign of God. A spirituality which is truly quickened by the Holy Spirit enables disciples to participate in the servant ministry of Christ in a way which proclaims a kingdom that is beyond the limits of earthly service.

The American bishops address the issues of service and witness in the life of Jesus with clarity and strength. Based on his example, they insist that ministry to the needs of this world and proclamation of the kingdom are so fused that they cannot be separated in an authentic Christian spirituality. Yet, the practical implications of this insight for a dynamic piety empowering social action need to be further developed, as will be stated in the evaluative comments in Chapter 8.

II. The Church as Social Agent and Eschatological Witness

Although the church is concerned with ultimate meanings and values, it is immersed in temporal concerns and the common culture.[30] Hence, its members are subject to both the benefits and the limitations of society. *The Spiritual Renewal of the American Priesthood* reminds priests that "the spiritual life is, above all, life."[31] It is ordinary, daily, and often uneventful. The bishops regard this concrete human foundation as crucial to contemporary spirituality. It is apparent that discussions about spirituality are welcome among priests if they deal with real life, that is, with authentic human concerns, and not with some otherworldly form of piety. This focus is appropriate indeed, since withdrawal is not the direction being set by the church today; instead identification with the sufferings and joys of humanity lies at the heart of an ecclesial spirituality.[32]

Chapter 6 made it clear that, by its very nature, the church has both a divine and a human character; its self-understanding must be rooted in both to be authentic. This chapter moves from concentration on the identity of the church to consideration of the relationship between its service to society and its ministry on behalf of history's eschatological goal. A new dynamic is, therefore, addressed: the interaction of efforts directed toward human betterment, on one hand, and toward the fulfillment of the reign of God, on the other. This section is divided into two parts: the first deals with the ways in which the transcendent goal of the church influences its earthly ministry; the second treats the reverse, the ways in which earthly ministry contributes to the attainment of its transcendent goal.

Since the church participates in the mysteries of Christ's incarnation and glorification, its temporal activity is permeated with an eschatological quality which gives vision to, empowers, and renders judgment on the community. Without a vision rooted in the transcendent the ecclesial community is not yet ready for authentic ministry. As an opportunity for discernment, prayer is a crucial activity directed at reading the signs of the times through the prism of the gospel.[33] Cardinal Bernardin says that prayer should not isolate one from the reality of social life, but lead to it: "Authentic prayer—that is, prayer which brings us into an intimate, loving union with God—will deeply affect how we perceive and deal with ourselves and with others."[34]

Bishop Clark proposes that the self-knowledge which is essential to Christian life and ministry is a consequence of prayer: "That wonderfully freeing gift helps us continually to walk from illusion to reality, to live in the present moment and to be at peace with ourselves as flesh and blood human beings."[35] In other words, human weakness is not to be denied or evaded; it is to be accepted as a place in which the loving power of God operates. Not only does authentic prayer promote an encounter with God; it is also an activity directed at increased personal and ecclesial self-understanding.

Prayer brings one closer to God only if it facilitates one's self-knowledge as a person and as a member of the church; it leads to God only if it promotes the discovery of communion with others.[36] In this way the kingdom, welcomed in prayer, lays bare the concrete earthly demands which are to be respected in an authentic spirituality. Since the transcendent kingdom sheds light on the true nature of present realities, prayer is essential to an accurate appraisal of daily life. This relationship between Christian prayer and earthly activity, then, is the first bond between transcendent goal and temporal tasks affirmed by the American bishops.

The bishops accentuate the need for prayerfulness by linking the well-being of society as a whole to the discovery of a transcendent vision. The first stage toward world peace lies in a spiritual rebirth. The wisdom arising from consciousness of the transcendent dimen-

sion of existence provides light by which temporal reality is interpreted. Since human beings have been raised to a level of existence
which transcends temporal reality as such, the institutions of society
must be founded on and guided by an accurate understanding of the
human person. In stressing this insight Cardinal Krol says: "The
dignity of the human person is the basic principle, the guiding norm
and the ultimate goal of the social doctrine of the gospel."[37] The
human community is bound together by its sense of fellowship with
God and the acceptance of a divine ordering of reality.[38]

Since the good news of Christ and a secular interpretation of
social progress are not necessarily the same, careful discernment is
necessary.[39] Archbishop Sanchez underlines the radical requirements of the gospel by citing three examples of the demands which
the Spirit makes on the Christian community: the church is to be
poor in reality, not only in spirit; the church is to serve and not to be
served; it is to give and not to receive. These values flow from a vision
of the kingdom rooted in a life of prayer—the archbishop declares
that it is imperative that Christ be listened to and known before he is
proclaimed to others. Because the vision and values of the church are
associated with worship, the conversion arising from prayer is an
essential element in the life of the pilgrim people of God, and therefore of those who lead it.[40]

Inasmuch as Christians often experience both a lack of congru-
ity between their lives and the example of Jesus, and a failure of
church structures adequately to reflect the ideals of the gospel, they
are constantly moved by the Spirit to self-criticism, purification and
renewal.[41] Sensitivity to the Spirit in prayer is the core of any movement toward revitalization of the activity of the church; in other
words, vision precedes action in an authentic ecclesial spirituality.

Renewed vision gives birth to a new way of life and generates
new personal and societal responsibilities which often run counter to
the values of contemporary culture.[42] While the American culture
makes a significant contribution to the ecclesial community, each of
its benefits must undergo purification if it is to serve the kingdom
and not become an end in itself. For example, the ecclesial community is enriched by the American zest for progress which gives rise to
healthy competition; yet the same cultural dynamic also engenders a
sense of invincibility which too easily substitutes endless possibilities
for growth for willingness to accept death as a necessary component
of coming to new life. Freedom, pluralism, and pragmatism are
values which can either serve the gospel or stand in the way of
legitimate authority, unity, and a more reflective approach to real-

ity.[43] The American experience, then, must be continually assessed in the light of the gospel.

The bishops consistently underline the fact that prayer enhances the conscious participation of the ecclesial community in the transcendent mystery which empowers its existence. John Roach, the archbishop of St. Paul and Minneapolis, sums up his teaching on prayer by declaring: "You surrender your life and your will to God. It's very simple but very hard."[44] Bishop Treinen describes prayer as the "release of self to the solicitation of the Holy Spirit," an experience which he says is marvelous to behold in others and glorious to experience in oneself.[45] Archbishop John Quinn asserts: "It is our search in prayer to enter into the mystery of the Lord's humiliation, suffering and death, the mystery of his love and obedience to the Father's will, that places in our hands the key to all meaning: the meaning of what we encounter in our ministry, the meaning of our personal struggles, the meaning of everything."[46] Thus, daily, prolonged personal prayer endows all aspects of ecclesial life with spiritual vision and a capacity for discernment.

True prayer is the word of God uttered by the Holy Spirit and welling up within the one praying.[47] It is rooted in that openness and emptiness of the human spirit before God which allows one to be imbued with the fullness of divine life, power and love. Prayer is a part of every Christian activity, at the same time that it is something which exists for its own sake. Although prayer and ministry should not be seen as separate realities, yet when everything is regarded as prayer so that worship ceases to be a distinctive activity, then nothing is prayer. Without explicit prayer the spiritual life of the community soon perishes.[48] *The Spiritual Renewal of the American Priesthood* says: "Service of God without living knowledge and love is service, but hardly prayer."[49] An authentic spirituality must involve an encounter with God and an experience of his presence.

Since prayer clarifies the deepest longings of humanity, it must lie at the heart of any true service offered to the human family. Prayer and ministry, then, are interdependent dimensions of ecclesial life. Prayer gives direction to ministry and service gives visible expression to prayer. Because of the close relationship between the two, Bishop Sullivan sees prayer as an apostolic matter, not as a leisure-time activity. He states quite bluntly that without mature prayer there cannot be mature ministry. He sums up his insights on prayer by saying: "It is the source of our vocation; it touches the essence of who we are and in some ways it defines the nature of our calling."[50] Growth in prayer always stimulates a strong desire to share more intimately in the work Jesus came to do.[51]

Not only does the transcendent provide vision; it also empowers ministry. Through hope-filled actions Christ continues to be present in history as the only true liberator of humanity. Because the American culture lends itself to feelings of omnipotence, the insistence of the gospel that, unaided, the church and its ministers are powerless to do anything to advance the kingdom of God is integrated into ministerial activity only with difficulty. Yet admission of powerlessness is the first requirement of a ministerial spirituality. Bishop Balke describes poverty of spirit as "the most fundamental truth of our being and becoming human."[52] Vulnerability is the meeting point of heaven and earth, the place where God and humanity embrace and the situation in which the Spirit is at work. The ecclesial community is called to acknowledge its poverty in three ways: first, it must affirm that it has no security other than the love of God; second, the community is called to pursue service to people rather than material enrichment; finally, the pilgrim church is to be poor so as to express solidarity with the poor. The goal of all of these aspects of ecclesial poverty is prayerful receptivity to God and ministerial availability to those in need.[53]

The bishops clearly teach, then, that the church is dependent on the transcendent not only for vision, but also for the power to act effectively. It is significant that Cardinal Bernardin tells a gathering of priests that the more aware they are of their own need for redemption and the more sensitive they are to the joys and sufferings of their people, the more profound will be their prayer of praise and thanksgiving.[54] The fundamental gospel value of poverty binds together responsiveness to humanity and openness to the power of God.

The way of life based on the vision of Jesus is quite radical when judged by contemporary standards.[55] For example, while Jesus taught that his disciples were to be free and fully human, he also insisted that they were not created to fulfill all their desires, but to live for others.[56] By encouraging the implementation of this teaching alone, priests make it clear that church membership, by definition, involves being counter-cultural. In fact, the bishops direct American Catholics ever farther from self-centered preoccupations. In response to the conciliar mandate that the church's attention be focused outward in a mission of service to the world, the ecclesial community is not to limit its efforts to concern for its own salvation.

Christians fulfill their vocation only by advancing the reign of God's peace and love in the total human community.[57] In the wake of the council, then, the human family has become the arena for Christian spirituality.

In this new global context, the bishops affirm not only that the transcendent and the temporal aspects of the Christian life complement one another, but also that the zeal for justice inherent in Christian spirituality flows from the church's experience of its eschatological Lord. The task committed to the ecclesial community, then, is the promotion of human development in a way which makes the divine image clear in each person. Cardinal Krol sums up the social thrust of the contemporary church by saying that the church in our time has grown in awareness of the fact that the promotion of human rights is required by the gospel and is, therefore, central to ecclesial ministry. He goes on to quote the Synod of 1971 which declared: "Anyone who ventures to speak to people about justice must first be just in their eyes."[58] Fostering human rights requires that the ecclesial community scrutinize and purify its own life, laws and policies. Being holy and at the same time sinful, the church must struggle to be faithful to its own identity as servant if it is to fulfill its worldwide mission.[59]

Even more striking is Bishop Hubbard's declaration that, since efforts on behalf of justice are a constitutive element of the Christian life, they are as much a part of an authentic spirituality as the proclamation of the word and the celebration of the sacraments.[60] Undertakings to alleviate human misery and to change the forces which cause it must be a part of the activity of each Christian and of the entire ecclesial community. In their joint statement *To Teach as Jesus Did,* the bishops declare: "The proclamation (of social teaching) must be forthright, even when forthrightness challenges widely accepted attitudes and practices. Even though Christians may at times err in their facts, interpretations, and conclusions about social issues, they must not fail to apply the gospel to contemporary life."[61] In the depersonalized climate which overshadows so much of society, a viable and visible ministry of service lends credibility to the ministry of word and sacrament.[62]

Raymond Lucker, the bishop of New Ulm, Minnesota, told the 1986 Collegeville Assembly that the church has a role in the social order. Quoting the Vatican II document *Apostolicam Actuositatem* he said: "The mission of the church is not only to bring to people the message and grace of Christ, but also to penetrate and perfect the temporal sphere with the spirit of the gospel."[63] He insisted that in

fulfilling this mission to the world the laity are of primary importance. Thus, lay people are called and consecrated, first of all, for the
Christian transformation of society. Secondarily, they may also share
a ministry within the ecclesial community itself. Because the laity are,
by definition, ordered to the service of the society in which they live,
the ordained, in turn, have the responsibility of encouraging, affirming, and supporting them in their ministry of transformation
in the social, political, cultural, scientific and economic spheres of
daily life.[64]

This aspect of the bishops' teaching is helpful in clarifying the
area of activity which is most suitable to the ordained: the development of the ecclesial community as such.[65] Just as service to the
temporal order is pivotal to the spirituality of the laity, so also ministry to the laity is central to the spirituality of the priests who are
their ecclesial leaders. Since the laity and the ordained participate in
the temporal and transcendent dimensions of ecclesial activity in
ways which are complementary to one another, it is only in the
interaction between them that the total mission of the church is
properly realized. Thus, the differentiation of ministries within the
ecclesial community and the bonding of these roles in correlated
service unite the baptized and the ordained, and render their mission
credible to the world.

In addressing the complex question of international peace as a
national conference, the American bishops clearly move Christian
ministry and spirituality beyond a narrow ecclesiastical vision and
into the forum of global humanitarian issues. They thereby affirm
both that the ministry of the clergy has a direct relationship to temporal issues, and that the eschatological kingdom should not be conceived as something belonging entirely to the future. And so they
offer a decisive challenge to the American people: "Christians are
called to live the tension between the vision of the reign of God and
its concrete realization in history. The tension is often described in
terms of 'already but not yet': i.e., we already live in the grace of the
kingdom, but it is not yet the completed kingdom."[66] The bishops
again wed eschatological values to authentic ministry in the human
community. This interrelationship is a pivotal tenet of post-conciliar
spirituality with implications for all aspects of ecclesial life.

This rapport between the temporal and the transcendent makes
the church a striking instrument of the kingdom of God in human
history. Since peace built on justice is one of the signs of the reign of
God, the effort of the ecclesial community to combat the consequences of sin in personal and social life makes the kingdom actively

present in the temporal order, advancing the cause of peace.[67] The American bishops teach that peace is both a divine gift and a human task; it is fostered by the interaction between prayer and work, thereby manifesting the necessary collaboration of God's grace and human ingenuity in its achievement.[68] This teaching on the interrelationship of social action and witness to transcendent values has made a notable contribution to American life; the development of a better integration of this dynamic into Christian spirituality will be commented on in Chapter 8.

Finally, the bishops insist that since the earthly church participates in the reality of the kingdom, its temporal activity stands subject to eschatological judgment. Therefore, the ecclesial community is accountable for the effectiveness of its life and institutions in witnessing to the kingdom it serves and prefigures.[69] The church has a duty to promote responsible stewardship among its members and ministers, and to provide opportunities for evaluation and enrichment.[70] Ecclesial accountability embraces both an acceptance of the imperfection of the human condition and an acknowledgement of the presence of God calling the community and its ministers to greater fidelity.

Thus, the teaching of the bishops has moved a step further; the activity of the church is not only imbued with vision and power by its relationship to the transcendent, it is also judged by it. Having learned from Jesus what it means to be a servant in the world, the church evaluates itself by his standards: feeding the hungry, clothing the naked, caring for the sick and giving comfort to victims of injustice.[71] Bishop Sullivan says that it is insufficient to have faith communities where the sacraments are well celebrated and people live together harmoniously unless these celebrations and experiences of fellowship break forth into service of others. Faith must engender love, action, and a thirst for justice.[72] In this same light, *The Program for Priestly Formation* affirms that education for social justice is an urgent aspect of all instruction in the church.[73] An appropriate ecclesial spirituality makes the community aware of its weakness and sinfulness, thereby moving it toward renewed vigor as an agent of the kingdom of God. It is clear that temporal ministry not only arises from a transcendent vision, but it also witnesses to the eschatological hope of the church. The pilgrim church points to the future not so much as a time which is yet to come, but more as the still to be completed culmination of the kingdom already initiated in the person of Jesus. Thus, ecclesial life and ministry already participate in the initial realization of the kingdom.[74] In every time and place, an authentic ecclesial spirituality challenges the community to seize opportunities for growth in response to the Spirit who already manifests the risen Lord.[75]

Archbishop Quinn brings the complex nature of the earthly church into clearer focus by describing it as the dawn which hints that the night is over, but does not yet proclaim the full light of day. He says: "The dawn dissipates the darkness and welcomes the light. Yet it holds both of them, darkness mixed with light."[76] As the eschatological companion of the pilgrim church, Jesus empowers his disciples to be daybreak and dawn for the world. The joyful fellowship characteristic of the early Christian communities suggests that a clear distinction between the two comings of Christ was not emphasized, since the lordship of Jesus was something already experienced in their lives.[77] Consequently the ecclesial community, in the very tenor of its life, is an eschatological witness.

Since the ecclesial community already participates in the dominion of the risen Christ during its earthly pilgrimage, it cannot be fully grasped in human terms or be adequately expressed in social-political categories.[78] Because the church is more God's work than the labor of the community, the life of the people of God is a mystery which eludes neat and final definitions.[79] Archbishop Mahony makes this point a very practical one by insisting that, at a time when clear job descriptions are important to avoid needless frustration among the members of a parish staff, an unclouded recognition of the difference between that which is God's responsibility and that which is the task of the community in fulfilling the mission of the church is even more critical.[80] Such clarity is impossible without constant reference to the transcendent. A sound spirituality, then, is essential in offering appropriate witness to the true source of the church's ministry.

Archbishop Mahony proposes that intercessory prayer is an important way in which the church witnesses to its eschatological hope. He suggests that regular prayer for those being served effects a profound transformation in ecclesial ministers, moving them away from Pelagian or messianic inclinations which produce great frustration and stress.[81] He insists that ministry is not simply or primarily a human activity; it is, first of all, the work of God. Prayer for those being served witnesses to an authentic understanding of the relationship between the divine and the human in the spiritual life. In the same light, both *The Spirituality of the American Priesthood,* and *As One Who Serves* see the Liturgy of the Hours as a normative prayer form for priests.[82] As a prayer shared with other members of the community and offered on behalf of the church, the Liturgy of the Hours expresses a profound intuition about the bond which exists between worship and ministry.

There is no doubt that the bishops view the eucharist as the staple of an ecclesial spirituality, since it most strikingly witnesses to the eschatological identity of the church by engendering communion with Christ among the members of the community.[83] In the eucharistic assembly, the people of God celebrates what it is becoming and is refreshed on its journey toward the culmination of the kingdom.[84] Through the eucharistic mystery Jesus stands among his people in his humanity, under the sign of his vulnerability and death. There, he is uniquely the living presence of the compassion of God offered in service to the community. In the celebration of the eucharist, Jesus most fully joins himself to the weakness and sinfulness, the fears and struggles, and the hopes and dreams of humanity.[85]

The church becomes a self-giving servant community through participation in the eucharist. Cardinal Bernardin affirms the connection between the eucharist and ministry by saying: "If our outreach to others becomes disconnected from the eucharist, it will lose its unique, compelling character . . . it will soon lose its spark, its inner dynamism, its capability continually to renew itself."[86] Since the ministers of the church must become bread which is broken and wine which is poured out for the life of the world, the eucharist must always be at the heart of their ecclesial experience. Cardinal Bernardin also quotes Pope John Paul II: "If our eucharistic worship is authentic, it must make us grow in awareness of the dignity of each person."[87] The eucharist, then, instructs and empowers the community in the servant love of the Christ who is offered equally to all.

The eucharist is both the clear invitation and the gifted capacity to live the values of the kingdom in the midst of the world. Its aim is radically to alter the community's understanding of the meaning of human existence, the dynamics of relationships with others, and the model of ecclesial ministry. As bread broken for others, the eucharist is designed to lead to a change in priorities and to courageous involvement in efforts to advance the kingdom of peace and justice. Bishop Hubbard declares quite forcefully: "A eucharist, then, which does not evoke within us a real identification with the other members of Christ's body, others who are in need, others who are suffering, is a eucharist which is celebrated according to our own mindset and not according to the mind of Jesus."[88] Since the risen Christ, whom the eucharist makes present, is the source of the servant-ministry of the church, this celebration witnesses to the eschatological reign of God by instilling a hunger for peace and justice in those who partake in it. Both in the eucharistic assembly and in the way of life which flows from it the eschatological kingdom and earthly service are united.

Consequently, the eucharist not only permeates the life of the ecclesial community by providing vision, empowering ministry, and judging actions, but it also witnesses to its hope by making eschatological fulfillment truly present in the person of the risen Christ. Inasmuch as the eucharistic mystery, in all its richness, is a fundamental component of an ecclesial spirituality, it must be pondered in prayer to be fully effective. Archbishop Quinn says that through prayer in the presence of the Blessed Sacrament, Christ communicates his own yes to the kingdom and empowers a like response in the church. He testifies that this form of prayer gives soul to preaching, strength to service, and joy and peace in suffering.[89] Cardinal Krol also highlights the council's endorsement of intimate, prayerful pondering of the eucharistic mystery, saying that not even liturgical activity can sustain a priest unless it is steeped in such prayer.[90] He recommends, not more prayers, but better prayer, that is, humble, constant, heartfelt personal prayer reaching from the human heart to the heart of God.[91] Archbishop Mahony draws attention to the positive cumulative effect of a daily eucharistic holy hour. He sees a close connection between time given to adoration of the eucharist and the ability of the preacher to open the heart of the word of God to the people.[92]

In conclusion, it is evident that although the popular mind often places concern for the present difficulties of humanity and attention to heavenly fulfillment in opposition to one another, the American bishops see them as essentially complementary aspects of an authentic ecclesial spirituality. Hence, faith in the transcendent God empowers service and deepens its meaning, while temporal ministry expresses the life of the kingdom and witnesses to it as the community moves toward eschatological fulfillment. A genuine ecclesial spirituality constantly seeks to nourish and sustain service with the vision, energy and hope found in communion with the transcendent God, at the same time that it consistently strives to make God's being and mission concrete in temporal acts of service to humanity.

Worship and ministry are not separate realities, then, but interdependent elements of being caught up in the mystery of Christ.[93] Any attempt to obscure the dynamic relationship between prayer and service strikes a devastating blow at the very heart of ecclesial existence. Contemplation and action are not realities set in opposition to one another, but constitutive dimensions of an integrated spiritual life. Therefore an authentic spirituality will always strengthen the bond between them.

III. Priests as Advocates for the Poor and Witnesses to the Kingdom

Since presbyteral spirituality is a distinctive expression of the self-understanding of the church, it flows from the same dynamic tension between the temporal and the transcendent which marks the life and activity of the ecclesial community. The treatment of this dimension of priestly life will be divided into three parts: the longest will consider the relationship between the kingdom and pastoral service in presbyteral spirituality; the two shorter parts will focus on service to the poor and priestly celibacy, respectively.

We begin with a consideration of the existential situation of priests to locate their openness to the kingdom of God in the poverty of the human condition. Cardinal Bernardin forcefully underscores this point of departure: "Despite our special identity and our unique role as priests of the new covenant, we remain human, subject to the same weaknesses and shortcomings as all our sisters and brothers."[94] The ordained are no less in need of forgiveness than other members of the community; therefore they should approach ministry with humility and compassion. Ever mindful of their own weakness, priests are challenged to deal mercifully with sinners.[95] The experience of human frailty, then, is the doorway both to the eschatological God of mercy and to the ecclesial ministry which God inspires.

Bishop Sullivan compares the ordained to the leper of the gospels: "We are weak, we are incompetent, we are desperately in need of help . . . the beginning of any authentic spiritual life is the realization that we, like the leper, are in need."[96] He, too, is convinced that recognition of one's wounded condition and inadequacy is the way to becoming the available instrument the Lord desires. Elden Curtiss, the bishop of Helena, Montana, says that "deficiency is an essential part of the vocation to priesthood."[97] To the characteristics desirable in priests he adds vulnerability to suffering, to failure, and to interior anguish. In the same light, *Human Sexuality and the Ordained Priesthood* pictures the ordained as compassionate fellow-strugglers, striving along with the laity to live up to difficult Christian ideals.[98]

The ordained carry the treasure of priestly service in fragile vessels of clay, showing, thereby, that the surpassing power of their ministry comes from God and not from themselves.[99] Archbishop

Borders even regards it as axiomatic that effective ministers must not fear making mistakes.[100] The first thing required of priests, according to Archbishop Quinn, is that they humbly and gratefully experience Jesus as the compassion of God in their own lives; as sinners they, too, must trust in his mercy and love. Moreover, since God has called those who are weak and count for nothing in the world to be ministers of the gospel, priests must constantly struggle to turn away from sin and to follow the Lord. In this way they are enabled, in turn, to be hope and compassion for others.[101] The people they serve are led to respond more wholeheartedly to their ministry of reconciliation as they see its effects in the lives of the ordained.[102]

Conversion, then, is an essential feature of a priestly spirituality firmly based in a shared experience of the human condition. Archbishop Mahony says that the ordained will be signs of repentance and witnesses to the grace of God at work in human weakness only if they have committed themselves to the lifelong process that conversion entails. He maintains that this means that priests must regularly experience the solace of the sacrament of reconciliation themselves.[103] The ordained need to meet the forgiving Lord, not only in prayer, but also in this healing sacrament.[104]

By recognizing their poverty and by accepting the mercy of the Lord, priests begin to realize that human weakness and God's gift are not incompatible elements of presbyteral spirituality; both lead them to conversion and make them apt mediators of the grace of reconciliation in others. *As One Who Serves* declares: "The priest brings to the sacrament of reconciliation not only the official ministry of the church, but also his own struggle to grow in the Lord."[105] The service rendered to the poor by the ordained starts, therefore, with the acceptance of their own poverty and with their personal availability to the kingdom of God.

Receptivity is an important aspect of presbyteral spirituality, since priests must be willing to receive the ministry of the ecclesial community as well as give it. Since they, too, are Christians in need of the ministry of others, priests who acknowledge their poverty are best equipped to be servants of the community.[106] The importance of this receptive capacity in ordained ministers is underscored in *The Continuing Formation of Priests:* "The priest of the future will be one who is himself evangelized by those with whom he works. He will learn what missioners have discovered about reverse-mission, that is, that the priest will receive healing and service, will be ministered unto, as he serves his sisters and brothers."[107] Priests are ministered to by the full ecclesial community, then, and not only by fellow presbyters. Their personal responsiveness to the ministry of others marks them as ecclesial persons and contributes an important element to their spiritual identity.

The bishops insist that the context of contemporary ministry imposes burdens that comprise an experience of poverty for many American priests. Bishop Quinn observes that a number of priests are "shellshocked" from the excessive demands made upon them. Some are broken, frightened, and feel useless and unable to cope.[108] The expectations are many, the number of priests has diminished, and the functions proper to the ordained are often unclear. Archbishop Roach draws attention to the pressures which arise from the lofty standards set for the performance of the priest: "In his own heart, and in the minds of his people, his life and ministry are measured by that of Christ."[109] Being asked to represent the Lord in a more public way than any other member of the ecclesial community generates an encounter with a special form of personal poverty. Since priests are frequently assessed by impossible criteria, they often disappoint themselves and others. Acknowledging weakness and failure, on one hand, and being misunderstood, on the other, are among the most painful elements of presbyteral spirituality.[110]

The asceticism to which the bishops draw attention arises from the nature of presbyteral existence itself. Since ordained ministry is always exercised imperfectly, those who are engaged in it must continue to grow in faith, in hope and in prayer.[111] In response to the developmental nature of every Christian vocation, the bishops urge priests to care for their growth needs in the spiritual, intellectual, emotional and relational aspects of their lives.[112] *The Continuing Formation of Priests* singles out honesty in facing loneliness, sexuality, intimacy, feelings of inadequacy and psychological immaturity.[113] Regular exercise and periodic physical examinations are also important in providing a healthy, holistic context for spiritual development.

Since areas of weakness persist in everyone, human growth is a lifelong process. An appropriate spirituality challenges priests to make a periodic assessment of their ministry in the light both of the Gospel and of ecclesial needs.[114] Here, the bishops add a challenging new dimension to presbyteral spirituality. The vulnerability which this inquiry into one's life and ministry demands may well raise doubts and fears. Precisely the openness which periodic assessment requires makes it a procedure which can lead to deeper conversion. In encouraging this and other processes for priestly renewal, the American bishops again underline the correlation between acknowledgement of human neediness, responsiveness to the ministry of others, and openness to the kingdom of God in an appropriate spirituality.

In accepting themselves as imperfect instruments, priests can discover joy, peace and renewed vision as authentic signs of God's presence in their lives. Archbishop John Quinn says very clearly: "When we finally have the humility to accept our limitations and to acknowledge our needs, then God can begin to work in our weakness."[115] Bishop Francis Quinn proposes that a significant dimension of growth in holiness is living a truly human life: "Some priests are working too hard. They do not take enough time for diversion and rest. Some do not ask the help they need in ministry from lay people."[116] He sees genuine holiness and true humanity as two sides of the same coin. Presbyteral spirituality, then, must make room for prayer, leisure, and friendship, as well as for hard work.

Balanced development lies at the heart of an appropriate spirituality; priests are encouraged to recognize the interaction between the personal and the communal, the rational and the intuitive, and the temporal and the transcendent in their lives. *The Continuing Formation of Priests* challenges the ordained to move beyond a purely functional understanding of their ministry and toward one that is more holistic.[117] In the same light, Cardinal Bernardin states that personal integrity and wholeness must be the goals of post-conciliar presbyteral spirituality: "To survive, to persevere in fidelity to the demands of this vocation means that much of the basic support and guidance must be found deep within each priest."[118] Therefore, external structures and material compliance are not sufficient foundations for contemporary spirituality. The values of the gospel must be internalized and the ideals of ministry must be personally appropriated.

The bishops challenge priests to more than acceptance of the poverty inherent in the human condition, as important as this attitude is; they also call them to a form of voluntary poverty which witnesses to the gospel they proclaim. Archbishop Weakland defines this poverty as not clinging to possessions, status and self-importance. As a key dimension of a mature spirituality, priestly simplicity of life invites the larger faith community to "let go" so that others may have what they need. It also awakens the community to the unavoidable truth about human existence contained in the finality of death itself. By seeking to permeate pastoral life with self-emptying love, the ordained herald that moment when all must be given over to Christ.[119]

In leading the family of God through Christ in the Spirit to the Father, the holiness of presbyters, as sacramental persons, has special significance. Archbishop Hickey says that the priest is called to a life of personal holiness, "for without a deep personal commitment to God—in prayer, in sacrifice, in a disciplined life—his ministry cannot be an authentic representation of Jesus' love for us."[120] Through holiness, realized in the sacramental life of the church and in dedication to pastoral care, the kingdom of God permeates priestly service. Bishop Wycislo proposes that priests seek "a towering and obvious sanctity" as the first requirement for their ministry.[121] Archbishop Hickey summaries the importance of presbyteral holiness by quoting François Mauriac: "The priest has remained for me what he was at the dawn of my life . . . he who, at the moment he raises his hands to absolve us, can no longer be distinguished from the Son of Man."[122] Priests stand in the midst of the human drama pointing to a new heaven and a new earth which are mysteriously being realized through the hidden power of God working in their ministry. Their time-bound words and actions manifest the healing and hope, the challenge and truth, the grace and salvation of the kingdom of God.[123]

Presbyteral spirituality is meant, then, to fashion truly sacramental persons who stand in full public view both to give service to the church community and to witness to the kingdom in the world at large. The bishops' 1969 statement on priestly celibacy says: "The priesthood is therefore, in a very special way, the church's witness to the mystery of Christ in service to the human community."[124] Specifically because of their relationship to the kingdom, priests are to be totally available for the work of building the human community. Since the ordained communicate the gospel by allowing their own prophetic self-understanding to enlighten others, their dying and rising with Jesus is a model for the ecclesial community in its interaction with society.[125] Hence, personal transformation in Christ for the sake of effective ministry is a spiritual imperative.[126]

In an ordination homily, Archbishop Quinn underscores the connection between holiness and ministry by declaring that being a priest today means "to be conformed to Jesus, the compassion of God."[127] The mission of priests of the new covenant is to bind up the wounds of the human heart, to proclaim liberation in the midst of the many afflictions which hold humanity prisoner, and to be a source of consolation.[128] The rite of ordination is a reminder that priests are empowered for their ministry by a reality outside of themselves. Archbishop Quinn asserts, therefore, that since the

Spirit conforms the ordained to Christ in his priestly headship, they have the responsibility of making their union with him a living communion, enabling them, not to work *for* the Lord, but *with* him as his companions.[129]

The bishops make it clear that presbyteral spirituality is rooted in a distinctive participation in Christ, the historical embodiment of the kingdom, through the sacrament of orders. In light of the American experience with the charismatic renewal and with the revitalization of religious life, an explicit treatment both of the charismatic endowment proper to the ordained and of the relationship between ordination and charism would have been helpful. This issue will be addressed again in Chapter 8.

Holiness, prayer and ministry have a direct relationship to one another in the articulation of presbyteral spirituality offered by the bishops. Because priests exist for the sake of serving the People of God,[130] the balance between prayer and work in the lives of the ordained is crucial to the welfare of the ecclesial community as well. Presbyteral spirituality calls for the integration of worship and activity, since as participants in the servant ministry of Christ, priests can effectively exercise their distinctive role only when they are prayerfully rooted in him.[131] This correlation between persistent prayer and effective ministry is a constant theme. *The Spiritual Renewal of the American Priesthood* comments: "Without actual communion with the Lord, the paschal mystery becomes less operative and cedes to worldly wisdom, the Spirit is muted, and one's ministry and personal life tend to be motivated by superficial and selfish considerations."[132] The experience of the transcendent through regular prayer is, therefore, essential to all presbyteral activities.

In the teaching of the American bishops, ministry and prayer are interrelated aspects of an appropriate priestly spirituality. *The Spiritual Renewal of the American Priesthood* very forcefully states: "Priestly ministry is the sham of a hireling unless it is rooted in a personal response to the efficacious word of Jesus."[133] The ordained comprehend their priestly identity and actualize their servant ministry only by seeking to abide with the Lord as his first followers did. Cardinal Krol quotes a saying of St. Charles Borromeo: "My brothers, you must realize that for us churchmen nothing is more necessary than meditation. We must meditate before, during and after everything we do."[134] Through prayer the ordained deepen their consciousness of dependence upon God, of the relationship between him and the work they do, and of the goal for which they strive. Meditation and spiritual reading are not only commendable practices, but are essential ones in an authentically Christ-centered spirituality.[135]

The significance of the foregoing statement is seen in Archbishop Weakland's affirmation that sensitivity to the kingdom of God is the most important impetus for priestly ministry. He says: "I don't see how we as priests can keep alive our motivation of service, if we don't have that strong sense . . . of the presence of God and his kingdom among us."[136] Conviction concerning the kingdom as the one thing which matters emancipates ordained ministry, and roots it in a relationship with the God who is loving, caring and forgiving.[137] Since spiritual conviction lies at the heart of priestly motivation, prayer is not merely an appendage to a busy ministry; it is the pulse of the living reality of the priesthood.[138]

A spirituality rooted in prayer unites awareness of the ultimate goal of ministry and sensitivity to its present demands. The bishops maintain that prayer is a necessary activity which must be rigorously pursued.[139] Cardinal Krol says: "The priest must consider prayer as the essential and irreplaceable work of his vocation. Prayer is not a restriction but an opportunity, and not an option, but a necessity if our ministry is to be effective."[140] Prayer is a hedge against the erosion of spiritual values. In a similar vein, Francis Hurley, the archbishop of Anchorage, Alaska, views prayer as a time which untangles the labyrinth of social and political pressures in contemporary ministry. The purpose of prayer is not to give priests an excuse for hiding from the world, but to enable them to be appropriately present in it.[141] By helping make sense of life, prayer promotes the spiritual growth of priests as servants of the ecclesial community.[142]

In light of the pivotal role which the bishops assign to prayer in renewing priestly identity and ministry, they make substantial recommendations to priests in this regard. After having only reluctantly made a thirty day retreat, Bishop Treinen comments: "During a retreat like this one learns that prayer is man's most important activity, his most fruitful work."[143] Using his own experience as an example, he reminds priests that there is no substitute for the time and silence which prayer demands.

Cardinal Bernardin also cites his own experience: "I have been ordained thirty-two years and it took me nearly twenty-five years to realize, in the deepest part of my being, that, if I wanted to be a truly successful priest and bishop—one who could walk with my people in the valley of darkness—I had to put Jesus first in my life, not merely in theory but also in practice."[144] In response to this insight he decided to spend a full hour in prayer each morning before leaving his room. The result has been a change in perspective: the activities of the day are seen as intimately related to the kingdom of God.[145] The value he attaches to his decision has endured; the cardinal testifies that the older he gets the more convinced he is of the need to root all the activities of life in prayer. He attests quite candidly: "To forfeit the quiet moments we should spend with the Lord, or to go about the ministry of word and table in a half-hearted way, is the surest way to rob our life and ministry of their inner strength, dynamism and creativity."[146]

Archbishop Quinn challenges priests to work toward an hour of prayer a day, in addition to the Liturgy of the Hours. He contends: "In the last analysis we are neither fulfilling the plan of Christ, following the example of Christ nor really doing much for our people unless prayer is a top priority every day in our lives."[147] Without prayer, judgments about the world and the church are dictated, gradually and imperceptibly, more by worldly standards than by the priorities of faith. Prayer is a fundamental exigency of the priesthood which keeps life centered on God and activity focused on service.[148] Since the Lord is the beginning and end of all things, priests must drink each day from the wellsprings of their existence through communion with God in prayer.[149] The archbishop insists: "To preach Christ Jesus means to let him speak in us and through us"; therefore, it is of little use to preach if the life of the preacher is not deeply founded in prayer.[150]

Cardinal Bernardin moves the discussion a step further by locating the challenge of ministry in the spiritual dynamic within priests themselves: "When all is said and done, the most important thing of all—the thing that will make sense of all we are and do, or rob our lives and ministry of their meaning and vitality; the thing that will make it possible for us to suffer with and for our people, to celebrate with them, to be creative in ministry and to be healers and reconcilers—is our relationship with the Lord."[151] Priests will never be the loving servants they are called to be unless they first experience the Lord's love for them. Ordained ministry, then, must be firmly anchored in intimacy with the Lord.

Because the first priority of presbyteral life is an ever deepening relationship with Christ, the ordained must blend their external activity with an internal spirituality.[152] Archbishop Quinn points to the fundamental principle of priestly spirituality found in the gospel passage in which Jesus calls the twelve to be his companions. He finds here both the primary object of the apostolic vocation and the first quality of the call to the priesthood, the desire "to be with him." The archbishop aptly remarks: "Unless discipleship is companionship, it will not endure its own costs."[153] Prayerful interaction with the Lord clothes the ordained in Christ, thereby enabling them to share his mind and heart with others.[154]

The capacity to offer fruitful ministry to others, then, is founded on intimate union with the Lord in prayer. Bishop Clark confirms this from his own experience: "Without prayer the life drains out of us. Our daily ministry becomes less an incarnation of the Lord's loving care and more an expression of our own egoism."[155] Bishop Brom points out that there is an ever-present danger that the ordained will be so immersed in harvesting for the Lord that they will fail to deepen their knowledge of the Lord of the harvest. To prevent their ministry from becoming ineffective, priests have as their first duty prayerful presence to Christ.[156] Cardinal Bernardin maintains that this spiritual imperative is reinforced by the simple fact that prayerful priests have an enormous impact on those they serve, even when they may be deficient in human gifts; those who are not perceived as prayerful fail to touch others in the same way.[157]

The essential prerequisite for ordained ministry, then, is thorough immersion in Christ. Bishop Quinn comments: "How hard it is for us as priests to learn to let Christ take over, to live 'now not I, but Christ lives in me.' To let go and let God."[158] Cardinal Krol draws the same conclusion by calling attention to St. John Vianney, a man of little natural endowment, yet of great sanctity. The point which the cardinal underlines is that while prayer was the soul of John Vianney's life, in no way was he remote from the people he served. In the year before his death 80,000 people came to Ars, a parish of 230 members, seeking his ministry.[159] Thus, the life-context of priests is an important part of their prayer. Archbishop Pilarczyk views the priest as one "who has been called to dedicate all his energies, all his talents till the very end of his earthly years to tending the needs of his people . . . he has been set apart *for* them."[160]

The bishops consider pain, brokenness and suffering special avenues both to an encounter with God, and to human growth. *The Priest and Stress* comments that much of the tension which the ordained experience comes from a lack of reflection on life and its disappointments and anxieties in the light of the paschal mystery. Prayer can transform the sufferings of pastoral ministry from causes for resentment into sources of life.[161] Cardinal Bernardin asserts that vulnerability can be a source of strength when priests no longer pretend that they are calling the shots or are in control.[162] Archbishop Quinn recommends meditation on the passion of Christ, because it enables the ordained to internalize God's standards, as it grounds and centers priestly existence and gives it meaning.[163] Prayer provides both a vision which reduces stress, and an energy which revitalizes zeal.

Archbishop Mahony broadens the context of priestly spirituality by viewing it against the background of a neo-pagan, narcissistic environment. In this setting, priests will not find a focus for their ministry either by simply being functionaries or by getting lost in frantic activity. They will do so only by maintaining a clear vision of the witness to which they have been called by Christ and the church.[164] The archbishop identifies prayer as the source of this sharpened understanding of ministry. He says that priests do not so much "bring" God to people, as they point out the Lord's presence because they have already discovered it in prayer. When ministry begins with prayer, then priests are able to offer religious leadership in its truest sense, that is, as a living articulation of the experience of God.[165]

While an appropriate spirituality embraces reflection and activity within a particular life-context, none of these factors, taken together or separately, is an adequate foundation for an authentic spiritual life. *The Spiritual Renewal of the American Priesthood* says that the awareness of oneself as a new creation in Christ is the integrating principle which brings together the various aspects of spirituality. Thus, consciousness of a new identity in Christ is proposed as the foundation for every facet of priestly life and ministry.[166] For this reason, Cardinal Krol underscores a great paradox in the spiritual journey of priests: the more time they devote to prayer and the stronger their relationship with God, the more effective will be their service to men and women in the world.[167]

The summit and source of all Christian prayer is the eucharist; this often affirmed principle of the spiritual life is applied to priests in separate homilies by both Cardinal Krol and Cardinal O'Connor, each commenting on a saying of St. John Vianney: "Holy communion and the holy sacrifice of the mass are the two most efficacious actions for obtaining the conversion of hearts."[168] The cardinals thereby emphasize that, since the eucharist is intimately related to a dynamic priestly spirituality, it lies at the heart of effective presbyteral ministry as well.

The previous statement is true because the kingdom penetrates the present world with unique force through the celebration of the eucharist. By quoting the ordination rite, Archbishop Quinn challenges priests: "Know what you are doing and imitate the mystery

you celebrate."[169] In the archbishop's mind this means drawing
strength from the eucharist to become the compassion of God as
Jesus was. Participation in the eucharist enables priests to be vulnerable with their people and to stand in solidarity with them in the midst
of fear and suffering.

Thus, the teaching of the American bishops on the relationship
between service to humanity and the reign of God reaches a cre-
scendo; they proclaim that the eucharist is the pivotal ecclesial activity bridging the temporal and the transcendent. Through it the
pilgrim church is both nourished on the glorified body of Christ the
servant, and, as those who already participate in the heavenly banquet, empowered to serve others. Moreover, the eucharist reveals
the relationship between these two dimensions of ecclesial existence.
Service to humanity and participation in the kingdom are inseparably
joined, since the life of the eschatological kingdom is available in the
eucharist, and temporal service flows from the eucharist. Because
the future reign of God is made present through service, a proper
understanding of the role of the eucharist is essential to empowering
deeper involvement of the community in the social-political realities
of daily life.

To serve all the baptized and to lead them to the kingdom is the
reason for presbyteral ordination. An appropriate spirituality, then,
must challenge priests to herald the future kingdom by assuming the
servant role which in the life of Jesus was a necessary prelude to its
realization.[170] Cardinal O'Connor very fittingly sums up the eschatological witness of priestly service: "In my first year of ordination I
was fortunate enough to ask an elderly priest for his advice. He said,
'I have only one word of advice: Be kind to the people, be kind to the
people, be kind to the people.' "[171] Kindness is a direct and simple
way of looking at the presence of God in human life; yet the cardinal
affirms that it is often not an easy undertaking for the ordained, even
though it belongs to the very nature of presbyteral ministry.

While priests must strive to be builders of a new world, they do
so as heralds of God's love and as sharers in the heartache and
drudgery of those they serve. Hence, they seek not merely to rear-
range the world, as if from above, but also to partake in the pain of
the community. Bishop Grady suggests that the eucharistic liturgy is
the event at which priests are most fully what they should be for the
people of God. He tells the ordained that as ministers of the eucharist they are sharers in the pain not only of Christ but also of the
people; priests join Christ's life and death and resurrection to that of
the community.[172] Presbyteral spirituality, then, challenges priests

to fashion a new world by involvement in the struggle of the present one.

Yet it is impossible for priests to remove all the pain from the lives of those they serve. While the ordained are obliged to do all they can to promote a better life in this world, Cardinal Bernardin notes that, in the final analysis, earthly accomplishments and immediate joys and sorrows are transitory. Priests also enable people to cope with the trials of life by helping them understand the present in the light of the future: "The ultimate fulfillment of all we attempt, the lasting remedy of all we suffer, lies in life eternal."[173] Archbishop Hunthausen echoes these thoughts, underlining the presence of the risen Lord as source of joy and peace amid the difficulties of the pilgrim journey.[174] Placing proper emphasis on the future is particularly difficult for American priests because of the material concerns of their society and its reluctance to deal with death.

The bishops show great consistency in their insistence on the relationship between eschatological hope and temporal service. When the eschatological promise of faith is properly proclaimed, the needs of the social order are served as well. Cardinal Krol brings these two dimensions of presbyteral spirituality together very succinctly: on one hand, the ministry offered by the ordained is rooted in the transcendent, being primarily a call to conversion and repentance; on the other hand, it leads people both to union with God, and to greater harmony with one another.[175]

In beginning the second part of this section, it is important to notice that an emphasis on prayer and conversion in no way weakens the stress which the American bishops put on the concrete service which priests are to offer especially to the poor. Bishop Balke insists that since the church has made a preferential option for the poor, an authentic spirituality must challenge priests to live out this same choice: "The priest should give the poor a certain priority over the non-poor by sharing himself, his life, and his time with the poor more than with the non-poor."[176] Furthermore, while the ordained may not be able to correct systemic injustices by themselves, they should be leaders in this area, constantly advocating the rights and upholding the dignity of the poor and the oppressed.[177]

Following the example of Jesus the servant, the ordained are to love people by walking with them in the dark valley of bodily sickness, moral dilemmas, oppressive structures and diminished rights. An appropriate spirituality will never allow priests to be detached professionals.[178] *The Continuing Formation of Priests* states: "As the priest becomes more acutely aware of the threats to humanity in the second half of our century—such as the horrible threat of nuclear war—he will want to find ways to speak to such issues that burden the hearts of men, women and children."[179] Bishop Sullivan stresses that by reading *Lumen Gentium,* he was challenged to love the poor, the infirm, the stranger and the homeless. For him this has meant changing ministerial priorities in order to address the full gamut of human needs stretching from outcasts and vagabonds at home to the plight of developing countries.[180]

In fact, the vision of the bishops reaches far beyond the Catholic community. Archbishop Quinn refuses to let priests rest within the confines of parish boundaries, but challenges them to look out at the colossal drama of suffering: hunger, poverty and want in the midst of a world of abundance, new forms of psychological slavery, deepening social and ideological conflicts, and the growing peril of total destruction through war.[181] At their ordination, the archbishop told a group of young religious: "It is in the midst of this city with its 'joys and hopes, its griefs and anxieties' that you must stand as priests."[182]

In suggesting a standard for assessing an authentic priestly spirituality, Archbishop Francis Hurley takes as his point of reference a draft of the bishops' pastoral on the economy. He proposes that, since care for the poorest segment of the population is the yardstick for measuring society itself, a good rule of thumb for evaluating pastoral ministry is the degree to which priests are involved with the poor and the deprived in the community.[183] *The Continuing Formation of Priests* states quite clearly: "Since justice is a constitutive element of the gospel and mission of the church, the priest strives to form his own conscience so that he may become more committed to the promotion of justice in the world."[184] Dedication to peace and reconciliation within and among families, races, classes and nations, and to the advancement of political, social and economic justice flows from the very nature of priestly ministry and, therefore, is an essential component of a sound presbyteral spirituality; it is not an option which can be left to other specially designated ministers.[185]

The bishops insist that involvement with the poor is not simply a modern addendum to the mission of the church, but a fundamental dimension of it. This is true because efforts on behalf of justice reveal and communicate the being of God; thus, undertakings which seek to permeate complex human relationships and social structures with the justice of the gospel express most fully the true nature of evangelization.[186] *Economic Justice for All* emphasizes the link between worship and social action: "The body of Christ which worshipers receive in communion is also a reminder of the reconciling power of

his death on the cross. It empowers them to work to heal the brokenness of society and human relationships and to grow in a spirit of
self-giving for others."[187] Seen in this light, the universal fellowship
which the gospel advocates prompts priests to take as their own
concern the plight of refugees, of victims of war, of those suffering
from economic discrimination, political oppression, or inhuman
working conditions and from other injustices.[188] *As One Who Serves*
further suggests that the ordained may need to make contact, directly or indirectly, with those having political or economic responsibility in the community both to safeguard their apostolic freedom in
teaching moral and religious principles on social matters, and also to
facilitate addressing grave public injustices, when necessary.[189] It is
clear, then, that in living out their spirituality, priests are not only to
work with the poor, but are also to challenge the ecclesial community
and the broader society on their behalf.[190]

Bishop Balke maintains that the promotion of justice by priests
is a stimulus to the laity in fulling their own distinctive ministry in the
social order. In this area, as in others, priests misunderstand their
role if they take all responsibility upon themselves; rather, they are to
help all members of the ecclesial community realize their own participation in the servant-ministry of Christ.[191] *The Program of Priestly
Formation* states that an important aspect of ordained ministry is "to
encourage Catholic laity in their vocation of restoring all things in
Christ."[192] Presbyteral spirituality, then, must challenge priests to
provide strong leadership in the church's ministry of justice and
peace, on one hand, but never to replace the efforts of the community itself, on the other.[193]

In summary, the bishops teach that the experience of the kingdom in prayer and the realization of the kingdom in service are
aspects of one and the same reality. "In worship and in deeds for
justice, the church becomes a 'sacrament,' a visible sign of that unity
in justice and peace that God wills for the whole of humanity."[194]
Therefore, ministry to the human community, when properly understood, is an expression of transcendent values. Conversely, liturgical and individual prayer, when properly conducted, stir Christians
to service. When integrated into an authentic spirituality, human
service empowered by prayer is a sign of the kingdom and its forceful
initial realization. Service to the human race and witness to its final
goal, then, are bound together as constitutive and interrelated dimensions of an appropriate priestly spirituality.

This final section focuses on priestly celibacy, reflecting the
importance which the bishops give to this gift as a sign of the unity

between temporal and transcendent dimensions of the Christian community. First of all, the bishops affirm that the exclusive dedication of Jesus to the kingdom is imaged in a special fashion through Christian celibacy. Some members of the church are called to share the servant-ministry of Jesus as distinctive witnesses to the anticipatory character of Christ's mission, exhibited in the present in-breaking of the reign of God. Archbishop Pilarczyk says that celibacy proclaims that the church, even now, participates in the final stage of salvation by the very fact that certain members of the community dedicate themselves to service in this distinctive way.[195]

The 1969 statement of the National Conference of Bishops on celibacy asks a challenging question: "Is not the priest more strikingly identified with the family of God as such, with the community of mankind as such, by his willingness to forgo a family of his own?"[196] The bishops, mindful that the present age is marked by revolution, speak about "the pilgrim spirit, the undomestic existence" which is required of those who completely identify with the radical message of the gospel. The promise of celibacy, according to this document, orients priests toward total involvement in generating and nurturing the body of Christ, the church. Thus, their time-bound commitment and ministry are aimed at building up the eschatological community on its historical pilgrimage.

The bishops affirm that the celibate priest should be willing to identify in a special way with Christ's kingdom on earth, "that is, with the service of God, mankind and the church, through a dedication of himself to the deepest concerns of the human family."[197] This distinctive way of living in solidarity with the entire family of God is meant to inspire renunciation of a particular family as his own. Paul Dudley, the bishop of Sioux Falls, South Dakota, says that celibacy is not an enemy, but a friend inviting the ordained priest to a total way of loving in sharing of all that he is and has.[198]

Archbishop Pilarczyk regards celibacy as a decisive way of embracing the kingdom: "It is not so much a matter of giving up marriage for the sake of giving up something, as it is a matter of extraordinary joy at finding a different treasure."[199] Viewed in this light, celibacy is a charism, a gift of the Spirit. Those who choose celibacy teach with their lives that, here and now, the future, in which all will be fully and definitively taken up in Christ, is already at hand. Celibacy, then, is focused on the endtime kingdom and witnesses to its influence on the present journey of the church.

Archbishop Weakland comments that priests will never be happy celibates if they have not discovered the kingdom as the pearl of great price, that is, as an undertaking so important that other possibilities and concerns do not distract them from their evangelical mission.[200] Celibate love has as its purpose "bringing humankind and God together, unifying all things in Christ."[201] Welcomed as a gift, celibacy intensifies love for the Lord and for those whom priests are called to serve in his name. Since celibate love is meant to render the church a loving community, Cardinal Bernardin reminds priests that when celibacy is properly understood, it frees them to better appreciate their sexuality, letting its power deepen within them the qualities of sensitivity, warmth, openness and respect.[202]

Archbishop Pilarczyk also understands the celibate way of life as a charism given to some for the sake of complete availability for apostolic service. He, therefore, accentuates an aspect of celibacy which was already suggested in Chapter 6—a means by which ordained ministers are more fully identified with the ecclesial community. Thus, certain members of the church are called to image Christ in a distinctive way by offering the bulk of their energies to the service of the community.[203] In this case, celibacy focuses attention on the need for dedicated service of the community in its pilgrim journey; it lends a practical bent to presbyteral spirituality.

Yet, when rightly understood, celibacy always points beyond service and toward the Lord in whose name ministry is undertaken. It not only opens priests to a deep pastoral love for the entire community, but also directs attention to the Lord, in whom alone celibacy finds its full meaning.[204] By the very nature of their lives, priests teach that the kingdom has not fully arrived and that earthly life is a transitory one awaiting a fulfillment which is yet to come. Archbishop Pilarczyk states that the celibate way of life seeks "to remind us all that even the holiest and most intimate of human relationships is secondary to what God has in store for us."[205] Priests not only lead those whom they serve on an earthly journey toward the kingdom, but also sacramentalize in their own lives the hunger of the whole community for its eschatological consummation.

Celibacy gives concrete expression, then, to the unity of the temporal and the transcendent dimensions of priestly spirituality. Archbishop Pilarczyk proposes it as a way of "falling so in love with Christ and the service of his church that one is willing to take the position that nothing else in life really matters."[206] On one hand, celibacy expresses a willingness to risk everything on immediate service to Christ and the church; on the other, it is a wager that work for the kingdom is valid and that eschatological expectations will certainly be fulfilled. Furthermore, even though an authentic interpretation of celibacy usually links temporal service and transcendent witness, the correlation between the two may be nuanced differently when associated with other charisms or experienced at various stages of life. Celibacy, therefore, is a dynamic spiritual reality requiring a personal response from those who assume it.[207]

The themes of ecclesial pilgrimage and anticipatory arrival come together, then, as the key motivations which engender the celibate commitment. The church has judged that celibacy is a fitting way of life for priests inasmuch as they have been ordained to be fully identified with a kingdom which is both present and still to come. Indeed, the reason for their ordination is that they might publicly serve the already extant kingdom in the ecclesial community and thereby lead it to its eschatological fulfillment. The bishops believe, then, that the spirituality arising from the mission inherent in ordination is enhanced by the celibate commitment.

The focus of celibacy on future fulfillment is not meant to remove priests from temporal concerns, since it is precisely in the name of the kingdom that they are called to be totally engaged in building the human community on earth.[208] The bishops regard celibacy, then, as "profoundly appropriate" because of its relationship to the struggle both to live the kingdom now, and to witness to its fulfillment which is yet to come.

The bishops instinctively realize that celibacy is marked by the frailty and vulnerability of all aspects of the church's earthly journey; yet, precisely because it is dependent on grace, celibacy creates an avenue to God. Cardinal Bernardin chooses "emptiness for God," the definition formulated by Thomas Aquinas, as his own approach to celibacy.[209] The human emptiness of the celibate life is meant to facilitate both an openness to the presence of God and an availability for service. Through their solitary lives, celibates focus attention on the God who is the source of all human thoughts and actions. Moreover, since celibacy bears witness to the state of poverty which is the condition of the whole church before God, celibates image the incomplete experience of the pilgrim community on its way to the kingdom of God. The conversion of emptiness and poverty into openness and hopefulness is the contribution which a presbyteral spirituality marked by celibacy offers the church.

As servants of the ecclesial community, celibates have their own particular burdens, pains and frustrations. These difficulties are not necessarily a sign that celibacy is an unjustly imposed burden created by human authority. Archbishop Pilarczyk succinctly comments: "All God's gifts, beginning with life itself, are heavy."[210] One way in which celibacy partakes in the difficulties of temporal existence is referred to in *Human Sexuality and the Ordained Priesthood*. This document asserts that, since chastity is mastered neither all at once nor without sacrifice, it may involve failures and regressions in the course of its development.[211]

In summary, celibacy highlights the struggle of the pilgrim church and its hope of future fulfillment. Since Christian celibacy derives meaning from both the temporal and the transcendent dimensions of ecclesial existence, priests aware of the eschatological character of the present times commit themselves to service and witness in the midst of the baptized. Celibacy is not a mere discipline imposed by law on certain ordained ministers; it is a charism contributing to ministerial effectiveness.[212] As such, celibacy must be more than passively tolerated; it is to root priestly spirituality in the dynamic tension between the present struggles of Christian existence and the new reality of the kingdom of God.

This chapter, in conclusion, has shown that the American bishops view priests both as champions of the poor and as ministers of the kingdom. The service which they offer to the ecclesial community is rooted in the incarnate and glorified Word who came to seek out the poor. The bishops strongly affirm that priestly ministry to human poverty is not opposed to service to the Kingdom of God, but is truly an expression of its in-breaking power. The priests of the United States, then, are invited by their bishops to regard service and proclamation, work and prayer, the social order and the kingdom not as separate realities, but as interrelated dimensions of their spirituality. While legitimate emphasis may be given to one or the other of these aspects of the presbyteral mission, yet they are not options to be chosen between, but constitutive elements of a whole which must be appropriately integrated.

8.

An Ecclesial Spirituality for American Priests

An Evaluation of the Teaching of the American
Bishops on Priestly Spirituality,
with Suggestions for Future Development,
and a Concluding Summary

The initial chapter of this study set a framework for all that followed by looking at the current situation of presbyteral ministry in the United States. Chapters 2 through 5 isolated and articulated the four major thrusts of the teaching of Vatican II on the ministerial priesthood: the ontological, the ecclesial, the social-political, and the eschatological. In this way, a context and a theological synthesis were provided for an analysis of the teaching of the American bishops.

Chapters 6 and 7 pinpointed the four themes of the council in the documents of the National Conference of Bishops and in the teaching of a cross-section of individual members of the American hierarchy, presenting them in terms of the two major tensions in the church in the United States. Chapter 6 dealt with the aspects of presbyteral identity arising from holy orders and baptism, respectively. Chapter 7 considered the two dimensions of presbyteral ministry, service to human need, on one hand, and the realization of the kingdom of God, on the other.

This final chapter will evaluate the implementation and development of the conciliar magisterium on presbyteral spirituality as found in the teaching of the American bishops since the close of the council. It will also make some suggestions about future directions for the spiritual formation of American priests based on a keener understanding of the presbyteral mission. A concluding section will summarize the bishops' teaching on priestly spirituality.

I. Priests as Participants in the Sacramentality of the Church

The church, as the family of God fired with a single ideal, is both the most immediate context of presbyteral spirituality and the existential milieu which generates, supports and complements priestly ministry; thus, an authentic understanding of the mystery of the church is crucial to an appropriate priestly spirituality. The council's aim in offering a broader ecclesiology by relating the hierarchy to the total community of the faithful has been carefully embodied in the contemporary thrust of Catholicism in the United States. This fundamental conciliar insight has borne abundant fruit. Not only do a

187

high percentage of American Catholics regularly participate in the liturgical life of the church, but vast numbers are also involved in either official or informal ministries. Vatican II, then, has led to a fresh burst of vitality in most American parishes.[1] The desire to serve the Lord and the church in some ministerial capacity has captivated a remarkable number of the faithful, the emergence of new ministries and the provision of ministry training programs for them being a major preoccupation of church life.[2]

The leadership of the American bishops has fostered a church which is alive and active, even if it is struggling for a more adequate understanding of its nature and mission so that the participation of an educated and eager laity may be facilitated.[3] In seeking universal participation in the mission of the church, American Catholics are being faithful to both the basic intention of the council and to the fundamental values of their culture. An ecclesial community to which all belong and in which all share decisions is a growing pastoral presumption. American Catholics regard the church as their own in a way which far surpasses passive involvement; they manifest a deep sense of ownership with regard to the structure and mission of the ecclesial community.[4]

The bishops insist that leadership of a sizable, educated and active lay community demands special skills on the part of priests, and they invite them to a spirituality which is both vital and practical, since growing numbers of American Catholics want to live the faith in which they were reared. Not only are the laity open to spiritual guidance from those who lead the ecclesial community, but they also expect priests to be models of a dynamic and maturing spiritual life. They seek from priests a spirituality which is faithful to the tradition of the church, yet tried and tested within their own culture. Lay people demand that presbyteral spirituality reflect the challenges of the present moment so that the whole community might be nourished, not only by the external ministry of priests, but also by their holiness.[5]

Like all members of the church, priests are called to holiness so that their example might serve others. Yet, as is apparent in the teaching of both the council and the American bishops, priests are not only baptized members of the church, but also those called to sacramentalize a distinctive aspect of ecclesial life, the servant-headship of Christ and the unifying work of his Spirit. This affirmation does not suggest that priests stand outside the community of the baptized, since all the sacraments, including orders, are signs of the church founded on baptism. It does indicate, though, that a more sophisticated understanding of the church would be a real service to American Catholicism. Inasmuch as the church is not only a community of those who share the same faith, baptism and mission, but also a complex organism which expresses itself differently in its various members, the articulation of a more nuanced ecclesiology should be a major concern of the American bishops in formulating a fitting priestly spirituality.[6]

A clearer theology of the church would affirm that while the ordained are baptized and draw their spirituality from the common ecclesial font of baptism, yet they are not simply the spokesmen of the baptized, but have a distinctive role in the life of the ecclesial community. Although baptism is fundamental to all ecclesial vocations, the reality described technically as the apostolic mission of authoritative leadership is not coextensive with the community of the baptized. The apostolic ministry which the sacrament of orders embodies is not simply a more public exercise of the office conferred by baptism, but a distinctive participation in the headship of Christ.[7]

Since the ordained participate in a distinct apostolic mission which sacramentalizes and mediates Christ's servant-headship in the community, they share in his identity and mission as servant-leader in a way which allows him to continue to lead the church through their words and actions.[8] Although all the baptized are called to various kinds of service and leadership, it is only the ordained who are constituted signs of Christ the servant-leader of the ecclesial community, as such. Priestly spirituality, then, is not shaped by service and leadership in general, but by these qualities offered as pastoral care to the community in the person of Christ the head of the church. Priestly duties, then, are not so much services offered to individuals in imitation of Christ, as they are signs which reveal the relationship between Christ the head and his body the church.

This more sophisticated ecclesiology highlights the necessary interaction between priests and laity in showing forth the full sacramentality of the ecclesial community, since the church itself is the fundamental sacrament of Christ.[9] Individuals within it embody aspects of Christ's ecclesial presence in the world, but only the interrelationship and interaction of the members of the church adequately reveal Christ as sacrament of the world's salvation. Although Christ's saving mission embraces the church, it also moves beyond it; therefore, Christ himself unites and correlates the ecclesiastical leadership of priests in the ecclesial community and the ministry of the laity in the total society. What Christ proposes to be for the world is fully operative only when every facet of the ecclesial community is given its proper emphasis, and each aspect interacts with the others in a way which contributes to the effectiveness of the whole.[10]

An appropriate spirituality reminds priests of their distinctive role as presbyters, while it insists that authentic priestly service is complemented by the ministry of the laity.[11] This more sophisticated understanding of the nature of the church challenges priests to offer a distinctive service, at the same time that it prevents them from grasping at the life of the church as if it were their own private preserve. Given the rapid development of the American Catholic community, attention to a properly balanced and clearly articulated ecclesiology is important if growth is to continue to be healthy. While all the elements of this ecclesiology are found in the teaching of the American bishops, seldom are they presented succinctly and forcefully. Greater ecclesiological sophistication would significantly enhance the magisterium of the bishops.

II. Priests as Leaders of the Ecclesial Community

The self-understanding embodied in presbyteral spirituality is necessarily tied to the office of Christ, the shepherd and head of the church. The theological identity and ecclesial role of priests needs to be clarified so that this can be easily grasped by clergy and laity alike. This does not mean that there are no riddles within the historical development of ordained ministry or that the contemporary ecclesial situation is a simple one.[12] It does affirm that there are fundamental concepts distilled from historical theology, the present magisterium and pastoral practice which provide the bases for a sound understanding of ordained ministry in an ecclesial context. Since all Christian spirituality is the practical implementation of a perceived identity in Christ, priests need a clear vision of their distinctive way of participating in the servant-ministry of Jesus if they are to attain spiritual maturity.[13]

While the American bishops insist upon the special character of the ministerial priesthood, they sometimes seem to allow the complexity of the situation to keep them from offering clear, concise and effective teaching about it, on one hand, or to be panicked into making ontological statements, which are true in themselves, but often immediately misunderstood, on the other.[14] At times they describe ordained ministry as an intensification of the holiness, discipleship, and ministry appropriate to all in the church. This movement toward viewing priesthood in terms of the mission common to all the faithful is indeed a helpful one, yet it does not adequately account for the distinctive identity and ministry of the ordained.[15]

Efforts to reassert the relationship of priestly ministry to the basic principles of the Christian life are important and presupposed to any discussion of the ordained. While needing constant emphasis, more attention has to be given to the frustration which arises in priests as a result of statements which begin as affirmations of the special significance of ordained ministry and in fact speak only of the universal call to discipleship, holiness and ministry. Since an effective spirituality is served best by a clear sense of identity, the distinctive, as well as the general, characteristics of presbyteral existence need to be carefully articulated.[16]

The ontological language of the council, often affirmed in the magisterium of the American bishops, attests to the belief of the faith community not only that priests perform distinctive functions because of their ordination, but that their special duties arise from their very identity as ecclesial persons. Thus, priestly ordination changes the identity of particular Christians relative to Christ and the Church in such a way that their activity has a distinctive authority and a new capacity in the life of the community. This change of identity is seen as a distinct way of participating in Christ and the church which adheres in the being of the ordained, and not just in their pastoral activities.[17]

Ordination, then, has more to do with who a person is for the church than what a person does. Since presbyters participate in Christ as the servant-head of the church in a special way, they also act in behalf of Christ and the community in a distinctive way. Ontological language asserts the priority of the gratuitous identity of the ordained as servant-leaders in the person of Christ which is given by the Spirit in ordination, over the individual functions which follow upon that identity.

Those hearing ontological affirmations about the ordained today often misunderstand, thinking that what is being asserted is that ordination produces a superior spiritual, moral, intellectual, psychological, or even human way of being. Simple observation refutes an affirmation of this kind, often resulting in the immediate rejection of such statements. Moreover, inasmuch as affirmations of ontological change are often perceived as a way of claiming a preferred status rather than a servant role, a fear of clericalism may also lie behind the rejection.[18] The bishops must deal with what people in fact hear when ontological language is so prominent a part of their explanation of ordained ministry. The common lay response to bald ontological affirmations about the special character of the ordained may well be: "Do you really think that priests are better than others?"

Obviously, the ontological difference intended by the bishops is not what the questioner understood, for the bishops are speaking of a distinctive identity based on participation in Christ and the church which has nothing to do with intellectual, psychological, or physical changes, and no guaranteed correlation with spiritual or moral transformation. While the language of "being" is important for theological clarity, it may not be the best way to present the significance of ordained ministry to the faithful.[19]

The language of sign or sacrament may be helpful in effectively explaining the distinctive character of the ministerial priesthood. This approach was suggested in Chapter 6, but it awaits further articulation by the bishops. The advantage of this approach is that the language of participation, sign and mediation seems to be both more accessible and acceptable to the majority of American Catholics than the categories of being, status and power.[20] An explicitly sacramental explanation of ordained ministry affirms that because of the special way in which presbyters participate in the identity and mission of Christ as servant-leader, they are enabled to signify and mediate the reality in which they share, thereby making the servant-leadership of Christ present in the ecclesial community.

The language, then, is not so much that of being, but of participation, symbol and effective mediation. At the same time, due to the incarnational realism of the sacrament of orders through which Christ is made present in the community as servant-leader in the words and actions of the ordained, the intention of the ontological language of the council is in no way compromised. Since presbyters have a sacramental identity which is rooted in Christ as head of the church and which mediates his servant-headship, the community looks to them expecting to find the words and actions by which Christ teaches, guides and sanctifies his church.

The benefits of a sign-centered approach to orders are several. First of all it preserves the priority given to being and identity over function and activity in the ontological statements of the council. That is, it maintains that before presbyters are ministers of the eucharist, preachers of the word or identified with any other of their functions, they are servant-leaders of the ecclesial community in the person of Christ the head of the church. At the same time it gives emphasis to the more dynamic notion of "participation" over that of "being," without compromising the latter. In this way function is given its proper importance. Just as all that Christ does is rooted in who he is, so, too, all that presbyters do is rooted in their sacramental identity. Yet, Christ is not a static being for the church, but a dynamic saving servant. The purpose of his identity as incarnate Word is found in his servant-ministry. In the same way, presbyteral identity is not an external status to be clung to, but an internal orientation to servant-leadership. Effective presbyteral activity is the purpose of ordained ministry and testifies to its nature.[21]

This sign-centered understanding of presbyteral ministry anchors priestly spirituality in a distinctive way of sharing in the reality of Christ as servant-leader, and grounds presbyteral ministry in the special character of his headship. If a distinctive participation in the servant-leadership of Christ is the foundation of all presbyteral activity, then any basis for action other than that which is found in him is unacceptable. This leads to the second advantage of this approach. Since in order to be sacramentally effective priests must make the one whom they represent concretely and visibly present, the spiritual life of priests, as such, is an important aspect of the signification of ordained ministry. Holiness is more than a desirable adjunct to otherwise valid ministerial functions. It is an essential part of the identity of ordained ministers.[22]

Finally, the sacramental identity of priests reminds them that since by definition they mediate the servant-ministry of Christ in word, pastoral care and sacred ritual for the sake of the church, presbyteral existence has its primary significance within the ecclesial community and its mission to the world. An authentic priestly spirituality, then, constantly invites the ordained to embrace and serve Christ and the church by deepening their relationship to both of these realities.

A clearer articulation of the nature of ordained ministry is a pressing need in the American church which the bishops have identified and have begun to address.[23] Using their magisterium as the source, a number of useful conclusions can be drawn about presbyteral ministry. All of the following are present in their teaching; greater focus and forcefulness in their presentation would add to their effectiveness.

First of all, presbyters are ordained to be effective signs of Christ in his role, specifically, as servant-head of the church. Since Christ is manifested in the ecclesial community in ways other than as servant-leader, care must be taken accurately to define the charism of ordained ministry in order to safeguard it, on one hand, as a necessary service to all the baptized, and, on the other hand, to clarify the proper dignity of the baptismal priesthood. Presbyteral ministry, then, captures one of the essential aspects of who Christ is for the church. Because the specific charism of the sacrament of orders is the mediation of Christ's servant-leadership, this distinctive participation in the mission of Christ enables presbyters to act *in persona Christi*—in a technical sense.[24]

Secondly, while leadership takes many forms in the Christian community and is exercised in many contexts, the presbyteral role involves the pastoral leadership of the community of faith as such.[25] Here, again, clarity is important since there are certainly forms of ecclesial leadership which are not proper to the recipients of the sacrament of orders. This is most obvious in the leadership which members of the laity exercise in the temporal, economic and social orders as an expression of the mission of the church. In some situations, there is admittedly a fine line between lay baptismal roles which are true manifestations of leadership within the community of faith, and those which are clearly *the* pastoral guidance of the community itself. What is certain, though, is that ordination designates and empowers those who are to be the pivotal servant-leaders in the Christian community when it is explicitly assembled and guided as the church.[26]

The functions assigned to the presbyterate in the teaching of the bishops help clarify the correlation between the servant-headship of Christ and the pastoral leadership of the community. Accordingly, when the community assembles explicitly as church, in the absence of the bishop, presbyters preside and exercise an essential role. The significance of presbyteral ministry is clearest in the eucharistic assembly in which priests proclaim the authoritative word, utter the eucharistic prayer and guide the gathering toward its mission. Since they are ordained to be servant-leaders of the church, they exercise their ministry in an intense way when the community achieves its highest visibility, unity and commissioning.

While many aspects of pastoral practice are changing and developing, three aspects of the bishops' magisterium on the ministerial priesthood are clear, essential, and in need of more effective delineation: priests are ordained to be effective signs of Christ the servant-head of the church, they offer a unifying and umbrella ministry of pastoral leadership to the ecclesial community as such, and they most clearly exercise their sacramental identity within the eucharistic assembly. Servant-headship, unifying leadership and eucharistic focus offer a solid foundation both for a concise catechesis on ordained ministry and for the development of an authentic priestly spirituality.

In an effort to reassert the distinctive character of the ministerial priesthood, some bishops have returned to portraying the priest as *alter Christus,* another Christ. While this is certainly a valid description which contains a great truth, it also presents certain difficulties. Perhaps the most apparent is a certain lack of clarity in a term which is often applied to all Christians.[27] Thus, a phrase which is affirmed of ordained priests with a particular significance in mind loses its distinctive meaning when it meets the popular understanding that the vocation of all Christians is to act like Christ, to make him present, and thereby to be another Christ.

More importantly, an indiscriminate use of *alter Christus* could blur the theological and spiritual focus of the community on the *one* Christ and on the centrality of his role. The situation is similar to that encountered in describing the eucharist as a sacrifice. While this certainly is true, the eucharist is not a new sacrifice or a different one, but the effective presence, here and now, of the one sacrifice of Calvary.[28] Thus, there are not many Christian sacrifices, but only one, truly made present in the eucharistic celebration. The eucharist powerfully communicates the paschal mystery which it sacramentally recalls, making the one sacrifice of Christ truly efficacious for the gathered community. In an analogous way, Christ the *one* priest is made present in presbyteral ministry.[29] Ordained ministers are called priests rightly enough, since the activity of Christ *the* priest becomes effectively present through their ministry. Yet this should not obscure the fact that there is in reality only one priest, Christ himself, and all other "priests" mediate his servant-ministry.[30]

The theology of presbyteral ministry and spirituality must seek to maintain a balance between two awesome realities. The first is that presbyters make Christ the head of the church present in their words and actions so that he truly teaches, guides and sanctifies his people through their ministry. This affirmation is a powerful one, indeed, and is consonant with the fundamental nature of the Christian community as a sacrament which continues to mediate Christ's saving presence in a variety of ways. The realization that the word they preach, the pastoral guidance they give and the sacraments they celebrate are the word of the prophetic Christ, the care of the shepherd Christ, and the ritual actions of the priestly Christ is to render priests open and responsive to the one they represent.[31] In this sense they are to be Christ for those they serve. On the other hand, when explained precisely presbyters are not other Christs, for there is only one; they are the personally responsible instruments through whom the one Christ is present and continues to work as servant-head of the ecclesial community. While it is true that the ministerial priest may be called "another Christ" in that he makes the one Christ present, this must not overshadow the fact that Christ himself is the head of the Christian community, and ordained ministers do not replace him as other Christs, but concretely mediate his unique presence.

Consequently, priests serve the church only through their identification with the one they represent, and apart from a transparent, sacramental relationship with him they have no ecclesial significance.[32] This must be kept in mind if a proper theological balance is to be maintained, since the ordained priest is not *alter Christus* in the same substantial sense that the eucharist is the presence of Christ. While certain sacramental actions are deemed valid without necessarily being accompanied by holiness in the minister, the full actualization of presbyteral effectiveness demands conformity to Christ in holiness of life. The humbling fact is that priests are not Christ, but those who are constantly being perfected in him. While they mediate his presence, they too must be sanctified by Christ if they are to achieve the purpose of their ministry. The affirmation that they are other Christs could leave priests too complacent in who they are, and not conscious enough of the urgency of the quest for holiness. Since there is only one Christ, priestly spirituality is a lifelong process of transformation into him.[33]

III. The Priest as Sacrament of the Holy Spirit

While the western church prefers christological images like "body of Christ," the theology and liturgy of the eastern church show a greater appreciation for the role of the Holy Spirit. The documents of Vatican II incorporate a growing consciousness of the role of the Holy Spirit in the life of the church. In an ecclesiology steeped in the teaching of the fathers, ecclesial relationships mirror the life of the Trinity and manifest grace as an experienced participation in the mystery of God. As already indicated, the Trinity demonstrates the collaboration of equal persons in diverse ways in a common mission.

Viewed from this perspective, the interaction of the Father, Son and Holy Spirit is the starting point in understanding the church and its ministry. Collaboration involves both equality and subsidiarity. Jesus said: "I and the Father are one" and "The one who sees me sees the Father." He also said: "The Father is greater than I." On one hand, Jesus was receptive, being conceived by the action of the Spirit and being empowered by the same Spirit in his ministry. On the other hand, Jesus was active in sending the Holy Spirit upon the church.

Since the entire church is empowered for a common saving mission, the Spirit operates through the whole body—and not only through the mediation of ordained ministry. In the wake of the council there have been many attempts to clarify the seminal ideas expressed in its documents.[34] Emerging parish structures point to three modes of church ministry empowered by the Spirit. First of all, the laity in general are consecrated as priest, prophet and shepherd in baptism and blessed with charisms too numerous to mention which are expressed in daily life.

The church also treasures charisms of lay leadership derived from baptism and exercised for the common good in a specific area of ministry within the ecclesial community. Sometimes these leadership roles flow from an official act or ritual of commissioning, as is the case with installed lectors and acolytes, eucharistic ministers, or chancellors and tribunal officials. At other times they result from implicit recognition that these people indeed represent the community. Catechists, pastoral ministers, and members of the parish pastoral council may fit into this grouping.

Ordained ministry, the third category, flows from baptism and the distinctive empowerment of sacramental ordination. Under the unifying umbrella of the proclamation, care and authority of ordained ministers the total community is gathered and ordered toward the one mission of the one church. Seen in this way, the sacrament of orders is an instrument of the Holy Spirit in the "holy ordering" of the church according to the saving purposes of God.

As a concrete manifestation of the work of the Spirit, the pastoral activity of the ordained is to epitomize the unifying gift proclaimed in the Preface for Christian Unity:

How wonderful are the works of the Spirit, revealed in so many gifts! Yet how marvelous is the unity the Spirit creates from their diversity, as he dwells in the hearts of your children, filling the whole Church with his presence and guiding it with his wisdom!

This understanding of ordained ministry emphasizes the relationship of all members of the faithful to the Spirit through baptism, and the resulting empowerment of all for the common good. It draws attention to the ordained as sacrament of the unifying Spirit, by whom the church is knit together, and away from a too constricted interpretation of the image of the ordained as sacrament of Christ the head, through whom all gifts are mediated. The two models offered by the council are not options, but interrelated aspects of a unified vision of the presbyteral mission. In offering both Vatican II reclaims the richness of the Catholic tradition, thereby opening the way for an explosion of lay ministries and recognizing the aspirations of many for a less structured and more relational church.

The American church has grown in wisdom through reflection on the experience of pastoral ministry. Parish ministers and ministry training programs have distilled emerging patterns of church life and made them an important force in shaping the future. Yet, these stirrings of the Spirit are too often expressed in psychological or sociological language alone. The American bishops would do a great service to the community by encouraging a theological interpretation of church life and ordained ministry which roots new insights more deeply in the trinitarian and sacramental traditions of the total church. In particular, the sacramental significance of their own ministry needs to be more clearly related to discernment, wisdom and unity flowing from the Holy Spirit whom they exemplify in a unique way in the community. In a context where many more lay people are conscious of their baptismal mission, ordained ministers who understand their significance as instruments of reconciliation and unity may well hold the key to healthy growth. An appreciation of ordained ministry as "sacrament of the unifying Spirit" holds promise which cries out for further development.

IV. The Relationship of Priests to the Ministry of the Bishop

The context of presbyteral spirituality is clearly both the ecclesial community and the ministry of the bishop; thus, the magisterium of the American bishops emphasizes the centrality of the diocesan church and the role of the bishop within that community. The identity and unity of the particular church in the person and ministry of the diocesan bishop is offered as a challenge to priests in seeing their own ministry as a part of a whole which transcends the parish community. This broader context for presbyteral ministry is a very helpful one. Not only do priests minister in union with the bishop, but they are accountable to him as the chief pastor of the diocese, and they are recipients of his pastoral care. An entrenched pattern of presbyteral isolation and individualism is countered by the insistence of the American bishops on the primacy of the diocesan church and on the pivotal significance of the ministry of the bishop.[35]

The bishops also point to episcopal ministry as the principal model for presbyteral service.[36] In doing so, they underline the similarities between the role of the bishop in the diocesan community and the ministry of the presbyter in the parish. This rethinking of ordained ministry has been beneficial to bishops and priests alike, for while it draws attention to that which these roles have in common, it also invites bishops to visualize their task in terms of pastoral involvement, and it challenges presbyters to see their position as that of coordinators of ministries and not as the sole servants of the local church.[37]

The pastoral significance of the bishop in the total diocesan church stands in need of further development and articulation; yet it is precisely because of the renewal of the episcopate that presbyters sense a lack of definition in their own ministry. Vatican II gave bishops greater prominence and highlighted the significance of the laity. In the subsequent episcopal magisterium priests are often told that they participate in the ministry of the bishop, on one hand, and that they are to serve the identity of the laity, on the other, with little attention being given to an articulation of the presbyteral role, as such. This is frustrating indeed for a priestly class which had been all too prominent, even self-important, in the past. In response priests crave a clear self-understanding.[38]

Since much has already been said about the rapport between ordained ministry and the baptismal community, the major challenge to be considered at this point lies in the area of properly articulating the relationship of presbyters to the bishop. In affirming the special role of the bishop as the leader of the diocesan church and the head of the presbyterate a number of bishops imply or simply state that priests are the *alter ego* of the bishop. This is certainly a forceful enunciation of an essential factor of presbyteral identity when posited as a necessary corrective to an ecclesial community which had lost an appreciation of the primal significance of the episcopacy, operating from an overly parochial concept of the Church; but as a general theological principle it could lack the subtleness which the council documents go to some length to preserve.

The history of the text of *Presbyterorum Ordinis* reveals movement toward softening a vision of priests as the vicars of the bishop. Thus, the very sentence in article 5 which speaks of priests making the bishop present is carefully nuanced, having been changed from an assertion that priests *"ab episcopo pendent,"* "depend upon the bishop," to priests *"cum episcopo hierarchice colliguntur,"* "are hierarchically united with the bishop." The reason given for the change in the *modi* is that the former text is *"nimis 'imperiosum,' "* "too commanding or imperious."[39] The use of *quodammodo,* "in a certain sense," in both texts where priests are said to make the bishop present suggests the same sensitivity to the complex theology of presbyteral ministry.[40]

It would appear that any consideration of the relationship between bishops and priests must take place with the history of the text of *Lumen Gentium* 28 in mind. In response to the intervention of a number of council fathers, the relationship of the presbyteral role to priestly ordination itself was strengthened considerably in the final version; thus, presbyters are said both to be dependent upon the bishops in the exercise of their power, and also to be joined to the bishops in sacerdotal dignity, since in virtue of the sacrament of orders they, too, are consecrated in the image of Christ the high priest to preach the gospel, shepherd the faithful, and celebrate divine worship as true priests of the New Testament.[41]

It is important, then, to distinguish carefully between a healthy insistence that priests are helpers of the bishop and identified with him in the exercise of their ministry, and an overemphasis on presbyters as representatives of the bishop. A balance must be maintained between the hierarchical relationship which is implied in the very definition of presbyteral ordination, demanding communion and collaboration with the bishop as well as obedience to him, and the sacramentality of priestly ordination itself. Priests are not only commissioned by the bishop to serve a particular community, they are ordained to do so. In the light of presbyteral ordination and within their ecclesial role, priests function *in persona Christi.*[42] Since it is Christ whom they make present, their primary identity is as sacrament of Christ the head of the church. They do so in a way which is related to the ministry of the bishop and subject to his authority, yet nowhere does the council propose that presbyters act *in persona episcopi* or in a strict sense sacramentalize his presence. Strong language of this kind is reserved to describe the ordained as representatives of Christ in his servant-leadership of the church.

It is crucial, then, that priests properly understand both the role of the bishop in the local church and their relationship to him in the exercise of their ministry. It seems equally important to an authentic presbyteral spirituality that hierarchical relationships be seen as constituting the necessary structure of the sacrament of orders, but not its focus as such. A carefully balanced theology insists that presbyteral spirituality revolves around conformity to Christ and ministerial activity in his name, at the same time that it demands effective communion with the bishop in the task which all members of the hierarchical community have in common.[43]

Since the fundamental purpose of ordained ministry is to extend the work of Christ in the local church, it is imperative that the presbyterate understand itself as a priestly community sharing in different ways in the same ecclesial mission and ministry as the bishop.[44] Priests do not multiply the presence and activity of the bishop; rather they point to him as a symbol of the unity in plurality which characterizes the Church as a communion in grace. This sacramental approach to relationships within the presbyterate is mentioned by a number of bishops, but left largely undeveloped. The elaboration of a spirituality based on this understanding would help correlate the Church as a communion, the complexity of contemporary ministry, the rich endowment of the presbyterate, and the necessary differentiation of roles within the ordained community.[45]

Much the same case can be made for this understanding of ordained ministry as St. Paul made for seeing the church as the body of Christ. The presbyteral community arising from the sacrament of orders shares a single ministerial thrust in the diocesan church and is enriched by the manifold gifts and talents of its members at the same time that it is responsive to the leadership of Christ the head made present in the person of the bishop. Since this articulation of ordained ministry emphasizes mutual relationships and shared responsibility at the same time that it values individual talents and distinctive roles, it engages and advances the maturity of its members and encourages their full involvement in the common enterprise.[46] By applying a basic scriptural image of the church to presbyteral spirituality, a climate is created which is less institutional, regimented and hierarchical in style, and, at the same time, supportive to the fundamental prerogatives which belong, by definition, to the role of the bishop.

The working relationships which implement an authentic understanding of the presbyterate develop only as they are lived and experienced. Latent suspicions about the autocratic tendencies of a bishop given a free hand yield slowly to a new experience of episcopal leadership in which priests trustingly expect him to be a strong and effective leader and a source of unity. Apprehension and uneasiness about priests who need to be controlled or held at bay yield slowly to new experiences within the presbyterate through which the bishop comes to expect priests to take initiative and act effectively, since they have become his trusted confidants and friends. Although such an idyllic state may seem a bit idealistic, it must be remembered that the presbyterate is a sign of the kingdom already present and active in the midst of a world of values different from its own. The shortcomings of the temporal journey should neither sabotage Christian witness nor hamper the quest for a more authentic life in Christ.[47]

The values which shape the identity and the spirituality of the presbyterate are neither those of the world nor those of a private spirituality, but ecclesial values which flow from the very nature of sacramental ordination.[48] Therefore, priests would benefit from hearing a clearer challenge from the bishops calling them to a way of life which is solidly based on the paschal mystery and the communion of grace found in both the ecclesial community and the distinctive ministerial relationships arising from the sacrament of orders. While contemporary management skills and processes, and psychological and developmental insights are powerful instruments in advancing ecclesial interaction and presbyteral effectiveness, they are servants of the faith community and not its lifestyle. This caveat seems to be in order in a culture which so easily substitutes structural reorganization and psychological growth for ecclesial relationships and spiritual renewal.[49]

Priests belonging to religious institutes in the United States have a special bond with the episcopacy arising from presbyteral ordination conferred by the bishops, and continuing in the ecclesial relationships inherent in the sacrament of orders. It is surprising, then, that so little attention is given to this very large and significant category of priests as such in the teaching of the American bishops. Moreover, the role of religious priests in the total ecclesial community needs to be looked at theologically as well as in terms of pressing pastoral needs. An appropriate theological consideration would have two components: the presbyteral identity of ordained religious, and the relationship of religious priests to the bishops.[50]

The ecclesial role associated with presbyteral ordination is clearly indicated in the council documents, even if it is not highly developed—servant-leadership in the pastoral care of a community, the proclamation of the gospel, and the celebration of the sacraments being focal concerns. While in many cases the apostolates undertaken by religious priests are quite different from those of the parish clergy, their activity should still embrace the fundamental concerns which flow from their ordination. This does not imply that appropriate presbyteral ministry cannot be exercised in a number of settings and ways, but it does propose that not all ministry is presbyteral, by definition. Religious priests need to be challenged to evaluate their activity in terms of their ordination to the presbyterate. In the same way, their spirituality should arise from their presbyteral ordination as well as from the charism of their religious institute. While, appropriately enough, much of the invitation to this kind of self-appraisal comes from within the religious institute itself, the bishops have a distinctive role in this regard arising from the relationship of presbyteral ordination to the episcopal order.[51]

Secondly, the relationship of the ministry of religious priests to the episcopal college is also an appropriate concern of the American bishops. Many statements of the bishops' magisterium indicate that they see an important role for religious priests in the diocesan presbyterate and that they very much want to make room for them there. As a result, religious priests are now a more integral part of the particular church.[52] At the same time, the trans-diocesan character of religious institutes could be more creatively integrated into the reflections of the bishops in documents intended for the American church as a whole. Little has been done to develop the theology implicit in *Presbyterorum Ordinis* 10, which insists that the spiritual gift which priests receive in ordination prepares them not only for a circumscribed ministry in the particular church, but for the universal mission of salvation. In this context the council hints at the possibility of ecclesial structures which augment and transcend the organization of the diocesan church, while respecting its normative character. *Christus Dominus* 34 picks up this same train of thought by maintaining that religious priests are prudent cooperators of the episcopal order as such.

As members of pontifical institutes, religious have effectively moved into apostolates and met needs which are broader than those of the diocesan church. The collegial nature of the episcopate as envisioned in the theology of the council seems to go a step further, inviting a better articulated pastoral relationship between the college of bishops and religious presbyters who move among local churches. More effective interaction on the regional or national levels between religious priests and a conference or grouping of bishops may well be more respectful of the trans-diocesan character of religious institutes, as well as a fruitful application of the universal pastoral

responsibility inherent in episcopal ordination. Thus, the largely un-
explored theological principle which lies behind the suggestion in
Presbyterorum Ordinis 10 needs further development and application.
If this were done, the spirituality of religious priests would flow more
obviously not only from a relationship to the local presbyterate, but
also from a special participation in the broader pastoral agenda of
the episcopal order as such.[53]

V. Priests and Ministry to the Poor

Both presbyteral identity and ministry relate priests to the poor.
It is not surprising, then, that the teaching of the American bishops is
very sensitive to the plight of the poor in articulating an appropriate
priestly spirituality. The National Conference has addressed issues
involving justice, compassion, human rights and the proper ordering
of society in major pastoral letters and massive national programs.
There is little doubt that their role as teachers in the area of social
morality has had a significant impact on the church as a whole, and
on priests in particular.

The consequences of their leadership for presbyteral spirituality
could be intensified with the help of a few clarifications. First of all,
priests, as members of the church, are called to be present to the
poor in loving service flowing from one human being to another with
all the vulnerability and earthiness which this implies.[54] While priests
should never be estranged from their ecclesial role, neither should
the cultural expectations surrounding their function separate them
from immediate contact with those they seek to serve. Clericalism is
one of the major impediments to effective ministry because it re-
moves priests from first-hand experience of the needs and struggles
of the community and somehow suggests that they are above the
sufferings of ordinary people.[55]

While an authentic priestly identity is essential, the continuing
existence of clericalism with its resultant isolation and supposed su-
periority is a serious problem affecting the effective witness of priests
to Christ as servant of humanity. The teaching and example of the
American bishops should indicate that while the role of the ordained
differs from that of the laity, their willingness to roll up their sleeves
as far as everyone else and get personally, even physically, involved
does not. Since effective ministry begins with authentic presence,
priests must learn to be servants in a true human sense before they
can be ministers of the gospel. The paralyzing effects of an inappro-

priate presbyteral culture and the harm done by flight from the poor to a safe clerical refuge need to be more forcefully addressed by the bishops if priests are to be faithful to the gospel and to give convincing witness to it.

Furthermore, the distinctive place of priests among the poor needs to be qualified by reference to their ecclesial role.[56] Since presbyters are leaders of the ecclesial community their presence among the poor should in some way be associated with their ministry in the community. While every Christian is to be involved with the poor as an expression of the power of the gospel and as a witness to the kingdom, priests, as leaders of the church, are there to proclaim a lived-word addressed to the ecclesial community itself about its identity and mission.[57] When priests are present among the poor, they always bring the ecclesial community with them, at least potentially, for they are there as leaders seeking to effectively illustrate the implications of the gospel. The difference between lay and presbyteral involvement in the social mission of the church is important for priestly spirituality in that it proposes a different focus. Lay ministry is an expression of baptismal responsibility for the renewal of the social order. Priests, on the other hand, seek to fulfill their responsibility for the ecclesial community as well by leading those they serve to an appreciation of the social consequences of the gospel. Therefore, priests are present among the poor not only as witnesses to the gospel, but also in a very explicit way as leaders and teachers of the community of the faithful.[58]

In addition, priests work among the poor to establish the ecclesial community there. While every act of service both expresses the life of the church and makes it present as a dynamic reality, presbyteral ministry has as its specific objective the founding, gathering and nourishing of the ecclesial community; thus, priestly service is related to the community generated by preaching, baptism and the eucharist.[59] Although the opportune time for inviting those being served to membership in the ecclesial community may be remote, this ultimate purpose can never be divorced from the service which priests render as ordained persons. Therefore, priests serve the poor in the way which is most proper to the ordained when they foster the ecclesial community among them.

While the American bishops challenge priests to embrace an essential component of the Christian life when they invite them to personal involvement in service to the poor, they could facilitate a more focused approach to presbyteral spirituality by highlighting the role of the ordained as ecclesial leaders who must bring the Christian community with them in this aspect of their ministry, and as pastors who seek to nurture the church among the poor whom they serve.

VI. Presbyteral Ministry as a Witness to the Kingdom

Presbyteral spirituality is related to the kingdom in both its present dynamism and its ultimate goal. In delineating the first of these, prayer is a constant theme in the teaching of the American bishops, since it is through prayer that the values, gifts and power of the kingdom are internalized and made operative in the ministry of the ordained. In fact, the insistence that a deep life of prayer is indispensable to a sound spirituality is one of the clearest elements in the bishops' magisterium. Yet the relationship between the charismatic endowment of particular members of the church and the grace of ecclesial office merits further development.[60] This is especially true in light of the American experience with the charismatic renewal which focuses attention on this area by seeking ministry from "the spiritually endowed" and not necessarily from ordained ministers as such, when the two do not appear to coincide.[61]

There is no doubt that the bishops see pastoral office and spiritual endowment as two sides of the complex character of presbyteral ministry, both of which are dependent on sacramental ordination.[62] While it is clear that office and the grace which accompanies it can not be disassociated, it is also apparent that the special natural and spiritual endowment which predisposes one for presbyteral ministry should not be overlooked either. There is a possibility of putting so much weight on the likelihood of change during the formation process or in response to the grace of state flowing from the sacrament of orders that the need to identify and ordain the right individuals is, in practice, denied.[63]

More attention needs to be given to the identification of suitable candidates for ordained ministry prior to and during formation. The consciousness of the total community, lay, religious and clergy, must be directed toward the recognition and development of the distinctive charism for leadership which ordained ministry embodies.[64] As was pointed out in Chapter 6, in the Catholic tradition the community participates in the identification and preparation of candidates even though it is the Spirit who empowers. Consequently, the involvement of the community in discernment and in the liturgical act of ordination are related to one another.[65] Since the Spirit acts in and through those chosen by the church, a community attuned to the manifestations of the Spirit, on the one hand, and involved in the selection and formation of candidates, on the other, is important if the faithful are to recognize a convincing unity of office and charism in those who serve them.

A distinctive feature of the teaching of the American bishops is the attention given to the lifelong formation of priests. Their concern that priests grow as apt instruments of the Spirit is expressed in two major national documents, implemented in a myriad of programs, and supported by their personal encouragement. In all of this the bishops maintain a careful balance between an affirmation of the assured efficacy of sacramental ordination and the need for conversion and greater openness to the kingdom on the part of the ordained. This thrust needs to be insisted upon and deepened, so that it becomes even more apparent that office and charism, structure and Spirit, sacramental grace and human development, truly complement one another.[66]

A crusade for ordained ministers at any price with little attention to the human and charismatic endowment of the aspirants tends toward magic, on one extreme, while a predilection for charism and talent apart from ecclesial structure and commissioning tends toward a cult of personalities, exaggerated self-importance and fragmentation, on the other. Even though ordained ministers, by definition, serve the kingdom of God, their optimum impact as ecclesial persons is related to unfailing docility to the Spirit and constant human development. The integration of the ontological, the human, and the charismatic dimensions of ecclesial leadership is difficult, yet absolutely essential.

In another sphere, while the bishops very effectively address many issues of public morality, a more expansive articulation of the relationship between social ministry and the eschatological Spirit empowering it would help resolve one of the great dichotomies in presbyteral spirituality.[67] Not only do episcopal statements tend to be highly structured, delineating scriptural insights, philosophical arguments and practical applications separately for the sake of logical development, but they tend to stay in the realm of logical discourse, not fully engaging the total person or the piety of the community.

Part of the problem lies in the fact that the bishops seem to see themselves primarily as teachers. This suggests an overly restricted interpretation of the relationship of the ministry of Jesus to the in-breaking of the kingdom. For example, as healer, Jesus touched humanity at the level of its pain and fear, thereby imparting a new life experience.[68] The rapid wane of interest in the peace pastoral after a very enthusiastic beginning suggests that it did not become a healing force, a way of life, a permanent part of the piety of a significant number of people.[69] A more vivid expression of ordained leadership rooted in the healing power of Jesus, in the lifestyle and ritual associated with the person of the bishop, and in the symbols and piety of the community, would greatly enhance the overall impact of the American bishops as dynamic witnesses to the influence of the kingdom on the social order. In going to jail in testimony to his beliefs, New York auxiliary Bishop Austin Vaughan recalls the power of ritual action in giving moral force to episcopal leadership. The bishops would greatly enhance their credibility by more clearly embodying the wisdom of the tradition—martyrdom, even in silence, is the most powerful word a bishop speaks to the church. A more wholistic approach to translating ideas into passionate concerns and doctrine into a forceful piety leading to action is crucial if the teaching of the bishops is to generate a new way of life.[70]

The difficulty being highlighted here is captured in another way by Avery Dulles in commenting on both the pastoral on peace and the one on the American economy. Having said that few American bishops enjoy a great reputation for their mastery of theology, liturgy or spiritual direction, he continues: "When the bishops devote so much attention to worldly affairs they can unwittingly give the impression that what is truly important in their eyes is not the faith or holiness that leads to everlasting life, but rather the structuring of human society. . . ."[71] Because religious authority comes from true human wisdom founded on rapport with the divine, while being neither piously simplistic nor coldly philosophical, the bishops must direct attention to the eschatological faith which enlightens the issue under consideration.[72] The insight the gospel gives, the power the Spirit imparts and the eschatological goal Christ sets lie at the heart of the social activity the bishops seek to inspire, as chapter 7 indicates; yet these are often placed alongside the human issue being addressed without sufficient attention being given to conversion not only of mind, but of the total person, to the in-breaking kingdom which alone makes the new ordering of humanity possible.[73] The benefits to presbyteral spirituality would be enhanced if the way in which the transcendent permeates and empowers social ministry were related more realistically to the dynamism which inspires and moves the Christian community to action.[74]

VII. Practical Concerns in Implementing the Bishops' Teaching

The question of who should be admitted to ordained ministry is a volatile one in the American church. The emotions which the issue arouses testifies to its importance to many people. While in no way minimizing the significance of this question, it is important for the bishops to find a way of separating it from a better articulation of the theology of ordained ministry as such.

An obvious conclusion from all that has preceded is that ordained ministry, by its very nature, is a constitutive element of the ecclesial community. Therefore, not only is it not going to disappear, but a diminution of its significance has a negative impact on the self-understanding and effectiveness of the community as a whole. For the good of all, ordained ministry must be properly understood, adequately chosen and authentically lived. Other related questions, including the requirements for ordination, lessen in comparison to an appropriate and courageous articulation of the identity and mission of ordained ministry in the ecclesial community. In fact, these questions have no meaning if ordination has little significance. Any fruitful discussion about qualifications for ordination must take place within the context of a proper understanding of the nature of this sacrament. This first, less complicated, and indispensable discussion needs to happen in the total Catholic community.

The actual impact of the teaching of the American bishops about presbyteral ministry on the church in the United States is a valid area of concern. Four areas merit attention: seminaries, priests, religious, and the total ecclesial community.

Seminaries offer an indispensable service in providing ordination candidates with a chance to learn about ordained ministry and to experience it in the midst of the ecclesial community. In the course of their education and formation seminarians are challenged by the constants and contradictions of history, and by a broad spectrum of theological reflections, as well as by diverse ministerial experiences. At times they are also exposed to the teaching of the local bishop, the most common occasions being homilies at ordinations or at the chrism mass. Some bishops have written longer pastoral statements which may be a part of a seminarian's background as well. But for the most part, the American bishops influence initial formation through those they have chosen as seminary administrators, professors and formation personnel. Because of their pivotal role in the local church, it seems proper to suggest that the bishops themselves must be a more effective part of seminary formation by their presence and teaching, as well as through those they appoint as permanent staff. Of course, the reverse is also true—since seminaries are a rich resource for reflection on ministry, the bishops could benefit by the exchange as well.

Priests are the second audience offering a special challenge to the implementation of the teaching of the American bishops. Perhaps the difficulty here is that priests are so close to the reality which the episcopal magisterium addresses that they are constantly distracted by the truth of their situation. A bishop who does not know his priests and has not experienced, at least vicariously, the complexity of their ministry will be written off as a dreamer and a teacher of abstractions. More time given to sharing pastoral experiences and to common reflection on the challenges of presbyteral life and ministry would provide bishops with words and examples which speak to priests at the same time that it would forge bonds of mutual understanding. The sacramentality of the presbyterate demands that bishops be clearly perceived as part of the body of priests they seek to lead and truly attuned to it.

The American bishops may need to take their own example more seriously as well. As indicated in Chapter 6, Archbishop Pilarczyk proposes the episcopate as the model for the ministry of priests. This seems to indicate that bishops teach as much by what they do as by what they say. While the articulation of a theology of ordained ministry in homilies, pastoral letters and diocesan policies is important, of even greater weight is the example which this body of teaching presupposes. Thus, the way that the bishops witness to the distinctive identity of the ordained, participative ministry, care for the poor, and relationship to the transcendent has more immediate and lasting effect than their teaching, since good example is the usual source of inspiration leading to a deeper spiritual life.

The need to address and involve religious priests in more creative ways has already been considered. Religious women offer a special challenge. While sisters were a strong influence on vocations to the priesthood in the past, now they often look at priests with an attitude of skepticism. The summary statement of the 1986 Collegeville Assembly indicated, in fact, that there is often tension between religious women and priests.[75] One of the great achievements of the bishops has been the ongoing dialogue with religious on the grassroots level in almost every diocese in the country. It may now be appropriate for the bishops to enter into a more focused discussion of vocations to the priesthood and of support for presbyteral ministry with religious women. This undertaking would demand candor, theological insight, patience and maturity from all involved. It would certainly have to include priests in some way if it were to be effective. It is all too obvious that a continuing, even growing, coolness between many priests and religious women is not helpful to the ecclesial community as a whole.

The final group needing attention is the full ecclesial community and the broad spectrum of lay ministers. "Final" in no way suggests least important. The communities which priests serve are not only the source of presbyteral vocations; they are also a major influence on priestly identity and a growing structure of support for the ordained. The American bishops must address this diverse community in a way which invites understanding, promotes mutual assistance, and elicits insight and encouragement. In this context, the concerns of women must also be responded to with sensitivity and respect. Since priests exist for service to the community, they will not achieve a vibrant ministry if they are not embraced and valued by those they serve.

Because the bishops understand priestly ministry in terms of pastoral service, it is fitting that parish communities be engaged in a theological and pastoral dialogue on the significance of presbyteral ministry in the contemporary church. The lay community, as a whole, needs to be a part of the reflection process if the laity are to be supportive of those who serve them. A growing number of ecclesial ministers are lay people who have chosen to serve the church in this way, and are committed to the development of lay ministerial initiatives as their primary focus. Others would seek ordination if the qualifications for presbyteral ministry were different. Both of these predispositions need to be taken into consideration in dialogue about vocations to the presbyterate and the healthy development of priestly ministry. The theology of ministry, ordained and lay, and the attitudes of ministers themselves must create the environment in which all can serve convincingly. Here, again, a discussion with lay ministers which is mutual, frank, theologically focused and realistic is important if priests are to function effectively as ordained representatives of the community, leading and coordinating the ministries of the church in the person of Christ.

These practical concerns contain a number of challenges for

priests themselves. The first involves a greater willingness on the part of priests to think theologically. In this context, theology is a spiritual discipline which helps define presbyteral identity and assists in determining the scope of ministerial activity. Priests who are unwilling to engage in theological reflection will soon lose a clear sense of who they are and what they are about. Since many priests brought little appreciation for the theological process with them from their seminary education, they currently suffer from the spiritual malady of insufficient self-definition. Only the mental discipline of a personally appropriated theology will prevent priests from being victimized by the variety of opinions, pressure groups and demands which contemporary ministry encounters.

The second challenge is to engage in dialogue. Since the ecclesial community is complex, priestly identity and ministry take shape in the interaction between theology and the various living components of the church. The ability to respond to the magisterium, personal experience, and the wisdom inherent in the community demands a maturity which is rooted in a dialogical approach to ecclesial life. Dialogue is a spiritual attitude and discipline which is essential to effective presbyteral ministry.

Finally, a truly vibrant presbyteral spirituality must impart courage. The American Church is a vital, energetic and self-assured community. Convictions are strong and positions often well defined. For priests to have and live a personally appropriated understanding of ordained ministry demands real strength. For them to enter into the current discussion on ministry in the broader community presupposes courage. The ability to assert an understanding of one's role after proper reflection and dialogue is an important characteristic of contemporary presbyteral spirituality.

VIII. An Ecclesial Spirituality for American Priests

It is now possible to delineate, from all that has gone before, an authentic presbyteral spirituality which is firmly based in the teaching of the bishops of the United States during the post-conciliar period, and also directly related to the framework proposed by the Second Vatican Council itself. In doing so, it is necessary to return to the summary offered in *Lumen Gentium* 28 and *Presbyterorum Ordinis* 6: Priests exercise, within the limits of their authority, the office of Christ, the shepherd and head. They assemble the family of God as a community fired with a single ideal, and they lead it through Christ, in the Spirit, to the Father. All the elements essential to an appro-

priate priestly spirituality are present here: animating spirit or dynamism, identity, context, activity, and goal. What remains is to specify
each of these a bit further, in the light of the foregoing chapters.

A. ANIMATING SPIRIT OR DYNAMISM

The role of the Spirit, as animating principle, is clear throughout the teaching of the bishops. Presbyteral ministry is not primarily
a human work; it is the work of God. Thus, it must be imbued with
the Spirit at its source, in its activity, and in the attainment of its goal.
Attentiveness to the Spirit is the most fundamental activity of the
priest, since the Spirit is not just a component of priestly ministry,
but its all-pervasive life force. In fact, priests are to be signs of the
Spirit uniting the church in one pastoral mission to the world.

Since the role of the Spirit is to bring about participation in the
life of the Father and the Son, priestly spirituality is indeed trinitarian—the Father being the goal of ecclesial life, and conformity to the
Son being the way to that goal. The activity of the Spirit is the
life-giving foundation and animating force which underlies all
aspects of the distinctive presbyteral mission.

B. IDENTITY

The self-understanding of priests establishes their basic spiritual
identity. This identity flows from the ways in which they participate in
Christ and, as such, precedes activity. Thus, the ways in which presbyters share in Christ's unique identity are to be the source of how
they act. The preceding chapters affirm that there are three dimensions to priestly identity. The first arises from humanity itself; as
members of the race priests share both the human condition with
Christ and his concern for its welfare. Secondly, presbyters share a
common identity with all baptized Christians, thereby being called to
participate in Christ in the holiness of the church and in the mission
of his ecclesial body to the world. This ecclesial identity includes
being representatives of the baptismal community as its publicly designated leaders. Finally, priests have a distinctive identity as participants in Christ the servant-head of the church. This identity arising
from the sacrament of orders enables them to act in the person of
Christ in relationship to the ecclesial community and its mission to
the human family, and also as representatives of the bishop and as
members of the presbyterate.

Clearly, the identity of priests is complex, and all aspects of it are
important in the formulation of an appropriate spirituality. The bish-

ops challenge priests to a self-understanding which embraces being human, baptized and ordained, all three. The interaction between these three aspects of presbyteral identity is essential to the authenticity to which American priests are being summoned. The implications of participation in Christ's servant-headship will be summarized here, the other two dimensions in what follows.

Ordination gives priests a new objective identity as participants in the servant-leadership of Christ; thus they share in the office of Christ as shepherd and head. It is crucial that they have an unclouded understanding of this objective reality. A proper appreciation of what they are empowered to be by ordination calls priests to subjective participation in Christ as well. Presbyteral spirituality involves an internalization of the values and attitudes of Christ manifested in his ministry as servant-head of the church. Acting in the person of Christ is itself the way to growth in that which priests were ordained to be. Hence, pastoral activity as an expression of presbyteral identity is a pivotal spiritual exercise.

C. CONTEXT

Since priests are ecclesial persons, the context of their spirituality is the life of the church and its mission to the world. Interaction with this faith community both as members and as leaders, then, provides the most immediate setting for their spiritual life. Because the bishops insist that the mission of the church is directed to the human family itself, presbyteral spirituality must enable priests to partake of the life of the ecclesial community and to lead it in both the internal and the global aspects of its mission.

Four characteristic ways in which priests are to be involved in the church form the core of presbyteral asceticism as recommended by the bishops. Participation comes first; the very identity of priests is shaped by participation in Christ and involvement in the ecclesial community, making the ability to be both member and participant, with the discipline and self-forgetfulness which this entails, a quality of immense importance. Consequently, presbyteral authenticity is largely the result of appropriate participation and membership.

Since both of these involve priests in a common ecclesial mission which is shared in diverse ways with other members of the community, collaboration is the second characteristic of presbyteral asceticism. This aspect of priestly spirituality is distinctively trinitarian in that it mirrors the collaborative relationships of the divine persons in the work of salvation. Thus, on every level, from participation in

Christ to involvement in the aspirations of humanity, priests both grow spiritually and become who they were ordained to be by collaborating with others.

Inasmuch as continuous involvement with others is the setting for presbyteral spirituality, discernment is a third aspect of priestly asceticism. This means that maintenance of a clear and effective identity in the midst of continual interaction with others, having their own proper ways of sharing in the common task, demands constant clarification of roles in the community. Finally, service is the overall characteristic which unites the others and orients them toward the special way in which presbyters are called to be involved in the mission of Christ and the church—as servants. Consequently, an ever deeper orientation to service must constantly purify priestly motivation.

In setting a direction for presbyteral spirituality, a number of strong statements can be made to illustrate the relationship between the self-understanding of priests as ordained persons and the context in which they exercise that identity. At the outset, it is clear that the first service priests offer those they lead is to truly become one of them; thus membership is a prerequisite for leadership. Furthermore, it is by involvement in the concrete interactions of the presbyterate that priests participate in Christ's servant-headship. Finally, it is by personifying the self-understanding of the community they serve that they exercise their most effective leadership. All of these underline the importance of the interaction between identity and context, leadership and membership, in an appropriate realization of presbyteral spirituality.

D. ACTIVITY

The characteristic actions ascribed to presbyters are to assemble and lead in the church and the world. In gathering and guiding people, priests are to focus on two objectives: service to human need, and witness to a kingdom which is present and still to come. Service and witness are intimately related and, when viewed properly, permeate and complete one another; thus the function of the spirituality articulated by the bishops is to guarantee that priests understand this relationship and are fortified by it.

A spirituality based on service must begin with a recognition of human need arising from the human condition itself, sin, limitations, lack of meaning and material poverty. Priests experience neediness too, and in acknowledging it they open themselves to being served by

Christ and the church. Thus, self-knowledge and receptivity are primal attributes of priestly spirituality, since in being served priests are enabled, in turn, both to recognize the poverty of others and to turn to them as agents of God's care.

Witness attests to the presence of God in the human condition as the one who enlightens and animates ecclesial life and ministerial activity. It affirms the unity existing between the worship of the community and its work in behalf of charity and justice. The bishops insist that prayer gives vision and power to ministry, and service to humanity gives tangible expression to the saving God encountered in prayer. The interrelationship between eschatological empowerment and authentic activity is pivotal to the spirituality which they formulate.

With insight which has profound significance for presbyteral spirituality, the bishops proclaim that the proclamation of the word, the celebration of the eucharist, and efforts in behalf of justice are interrelated and constitutive elements of the Christian life. Thus, they affirm that there is a dynamic and necessary relationship between preaching, the sacraments and service to the human family. This intuition has tremendous potential for unifying presbyteral ministry and spirituality.

There are a number of consequences flowing from this for priestly life. It is obvious, first of all, that the proclamation of the word, the sacrament of penance and the eucharist are meant to lead priests to the poor; and, inversely, every encounter with human need has the potential of leading priests back to the worship life of the church. This fundamental dynamism of ecclesial existence must lie at the heart of an authentic presbyteral spirituality. Since ministerial activity teaches others about the loving God whom priests encounter in prayer, better integration of contemplation and action in the lives of the ordained leads to greater understanding in the community they serve. Finally, because the gospel is to be proclaimed and worship is to be offered in a concrete ecclesial setting, the service which priests give must have a tangible character as well, addressing both situations and structures which must change when enlightened by the values of the kingdom.

E. GOAL

The goal of presbyteral spirituality is to bring the family of God through Christ to eschatological completion in the Father. This goal has two phases: the first is coextensive with the temporal journey of the church, and the second will be accomplished only when Christ comes again. Since this goal is already being realized through the service and witness of presbyteral ministry, the future truly permeates the present. This is most obvious in the rhythm of worship and charity which both characterizes the present condition of the church and foreshadows its fulfillment.

The goal of presbyteral spirituality, then, is not bound to a nebulous future happening; it is already being realized, but in a way which is to be brought to perfection beyond the historical process. This fact gives further unity to presbyteral spirituality, for the worship and charity which are the present focus of priestly ministry are its ultimate goal as well. Consequently, while the hereafter is out of reach, the present both expresses a future way of life and works toward it; thus, priestly spirituality is an expression of the life of the kingdom, as well as a witness to its final character. Since the bishops see both presbyteral ministry and lifestyle as important, they propose priestly celibacy as a fitting way of enhancing temporal service, on the one hand, and as an eschatological witness, on the other.

Jesus is proposed as the model for humanity in both phases of its journey, since his life, death, and resurrection most fully expresses the worship and charity of the kingdom, thereby initiating eschatological fulfillment. The bishops offer a spirituality to priests based on the paschal mystery, then, for it is only in living out the present reality of the kingdom in association with the dying and rising of the Lord that they can effectively herald the kingdom and bring the people of God to its consummation.

There are several consequences of the eschatological orientation of presbyteral spirituality. To begin with, priestly ministry has two goals, that the Kingdom be realized in the present through particular acts of service, and that every ministerial action move the people of God toward eschatological fulfillment. While the two are closely related to one another, the tension between them keeps presbyteral spirituality appropriately stretched between thanksgiving for what already is and petition for what is yet to come. A clear articulation of the eschatological orientation of the Christian life underlines the ultimate goal of presbyteral ministry—that Christ come again in glory and that his people realize their full potential by becoming saints. Accordingly, the definitive goal of presbyteral spirituality is full communion in truth, love and worship. The eucharist, as the foretaste and promise of the kingdom, is the pivotal activity of priestly ministry and the centerpiece of presbyteral spirituality, since there presbyters deepen communion among the people of God as shepherds, proclaim the saving presence of the Lord as prophets, and foster worship and active charity among them as priests.

Faithful to the insistence of Vatican II that priestly spirituality is essentially related to the presbyteral mission, the American bishops have effectively articulated the relationship between priestly identity and ecclesial membership, and service to humanity and eschatological witness; thus they have made an important contribution to the spiritual well-being of the priests of the United States.

Notes

1. The American Priest in Context

1. Richard Schoenherr, in *Laborers for the Vineyard: Proceedings of a Conference on Church Vocations* (Washington, D.C.: United States Catholic Conference, 1983), p. 57.
2. Ibid. p. 61.
3. Dean Hoge, Joseph Shields and Mary Jeanne Verdieck, "Attitudes of American Priests in 1970 and 1985 on the Church and Priesthood," Report No. 4 (Washington, D.C.: Department of Sociology of the Catholic University of America, 1986), p. 20.
4. Andrew Greeley, *American Catholics Since the Council: An Unauthorized Report* (Chicago: Thomas More Press, 1985), p. 121.
5. Richard Schoenherr, in *Laborers for the Vineyard*, p. 62.
6. Ibid.
7. Karl Rahner, "Secular Life and Sacraments: 1," *The Tablet* 225 (March 6, 1971): 237.
8. Joseph Laishley, "What Is a Priest?" *The Way Supplement.* 47 (Summer 1983) pp. 9–11.
9. John Tracy Ellis, ed., *The Catholic Priest in the United States: Historical Investigations* (Collegeville, Minnesota: St. John's University Press, 1971), pp. 11–14.
10. Louis Abelly, *La Vie du Vénérable Serviteur de Dieu, Vincent de Paul* (Paris: Lambert 1664) Sec. 1.213, quoted in Ellis, pp. 12–13.
11. Ellis, p. 13.
12. *Schema Decretorum Concilii Plenarii Baltimorensis Tertii,* as summarized in Ellis, p. 47.
13. Ellis, p. 14. The ready compliance of the American church with the decree of Leo XIII in *Aeterni patris* is particularly significant: "We desire and we order that in teaching the philosophical and theological disciplines all professors follow studiously and faithfully in the footsteps of the Angelic Doctor . . ." as quoted by Ellis, p. 47.
14. Dean Hoge, "Demographic Changes and Their Impact on the

Church," in *Bishops' Assembly for Prayer and Reflection on Episcopal Ministry in the United States: Background Paper, Part Two—Selected Trends and Assumptions in American Society and the Church* (Washington, D.C.: United States Catholic Conference, 1981), p. 95 (private circulation).

15. *The Gallup Report 236* (Princeton, New Jersey: The Gallup Report, May 1985), p. 50.

16. Richard Neuhaus, "After the Mainline in Post-Secular America," in *Bishops' Assembly for Prayer and Reflection: Background Paper*, p. 107.

17. George Tavard, *Catholicism U.S.A.* (New York: Newman Press, 1969), pp. 118–119. The growth of ecumenical dialogue has both enriched the American priest with the experience of other traditions and sharpened his consciousness of gospel models of leadership.

18. Richard McBrien, *Catholicism* (Minneapolis: Winston Press, 1980), 2: 1058.

19. Andrew Greeley, *The Catholic Priest in the United States: Sociological Investigations* (Washington, D.C.: United States Catholic Conference, 1972), pp. 73–74.

20. Andrew Greeley, *Priests in the United States: Reflections on a Survey* (Garden City, New York: Doubleday and Company, 1972), p. 58. In this discussion, it is important to remember that the obligation to pray the Liturgy of the Hours is stated in much more nuanced language in the "General Instruction of the Liturgy of the Hours." *The Liturgy of the Hours* (New York: Catholic Book Publishing Company, 1975) I:38.

21. Ibid. pp. 60–61.

22. Charles E. Curran, "Crises of Spirituality in Priestly Ministry," *The American Ecclesiastical Review* 166 (February 1972): 96–97.

23. Karl Rahner, *Theological Investigations* (New York: Crossroad, 1981), 20: 149.

24. Andrew Greeley, *New Horizons for the Priesthood* (New York: Sheed and Ward, 1970), p. 139.

25. Desmond Mullan, "Spiritual Life of the Pastoral Priest," *Furrow* 27 (December 1976): 657.

26. "Report of Regional Meetings on the Ministerial Priesthood," in *Documentation for General Meeting of National Conference of Catholic Bishops* (Washington, D.C.: United States Catholic Conference, April 27–29, 1971): 83. (A private circulation document in which the sections are not numbered consecutively.)

27. Eugene Kennedy, chairman, "Report of Subcommittee on Psychology," in *Documentation for General Meeting of National Conference of Catholic Bishops*, p. 99. The complete results of this study later appeared as Eugene Kennedy and Victor Heckler, *The Catholic Priest in the United States: Psychological Investigations* (Washington, D.C.: United States Catholic Conference, 1972).

28. Ibid. p. 105.

29. Ibid. p. 108.

30. Thomas Merton, *New Seeds of Contemplation* (New York, New Directions Books, 1961), p. 32.

31. Thomas Morgan, "The Pastor and Holiness," *Priest* 40 (May 1984): 34–36.

32. Eugene Kennedy, "Report of Subcommittee on Psychology," in *Documentation for General Meeting*, p. 118.

33. *Schema Decretorum Concilii Plenarii Baltimorensis Tertii*, pp. 44–45 (Baltimore: privately printed by Foley Brothers, 1884). The direction set in the draft decrees on major seminaries was for the most part the direction followed by the bishops. Ellis, p. 48; James Gibbons, *Decreta Concilii Plenarii Baltimorensis Tertii* (Baltimore: Joannis Murphy, 1886), Caput II, 160, p. 82: *"Munus suum ita cordi habeant, ut ne zeli quidem apostolici opera, quibus ab illo distrahi possint, extra seminarium aggrediantur."*

34. Gibbons, Caput II, 159, p. 81: *". . . qui juvenes clericos humilitatem, mundi fugam, laboris et solitudinis amorem, orationis assiduam praxim exemplo non minus quam verbo edoceant. . . ."*

35. Tavard, *Catholicism U.S.A.*, p. 15.

36. Bill Pruett, "Toward a Spirituality for Diocesan Priests," *Priest* 35 (September 1976): 19; William Hogan, "The Spirituality of the Diocesan Priest," *National Catholic Education Association Bulletin* 62 (August 1965): 86–93.

37. John Sheets, *To Believe Is To Exist* (Denville, New Jersey: Dimension Books, 1986), pp. 282–283.

38. "Report of Regional Meetings on the Ministerial Priesthood," in *Documentation for General Meeting*, p. 6.

39. Ibid. p. 96.

40. Paul Williamson, *Contemporary Approaches to the Ordained Priestly Ministry in Theology and the Magisterium: A Study of Selected Writings of Edward Kilmartin, S.J., Hervé-Marie Legrand, O.P. and Edward H. Schillebeeckx, O.P. in the Light of the Second Vatican Council and Subsequent Magisterium* (Rome: Pontificia Universitas Gregoriana, Facultas Theologiae, 1983), pp. 357–372 (doctoral dissertation); Peter Drilling, "Fellow Pil-

grim and Pastoral Leader: Spirituality for the Secular Priest,"
Spirituality Today 35 (Winter 1983): 319–335.

41. René Latourelle, *Christ and the Church: Signs of Salvation* (Staten Island, New York: 1972), p. 72.

42. Jn 3:28–30.

43. Philip Rosato, "The Spirituality of the Diocesan Priest," *Way Supplement* 39 (Winter 1980): 83–96.

44. "De Ordinatione Presbyterorum," in *Pontificale Romanum: "Accipe oblationem plebis sancte Deo offerendam. Agnosce quod ages, imitare quod tractabis, et vitam tuam mysterio dominicae crucis conforma."*

45. Richard McBrien, 2:1073.

46. Thomas Merton, pp. 39, 78.

47. Matthew Fox, *Humpty Dumpty and Us* (Minneapolis: Winston Press, 1979), p. 268.

48. (Notre Dame, Indiana: University of Notre Dame Press, 1964).

49. "Report of Regional Meetings on the Ministerial Priesthood," in *Documentation for General Meeting,* p. 89.

50. Ibid. p. 96.

51. Ibid. pp. 54, 51.

52. Ibid. p. 111.

53. Bill Pruett, p. 21.

54. Peter Drilling, p. 322.

55. *The Gallup Report 236,* p. 50.

56. Ibid. p. 13.

57. Ibid. p. 45.

58. Ibid. p. 13.

59. Ibid. p. 5.

60. Ibid. p. 9.

61. George Gallup, Jr., and Jim Castelli, *The American Catholic People* (Garden City, New York: Doubleday, 1987), p. 2.

62. Andrew Greeley, *American Catholics Since the Council,* p. 126.

63. Dean Hoge, Raymond Potvin, and Kathleen Ferry, *Research on Men's Vocations to the Priesthood and the Religious Life* (Washington, D.C.: United States Catholic Conference, 1984), p. 41.

64. George Gallup, *The American Catholic People,* p. 44.

65. Ibid. pp. 43–44.

66. Ibid. pp. 26–28.

67. Robert Bellah, et al. (New York: Harper and Row, 1985), p. 65.

68. Aubert Clark, "Leadership and Authority," in *The Bishops' Assembly for Prayer and Reflection: Background Paper,* p. 164.

69. Raymond Potvin, "Privatization in Religion and Life," in *Bishops' Assembly for Prayer and Reflection: Background Paper*, p. 152.

70. Jackson Carroll et al., *Religion in America, 1950 to the Present* (New York: Harper and Row, 1979), quoted in *The Gallup Report 236*, p. 4.

71. Raymond Potvin, p. 152.

72. Andrew Greeley, *An Unauthorized Report*, p. 118.

73. *The Gallup Report 236*, p. 8.

74. Richard Schoenherr, in *Laborers for the Vineyard*, p. 61; 2.6 percent of the priests ordained between 1943 and 1966 had left active ministry by the latter date. During the decade following the council approximately 13 percent of the active diocesan clergy resigned. Richard Schoenherr, "From the Second Vatican to the Second Millennium" (p. 27). Most of the current decline in resignations is the result of the reduced number of ordinations (ibid. p. 28). The resignation rate among religious priests seems to be significantly higher, since in 1970 the median ages of diocesan and religious priests were similar, and in 1985 religious priests tended to be a good bit older. Dean Hoge, "Attitudes of American Priests," p. 7. Resignation rates will lessen during the final quarter century due largely to growing conservatism in the international church, the aging of the clergy, and the conservatism of current seminarians. Richard Schoenherr and Annemette Sorensen, "Social Change in Religious Organizations: Consequence of Clergy Decline in the U.S. Catholic Church." *Sociological Analysis: a Journal in the Sociology of Religion* 43 (Spring 1982): 36.

75. Richard Schoenherr, *Sociological Analysis*, p. 44.

76. Richard Schoenherr and Annemette Sorenson, *From the Second Vatican to the Second Millennium: Decline and Change in the U.S. Catholic Church*, CROS Respondent Report: 5 (Madison, Wisconsin: University of Wisconsin, 1981), p. 13.

77. Patricia Gries, Symposium on Staffing Today's Parish (Glenview, Illinois, May 4–7, 1986) p. 10.

78. Andrew Greeley, *An Unauthorized Report*, 114.

79. Dean Hoge, "Attitudes of American Priests," p. 19.

80. George Gallup, *The American Catholic People*, p. 181.

81. David O'Brien, *The Renewal of American Catholicism* (New York: Oxford University Press, 1972), p. 58.

82. Robert Leckie, *American and Catholic* (Garden City, New York: Doubleday, 1970), p. 319.

83. William McCready sees the situation as a serious one for vocations to the priesthood: "The vocation crisis is, I believe, intimately linked with the relationships between Catholic women and their Church," in *Laborers for the Vineyard*, p. 47.

84. George Gallup, *The American Catholic People*, pp. 46–47.

85. James Gibbons, *The Ambassador of Christ* (Baltimore: John Murphy Co, 1896), p. 249; It is interesting that Cardinal Gibbons was also involved in the labor movement. George Gallup, *The American Catholic People*, p. 67.

86. *The Challenge of Peace: God's Promise and Our Response* (Washington, D.C.: United States Catholic Conference, 1983); *Economic Justice for All* (Washington, D.C.: United States Catholic Conference, 1986).

87. An outstanding example is found in *Ethics and the Search for Christian Unity* (Washington, D.C.: United States Catholic Conference, 1981).

88. Quoted in Robert Leckie, p. 193.

89. George Tavard, *Catholicism U.S.A.*, pp. 30–31.

90. William Barrett, *Irrational Man* (Garden City, New York: Doubleday, 1958), pp. 24–25.

91. Ben Stein (New York: Basic Books, 1979).

92. Robert Bellah, *Habits of the Heart*, pp. 47–48.

93. Christian Duquoc, "Preface," in Duquoc, editor, *Secularization and Spirituality* (Concilium Vol. 49) (New York: Paulist Press, 1969), pp. 2–3.

94. Charles E. Curran, "Crises of Spirituality in Priestly Ministry" (March 1972): 97–98.

95. Christian Duquoc, p. 2.

96. Pope Paul VI, *Ecclesiam Suam* (Washington, D.C.: National Catholic Welfare Conference, 1964).

97. Andrew Greeley, *American Catholics Since the Council*, pp. 99, 93–94.

98. George Gallup, *The American Catholic People*, p. 83.

99. Ibid. pp. 89, 77–78.

100. Ibid. pp. 76, 67.

101. Ibid. pp. 48, 62.

102. Andrew Greeley, *An Unauthorized Report*, pp. 83–84.

103. Ibid. p. 51.

104. George Gallup, *The American Catholic People*, p. 93.

105. Andrew Greeley, *An Unauthorized Report*, p. 83.

106. Richard Shaull, *Heralds of a New Reformation* (Maryknoll, New York: Orbis Books, 1984), pp. 76–100; Jon Sobrino, *The True*

Church and the Poor (Maryknoll, New York: Orbis Books, 1984), pp. 276–280; Bakole Wa Ilunga, *Paths of Liberation: A Third World Spirituality* (Maryknoll, New York: Orbis Books, 1984).

107. Thomas Clarke, "Finding Grace at the Center," in Thomas Keating et al., *Finding Grace at the Center* (Still River, Massachusetts: St. Bede Publications, 1978), p. 59.

108. Tanquerey, *The Spiritual Life* (New York: Desclée, 1930) p. 5.

109. Ernest Larkin, "Asceticism in Modern Life," in *Spirituality in the Secular City* (Concilium Vol. 19) (New York: Paulist Press, 1966), p. 103.

110. Teilhard de Chardin, *"Domine, fac ut Te videam, ut Te omnipraesentem, et omnianimantem videam et sentiam,"* quoted by Pierre Reginald Cren, "The Christian and the World According to Teilhard de Chardin," in *Spirituality in the Secular City* (Concilium Vol. 19) (New York: Paulist Press, 1966), pp. 76–80.

111. William F. Hogan, "The Spirituality of the Diocesan Priest," *National Catholic Education Association Bulletin*, Vol. 62, August 1965, p. 91.

112. J. Dalrymole, "Some Reflections on the Spirituality of Secular Priests," *The Clergy Review* 52 (March 1967): 171.

113. Richard McBrien, *Catholicism*, 2:1078.

114. Thomas Gannon and George Traub, *The Desert and the City: An Interpretation of the History of Christian Spirituality* (Chicago: Loyola University Press, 1969), pp. 289–290.

115. Charles E. Curran (March 1972): 171.

116. James Nelson, *Embodiment: An Approach to Sexuality and Christian Theology* (Minneapolis: Augsburg Publishing House, 1978), pp. 34–35.

117. *Spiritual Pilgrims* (New York: Paulist Press, 1982), p. 178.

118. Keith Clark, *Being Sexual and Celibate* (Notre Dame, Indiana: Ave Maria Press, 1986), pp. 175–182.

119. George Gallup, *The American Catholic People*, p. 55.

120. Andrew Greeley, *The Catholic Priest in the United States: Sociological Investigations*, p. 233. The overall number of priests who say that celibacy is a great problem for them personally, on a day to day basis, increased by 3 percent to 14 percent between 1970 and 1985. Those age 36 to 45 experienced the greatest jump, a 10 percent increase to 25 percent. Dean Hoge, "Attitudes of American Priests," Table 9, p. 1.

121. Richard Schoenherr, *From the Second Vatican to the Second Millennium*, p. 22; Andrew Greeley, *American Catholics Since the Council*, p. 118.

122. Robert Lauder, *The Priest as Person: A Philosophy of Priestly Existence* (Whitinsville, Massachusetts: Affirmation Books, 1981), pp. 27, 46.
123. Ibid. p. 113.
124. Eugene Kennedy, *Psychological Investigations,* p. 11.
125. Richard Neuhaus, p. 108.
126. Robert Kinast, "The Developing Role of the Laity," in *Bishops' Assembly for Prayer and Reflection: Background Paper,* p. 231.
127. Rosemary Haughton, *The Passionate God* (New York: Paulist Press, 1981), pp. 74–88. Monika Hellwig, *Jesus, The Compassion of God* (Wilmington, Delaware: Michael Glazier, 1983).

2. Participants in Christ the Head of the Church

1. *Presbyterorum Ordinis* 2.
2. *Lumen Gentium* 21.
3. *Lumen Gentium* 21.
4. When the subcommission charged with the development of the text of *Lumen Gentium* was asked why the chapter on the people of God was placed immediately after the one on the mystery of the church and ahead of a consideration of the hierarchy, they responded that, although the hierarchy could in a certain sense be considered first because of its role in forming the community, yet the clergy and faithful alike belong to the same people and are directed to the same end. Thus it is proper that the whole be treated first to make it clear that both clergy and laity have diverse, but important, responsibilities in the common enterprise. *Acta Synodalia: Sacrosanctum Concilii Oecumenici Vaticani II.* "Relatio Generalis" (Congregatio Generalis LXXX: September 15, 1964) (Typis Polyglottis Vaticanis, 1978), vol. 3, part 1, pp. 209–210.
5. *Lumen Gentium* 1. The usage "all men" is quoted here and throughout. It is retained for the sake of simplicity only. The author does not intend any exclusive or sexist meaning.
6. Aloys Grillmeier. "Dogmatic Constitution on the Church," Chapter 1, *Commentary on the Documents of Vatican II,* ed. Herbert Vorgrimler (New York: Herder and Herder, 1967), vol. 1, p. 157.
7. *Lumen Gentium* 10.
8. *Lumen Gentium* 62. The priesthood of Christ is shared in various ways both by ordained ministers and by the faithful.
9. *Lumen Gentium* 10.

10. *Lumen Gentium* 40.
11. Aloys Grillmeier in *Commentary on the Documents of Vatican II,* I:123.
12. *Lumen Gentium* 40.
13. *Lumen Gentium* 62.
14. *Presbyterorum Ordinis* 2. The consideration of the nature of the ministerial priesthood begins by affirming that "all the faithful are made a holy and kingly priesthood. . . ."
15. *Lumen Gentium* 48. ". . . the pilgrim church, in its sacraments and institutions which belong to this present age, carries the mark of this world which will pass, and she herself takes her place among the creatures which groan and travail yet and await the revelation of the sons of God."
16. *Lumen Gentium* 7; Col 1:15–18.
17. *Dei Verbum* 4.
18. Jn 14:6.
19. *Acta Synodalia,* "Relatio Generalis" (Congregatio Generalis CLXVI: December 2, 1965), 2, part 7: 108.
20. Roman Missal, Eucharistic Prayer IV.
21. Jn 19:30; *Sacrosanctum Concilium* 5: "For it was from the side of Christ as he slept the sleep of death upon the cross that there came forth 'the wondrous sacrament of the whole Church.' "
22. *Lumen Gentium* 2.
23. *Lumen Gentium* 7.
24. *Lumen Gentium* 50.
25. 1 Cor 4:15–16; Phil 3:1.
26. *Lumen Gentium* 7.
27. *Lumen Gentium* 5.
28. *Optatam Totius* 4; 9.
29. Jn 12:32; *Lumen Gentium* 3.
30. Roman Missal, Eucharistic Prayer of Reconciliation I.
31. *Lumen Gentium* 9.
32. *Lumen Gentium* 50.
33. *Lumen Gentium* 51.
34. *Sacrosanctum Concilium* 10.
35. *Lumen Gentium* 28.
36. *Lumen Gentium* 28.
37. *Lumen Gentium* 24.
38. *Presbyterorum Ordinis* 6.
39. *Presbyterorum Ordinis* 13.
40. *Lumen Gentium* 35.
41. *Lumen Gentium* 12.

42. In *Lumen Gentium* 25, the endorsement of preaching is equally strong when applied to bishops: "Among the more important duties of bishops that of preaching the gospel has pride of place." The transmission of divine revelation is intimately tied to the office of bishop, and, by association, also to priests. See *Dei Verbum* 7.

43. *Presbyterorum Ordinis* 4.

44. *Lumen Gentium* 21; also *Presbyterorum Ordinis* 5.

45. *Lumen Gentium* 29 states that deacons "receive the imposition of hands 'not unto the priesthood, but unto the ministry.'" The degree to which the council wishes to relate deacons to the role of sanctification through celebration of the sacraments is not fully developed. The solemn conferral of baptism is a deaconal role.

46. *Presbyterorum Ordinis* 5.

47. *Lumen Gentium* 28.

48. In explanation of the emended text the following appears: "*In hac tamen missione adimplenda, fideles nullam potestatem proprie dictam ipsius Christi Capitis in Corpus suum quod est Ecclesia (cf. Col. 1, 24) exercere valent, eaque tantum consecratione signantur qua in initiationis christianae sacramentis 'regio et sacerdotali propheticoque honore perfusi' sunt.*" Sacrosanctum Oecumenicum Concilium Vaticanum Secundum. *Scehema Decreti De Ministerio et Vita Presbyterorum: Textus Emendatus et Relationes* (Typis Polyglottis Vaticanis, 1964), p. 7.

49. Giuseppe Rambaldi, "Natura e Missione del Presbiterato Nel Decreto 'Presbyterorum Ordinis,'" *Gregorianum* 50 (1969): 243. The significance of the phrase "in the person of Christ" is underlined by its usage in the revised Code of Canon Law. The task of the revision of the code was to apply the theology of the council to the life of the church. The code uses the phrase three times, most significantly in the definition of the sacrament of orders. See Canons 899.2, 900.1, and 1008.

50. *Lumen Gentium* 10.

51. *Presbyterorum Ordinis* 2.

52. *Acta Synodalia* (Congregatio Generalis CLIX: November 12, 1965), 4, part 6:342.

53. *Presbyterorum Ordinis* 12.

54. *Lumen Gentium* 10; *Lumen Gentium* 28; *Presbyterorum Ordinis* 13.

55. *Lumen Gentium* 28.

56. *Sacrosanctum Concilium* 7.

57. *Lumen Gentium* 21.
58. *Sacrosanctum Concilium* 14.
59. *Presbyterorum Ordinis* 13.
60. *Presbyterorum Ordinis* 14.
61. *Lumen Gentium* 18.
62. *Lumen Gentium* 19.
63. *Lumen Gentium* 20.
64. *Lumen Gentium* 18.
65. *Lumen Gentium* 21. *The Documents of Vatican II*, ed. Walter Abbott (New York: Guild Press, 1966). The Abbott translation is cited here because it is significantly more faithful to the Latin text.
66. *Christus Dominus* 15.
67. *Lumen Gentium* 21.
68. *Sacrosanctum Concilium* 41; *Lumen Gentium* 26.
69. *Presbyterorum Ordinis* 2. The Latin text speaks of the presbyterate as a subordinate grade or level: "*Episcopos, quorum munus ministerii, subordinato gradu, Presbyteris traditum est ut in Ordine presbyteratus constituti, ad rite explendam missionem apostolicam a Christo concreditam, Ordinis episcopalis essent cooperatores.*" The footnote in the text directs attention to *Lumen Gentium* 28 which further explains that ". . . *eorum successores, videlicet Episcopos participes effecit, qui munus ministerii sui, vario gradu, variis subiectis in Ecclesia legitime tradiderunt.*" The statements of the council are somewhat ambivalent in this regard, as will be shown later. "Subordinate" should not be interpreted as an attempt to minimize the true sacramental significance of presbyters.
70. *Presbyterorum Ordinis* 2.
71. *Christus Dominus* 34.
72. In the revision of *Presbyterorum Ordinis* there was an effort to rename the document "*De Ministerio et Vita Presbyterorum speciatim diocesanorum.*" This suggestion was rejected in that the document deals with presbyteral ministry, as such, and the life which flows from it. In this sense it applies to all ordained to that ministry. *De Presbyterorum Ministerio et Vita: Textus Recognitus et Modi* (Typis Polyglottis Vaticanis, 1965), pp. 14–15.
73. *Presbyterorum Ordinis* 7.
74. *Lumen Gentium* 41.
75. *Gaudium et Spes* 24: ". . . the Lord Jesus, when praying to the Father 'that they may all be one . . . even as we are one' (Jn 17:21–22), has opened up new horizons closed to human rea-

son by implying that there is a certain parallel between the union existing among the divine persons and the union of the sons of God in truth and love." This text confirms the trinitarian parallel suggested.

76. *Presbyterorum Ordinis* 5: "Priests are hierarchically united with the bishop in various ways and so make him present in a certain sense in individual assemblies of the faithful." (*"Presbyteri diversis rationibus cum Episcopo hierarchice colliguntur, et sic eum in singulis fidelium congregationibus quodammodo praesentem reddunt."*) The usage of "in a certain sense" seems to be a caution in the text against making the affirmation too strong. Priests make Christ present, and in a certain, yet very different, sense they make the bishop present as well. The text appeared first in *Lumen Gentium* 28. Here, also, the same "in a certain sense" (*"quodammodo"*) appears. This matter is treated further in chapter 8.

77. *Presbyterorum Ordinis* 12. This same text affirms that presbyters are cooperators with the episcopal order. The words *"tamquam Ordinis episcopalis cooperatores"* were maintained when challenged by four council fathers as unnecessary. It is clear from the development of the text that while the sacrament of orders involves configuration to Christ, presbyteral ordination is qualified by an essential relationship to the episcopal order. *De Presbyterorum Ministerio et Vita: Textus Recognitus et Modi* (1965), p. 93. *Lumen Gentium* 28 maintains that presbyters are "true priests of the New Testament."

78. *Presbyterorum Ordinis* 7.
79. *Presbyterorum Ordinis* 8.
80. *Presbyterorum Ordinis* 8.
81. *Christus Dominus* 28.
82. *Lumen Gentium* 41.
83. *Lumen Gentium* 8.
84. *Lumen Gentium* 6.
85. *Optatam Totius* 9.

3. Members and Representatives of the Local Church

1. *Lumen Gentium* 3.
2. *Lumen Gentium* 1.
3. *Lumen Gentium* 8.
4. *Lumen Gentium* 1.
5. *Lumen Gentium* 3, 8; *Gaudium et Spes* 21: ". . . it is the function

of the church to render God the Father and his incarnate Son present and as it were visible, while ceaselessly renewing and purifying herself under the guidance of the Holy Spirit."

6. *Lumen Gentium* 13.
7. *Lumen Gentium* 9; *Lumen Gentium* 32: "There is, therefore, one chosen people of God: 'one Lord, one faith, one baptism'; there is a common dignity of members deriving from their rebirth in Christ, a common grace as sons, a common vocation to perfection, one salvation, one hope and undivided charity."
8. The ontological foundation for membership in the people of God arising from baptism also relates Catholics to other Christian communities. Ecumenism, therefore, is an important aspect of the work of the Council. *Unitatis Redintegratio* 22.
9. *Lumen Gentium* 10.
10. *Lumen Gentium* 9.
11. *Lumen Gentium* 30.
12. *Lumen Gentium* 31.
13. *Code of Canon Law,* Latin-English edition (Washington, D.C.: Canon Law Society of America, 1983). The law flowing from the theology of the council affirms this vision:
    Canon 204 "The Christian faithful are those who, inasmuch as they have been incorporated in Christ through baptism, have been constituted as the people of God. . . ."
    Canon 207 "Among the Christian faithful by divine institution there exist in the Church sacred ministers, who are also called clerics in law, and other Christian faithful, who are also called laity."
    Canon 208 "In virtue of their rebirth in Christ there exists among all the Christian faithful a true equality with regard to dignity and the activity whereby all cooperate in building up the Body of Christ in accord with each one's own condition and function."
14. *Lumen Gentium* 11.
15. *Lumen Gentium* 11.
16. Roman Sacramentary, Priesthood Preface (Chrism Mass).
17. *Apostolicam Actuositatem* 4.
18. *Lumen Gentium* 7; 1 Cor 12:12.
19. This image is also used to explain the diversity of liturgical rites and traditions within the church and to praise their contribution to the enrichment of the whole. *Orientalium Ecclesiarum* 2.
20. *Apostolicam Actuositatem* 2.
21. *Presbyterorum Ordinis* 2.

22. *Lumen Gentium* 7.
23. *Lumen Gentium* 12.
24. *Presbyterorum Ordinis* 2.
25. 1 Kgs 3:9.
26. *Lumen Gentium* 12.
27. *Presbyterorum Ordinis* 9.
28. *Lumen Gentium* 6.
29. *Lumen Gentium* 65.
30. *Lumen Gentium* 4.
31. *Lumen Gentium* 7; Eph 5:23–28.
32. *Lumen Gentium* 39: "The church, whose mystery is set forth by this sacred council, is held, as a matter of faith, to be unfailingly holy. This is because Christ, the Son of God, who with the Father and the Spirit is hailed as 'alone holy,' loved the church as his bride, giving himself up for her so as to sanctify her; he joined her to himself as his body and endowed her with the gift of the Holy Spirit for the glory of God."
33. *Lumen Gentium* 9.
34. *Dei Verbum* 8.
35. *Sacrosanctum Concilium* 7.
36. *Lumen Gentium* 26.
37. *Lumen Gentium* 11.
38. *Lumen Gentium* 44; *Perfectae Caritatis* 12.
39. *Presbyterorum Ordinis* 16; *Perfectae Caritatis* 12.
40. *Lumen Gentium* 23.
41. *Lumen Gentium* 22: *Collegium hoc quatenus ex multis compositum, varietatem et universalitatem Populi Dei, quatenus vero sub uno capite collectum unitatem gregis Christi exprimit.* The Latin text is clearer than the Flannery translation usually cited in this work.
42. *Presbyterorum Ordinis* 11.
43. *Lumen Gentium* 22.
44. This is not to say that there are not situations in which a priest from another country or cultural background is called to lead a local community. Cross-cultural experiences can be a healthy expression of the universality of the church. They are the exception, though, and not the rule.
45. This is also true of religious priests who belong to geographically defined provinces and, for the most part, minister within a defined inter-diocesan community with which they have an enduring relationship.
46. *Lumen Gentium* 26.
47. *Lumen Gentium* 28.

48. *Sacrosanctum Concilium* 42. The text cited modifies the participation of the parish community in the total reality of the church with the words "in some way." It does this in acknowledgment of the fact that only in the community gathered around the bishop does the local church attain full stature.
49. *Gaudium et Spes* 44.
50. *Gaudium et Spes* 58.
51. *Gaudium et Spes* 32.
52. *Christus Dominus* 13. The footnote to this section in the council document refers to *Ecclesiam Suam,* Pope Paul VI's encyclical letter which was written during the course of the council. The encyclical deals with the responsibility of the church to enter into dialogue with its environment.
53. *Lumen Gentium* 3.
54. *Presbyterorum Ordinis* 3.
55. *Lumen Gentium* 28.
56. *Presbyterorum Ordinis* 2.
57. *Presbyterorum Ordinis* 9, 12.
58. *Presbyterorum Ordinis* 18.
59. *Lumen Gentium* 41.
60. *Dei Verbum* 25: "For it must not happen that anyone becomes 'an empty preacher of the word of God to others, not being a hearer of the word in his own heart,' when he ought to be sharing the boundless riches of the divine word with the faithful committed to his care, especially in the sacred liturgy."
61. *Presbyterorum Ordinis* 12.
62. *Lumen Gentium* 32. Also see *Apostolicam Actuositatem* 25; *Presbyterorum Ordinis* 9.
63. *Presbyterorum Ordinis* 3; also Rom 9:19–23.
64. *Presbyterorum Ordinis* 3; also Heb 2:17.
65. *Presbyterorum Ordinis* 3.
66. *Presbyterorum Ordinis* 9. The laity are told "they should also share their priests' anxieties and help them as far as possible by prayer and active work so that they may be better able to overcome difficulties and carry out their duties with greater success."
67. *Presbyterorum Ordinis* 6.
68. *Presbyterorum Ordinis* 6.
69. *Apostolicam Actuositatem* 7.
70. *Apostolicam Actuositatem* 10 and 25. *Lumen Gentium* 31 states: ". . . the faithful who by baptism are incorporated into Christ, are placed in the people of God, and in their own way share the

priestly, prophetic and kingly office of Christ, and to the best of their ability carry on the mission of the whole Christian people in the church and in the world."

71. *Lumen Gentium* 37.
72. *Presbyterorum Ordinis* 2.
73. *Presbyterorum Ordinis* 9.
74. *Presbyterorum Ordinis* 9.
75. *Presbyterorum Ordinis* 4.
76. *Gaudium et Spes* 43.
77. *Presbyterorum Ordinis* 5.
78. *Presbyterorum Ordinis* 2.
79. *Sacrosanctum Concilium* 33.
80. *Presbyterorum Ordinis* 5.
81. *Sacrosanctum Concilium* 83–85; *Presbyterorum Ordinis* 13.
82. *Sacrosanctum Concilium* 88.
83. *Sacrosanctum Concilium* 99.

4. Servants of the Poor in Society

1. *Gaudium et Spes* 36.
2. *Gaudium et Spes* 76.
3. *Gaudium et Spes* 74.
4. *Gaudium et Spes* 42.
5. *Gaudium et Spes* 76.
6. *Gaudium et Spes* 76.
7. *Gaudium et Spes* 43.
8. *Gaudium et Spes* 42: "Christ did not bequeath to the church a mission in the political, economic, or social order: the purpose he assigned to it was a religious one." *Apostolicam Actuositatem* 5 states: "The work of Christ's redemption concerns essentially the salvation of men; it takes in also, however, the renewal of the whole temporal order. The mission of the church, consequently, is not only to bring men the message and grace of Christ but also to permeate and improve the whole range of the temporal. The laity, carrying out this mission of the church, exercise their apostolate therefore in the world as well as in the church, in the temporal order as well as in the spiritual." There seems to be lack of harmony between these two affirmations of Vatican II, since it is difficult to see how the laity can undertake the task assigned to them without exercising a mission to the political, economic or social order. If interpreted too narrowly, the text from *Gaudium et Spes* would raise a question about the

way in which the apostolate of the laity is a part of the mission of the church. A more developed theology of the role of the laity within the mission of the church would probably make a distinction between institutional mission and the mission of members of the church as participants in society. Both are a part of the full mission of the church, but in different ways.

9. *Ad Gentes* 3.
10. *Ad Gentes* 3; *Lumen Gentium* 8; *Lumen Gentium* 42; *Presbyterorum Ordinis* 17.
11. *Lumen Gentium* 57.
12. *Lumen Gentium* 46; *Presbyterorum Ordinis* 6.
13. *Lumen Gentium* 55.
14. *Lumen Gentium* 46; *Lumen Gentium* 50. Vatican II associates poverty and celibacy in a number of contexts. *Perfectae Caritatis* 1 states: "They (religious) follow Christ who, virginal and poor, redeemed and sanctified men by obedience unto death on the cross."
15. *Presbyterorum Ordinis* 17.
16. *Lumen Gentium* 42.
17. *Ad Gentes* 12; *Apostolicam Actuositatem* 8; *Presbyterorum Ordinis* 6.
18. *Lumen Gentium* 5; Mk 10:45.
19. Mk 10:42–45.
20. *Lumen Gentium* 8; Phil 2:5–8.
21. *Roman Missal:* Easter Vigil, *Exultet.*
22. Jn 13:1–17. The summary portion of this chapter of John (13:34–35), which flows from the example of Jesus in the washing of the feet, is often cited in the Vatican II documents as a call to service: *Apostolicam Actuositatem* 8; *Christus Dominus* 30; *Gaudium et Spes* 93; *Lumen Gentium* 9; 40.
23. *Ad Gentes* 3.
24. *Gaudium et Spes* 63; 81; 88; 90.
25. *Gaudium et Spes* 90.
26. *Lumen Gentium* 4.
27. *Gaudium et Spes* 22.
28. *Gaudium et Spes* 45.
29. *Gaudium et Spes* 13.
30. *Gaudium et Spes* 19.
31. *Ad Gentes* 5.
32. *Lumen Gentium* 8.
33. *Lumen Gentium* 41; 42; *Gaudium et Spes* 37: "Man thanks his divine benefactor for all these things, he uses them and enjoys

them in a spirit of poverty and freedom: thus he is brought to a true possession of the world, as having nothing yet possessing everything."

34. *Apostolicam Actuositatem* 4. The Flannery translation originally read: "Following in his poverty, Jesus. . . ." The words have been rearranged for a better reading.

35. *Gaudium et Spes* 72.

36. The participation of the ordained in the identity of the poor Christ will be treated in the last section of this chapter. The call of religious is considered in *Lumen Gentium* 42, as well as in *Perfectae Caritatis* 13.

37. *Lumen Gentium* 8.

38. *Lumen Gentium* 8; *Gaudium et Spes* 21.

39. *Gaudium et Spes* 19.

40. *Dei Verbum* 8.

41. *Lumen Gentium* 8.

42. *Gaudium et Spes* 1; *Ad Gentes* 12.

43. *Gaudium et Spes* 88.

44. *Gaudium et Spes* 88.

45. *Gaudium et Spes* 93.

46. *Apostolicam Actuositatem* 8.

47. *Gaudium et Spes* 69.

48. Ibid.

49. *Apostolicam Actuositatem* 5. The mission of the church is the renewal of society "in the spirit of the gospel." The Flannery translation is defective at this point, leaving *"spiritu evangelico"* untranslated.

50. *Ad Gentes* 12.

51. *Apostolicam Actuositatem* 7.

52. *Lumen Gentium* 36. The Latin text reads: *"In quo officio universaliter adimplendo laici praecipuum locum obtinent."* The laity have "the" principal role in ordering secular reality to God. The Flannery translation, usually cited, weakens the impact of the Latin text. The Italian translation reads: ". . . *i laici hanno il posto di primo piano."*

53. *Lumen Gentium* 36.

54. *Gaudium et Spes* 43: "It is to the laity, though not exclusively to them, that secular duties and activity properly belong."

55. *Gaudium et Spes* 29.

56. *Lumen Gentium* 28; Heb 5:7–9.

57. *Gaudium et Spes* 22.

58. *Gaudium et Spes* 43.

59. *Gaudium et Spes* 22.
60. *Lumen Gentium* 9. The Flannery translation omits the reference to the Holy Spirit which appears in the Latin text: "*et sub actione Spiritus Sancti, seipsam renovare non desinat.*" Therefore the reference to the Holy Spirit has been added to the English text as quoted.
61. *Lumen Gentium* 27. The Latin text reads: "*Assumptus ex hominibus et circumdatus infirmitate. . . .*" The Flannery translation reads: "Taken from among men and oppressed by the weakness that surrounds him. . . ." Since the Latin is itself a bit ambiguous, I have relied on the context of the text in Hebrews (5:1–2), and on the alternate translation offered by Abbott, as well as on the Italian: "*Preso di mezzo agli uomini e soggeto a debolezze. . . .*" Thus the bishop is not only surrounded by weakness, but also himself beset with it.
62. *Presbyterorum Ordinis* 17; Acts 2:42–47.
63. *Presbyterorum Ordinis* 17.
64. *Presbyterorum Ordinis* 20.
65. *Optatam Totius* 8.
66. *Christus Dominus* 13.
67. *Christus Dominus* 30.
68. *Gaudium et Spes* 29: "It is regrettable that these basic personal rights are not yet being respected everywhere, as is the case with women who are denied the chance freely to choose a husband, or a state of life, or to have access to the same educational and cultural benefits as are available to men." *Gaudium et Spes* 60: "It is up to everyone to see to it that woman's specific and necessary participation in cultural life be acknowledged and fostered."
69. *Lumen Gentium* 23.
70. *Presbyterorum Ordinis* 6.
71. *Presbyterorum Ordinis* 17.
72. *Apostolicam Actuositatem* 7: "Pastors have the duty to set forth clearly the principles concerning the purpose of creation and the use to be made of the world, and to provide moral and spiritual helps for the renewal of the temporal order in Christ."
73. *Gaudium et Spes* 69.
74. *Ad Gentes* 37; *Presbyterorum Ordinis* 20. The council recommends: ". . . priests' remuneration should be such as to allow the priest a proper holiday each year. The bishop should see to it that priests are able to have this holiday." Travel may offer

special opportunities in obtaining the breadth of vision which supports ministry to those in need.

75. *Gaudium et Spes* 88; *Lumen Gentium* 28.
76. *Gaudium et Spes* 13.
77. *Presbyterorum Ordinis* 5; Mt 4:17.
78. *Lumen Gentium* 7.
79. *Presbyterorum Ordinis* 5.

5. Witnesses to the Kingdom in the World

1. *Lumen Gentium* 6.
2. *Gaudium et Spes* 10.
3. *Gaudium et Spes* 14.
4. *Gaudium et Spes* 16.
5. *Gaudium et Spes* 17.
6. *Gaudium et Spes* 41.
7. *Gaudium et Spes* 18.
8. *Gaudium et Spes* 38.
9. *Gaudium et Spes* 39.
10. *Sacrosanctum Concilium* 5: "He achieved his task principally by the paschal mystery of his blessed passion, resurrection from the dead, and glorious ascension, whereby 'dying, he destroyed our death, and rising, restored our life.' " The quotation cited by the document is from an Easter Preface of the *Roman Missal*.
11. *Gaudium et Spes* 22.
12. *Gaudium et Spes* 45; Rev 22:12–13.
13. *Gaudium et Spes* 22.
14. *Gaudium et Spes* 36.
15. *Gaudium et Spes* 41.
16. *Gaudium et Spes* 22.
17. The council also speaks of an "in between" stage of purgation. It is a passive mode of ecclesial existence which prepares some members of the earthly church for entry into the heavenly community. By definition, it is not absolutely necessary for the Christian journey, as are the earthly and heavenly communities.
18. *Lumen Gentium* 51.
19. *Gaudium et Spes* 22.
20. *Lumen Gentium* 13; *Gaudium et Spes* 32.
21. *Lumen Gentium* 3.
22. *Gaudium et Spes* 38.
23. *Lumen Gentium* 3; 1 Cor 10:17; 11:26.

24. *Lumen Gentium* 26; *Sacrosanctum Concilium* 6; 8; 10.
25. *Lumen Gentium* 50.
26. *Lumen Gentium* 48.
27. *Lumen Gentium* 6, Col 3:1–4.
28. *Lumen Gentium* 49.
29. *Lumen Gentium* 48, *Gaudium et Spes* 39.
30. *Lumen Gentium* 48, *Gaudium et Spes* 45.
31. *Lumen Gentium* 48.
32. *Gaudium et Spes* 39.
33. *Gaudium et Spes* 39; 40.
34. *Lumen Gentium* 48; 8; *Gaudium et Spes* 40.
35. *Sacrosanctum Concilium* 2.
36. *Gaudium et Spes* 40.
37. *Lumen Gentium* 5.
38. *Sacrosanctum Concilium* 33.
39. As was stated earlier, in saying that the church does not have a mission in the social, economic or political order, it is necessary to take into consideration the affirmation of the council that the laity have as their apostolate the renewal of the temporal order (see the comments in Chapter 4, note 8).
40. *Gaudium et Spes* 42; 76; *Lumen Gentium* 8.
41. *Gaudium et Spes* 45.
42. *Lumen Gentium* 13; *Gaudium et Spes* 1.
43. The documents *Orientalium Ecclesiarum* and *Unitatis Redintegratio* treat of this concern. Furthermore, the responsibility of Catholics to enter into fruitful relationships with all religions is placed in an eschatological context by *Nostra Aetate* 1.
44. *Lumen Gentium* 8; 9; 14.
45. *Apostolicam Actuositatem* 4.
46. *Gaudium et Spes* 22.
47. *Gaudium et Spes* 38.
48. *Gaudium et Spes* 43.
49. *Gaudium et Spes* 38. The Flannery translation is not clear at this point. ". . . *omnibusque terrenis viribus in vitam humanam assumptis, . . .*" is translated "and integrate earthly resources into human life." The Abbott translation is more faithful to the Latin: ". . . and bringing all earthly resources into the service of human life."
50. *Lumen Gentium* 44.
51. *Perfectae Caritatis* 15: "A community gathered together as a true family in the Lord's name enjoys his presence. . . . For love sums up the law and is the bond which makes us perfect; by

it we know that we have crossed over from death to life. Indeed, the unity of the brethren is a symbol of the coming of Christ and is a source of great apostolic power.''

52. *Lumen Gentium* 44.
53. *Perfectae Caritatis* 12.
54. *Perfectae Caritatis* 2.
55. *Lumen Gentium* 43.
56. *Gaudium et Spes* 39.
57. *Lumen Gentium* 49.
58. *Lumen Gentium* 4.
59. *Lumen Gentium* 50.
60. *Lumen Gentium* 50.
61. *Lumen Gentium* 49.
62. *Lumen Gentium* 62.
63. *Lumen Gentium* 63.
64. *Lumen Gentium* 68: ''. . . the mother of Jesus in the glory which she possesses in body and soul in heaven is the image and beginning of the church as it is to be perfected in the world to come.'' *Sacrosanctum Concilium* 103: ''In her the church admires and exalts the most excellent fruit of redemption, and joyfully contemplates, as in a faultless image, that which she herself desires and hopes wholly to be.''
65. *Lumen Gentium* 66.
66. *Lumen Gentium* 50.
67. *Gaudium et Spes* 45.
68. *Lumen Gentium* 7.
69. *Lumen Gentium* 48; 50.
70. *Lumen Gentium* 51.
71. *Gaudium et Spes* 39.
72. *Gaudium et Spes* 76.
73. *Lumen Gentium* 41.
74. *Presbyterorum Ordinis* 15.
75. *Gaudium et Spes* 22.
76. *Sacrosanctum Concilium* 5; 6.
77. *Gaudium et Spes* 22; 38.
78. *Optatam Totius* 10.
79. *Presbyterorum Ordinis* 16.
80. *Optatam Totius* 10; *Perfectae Caritatis* 12; *Presbyterorum Ordinis* 16.
81. *Lumen Gentium* 28; *Presbyterorum Ordinis* 6.
82. *Gaudium et Spes* 40.
83. *Presbyterorum Ordinis* 2.

84. *Sacrosanctum Concilium* 8.
85. *Sacrosanctum Concilium* 2.
86. *Sacrosanctum Concilium* 6–9.
87. *Lumen Gentium* 50: "*Nobilissima vero ratione unio nostra cum Ecclesia coelesti actuatur, cum, praesertim in sacra Liturgia, in qua virtus Spiritus Sancti per signa sacramentalia super nos agit, divinae maiestatis laudem socia exultatione concelebramus, et universi in sanguine Christi ex omini tribu et lingua et populo et natione redempti atque in unam Ecclesiam congregati, uno cantico laudi Deum unum et trinum maginificamus.*" The Flannery translation of this passage usually cited is very unclear.
88. *Gaudium et Spes* 32.
89. *Gaudium et Spes* 38.
90. *Presbyterorum Ordinis* 2.
91. *Lumen Gentium* 51.
92. *Presbyterorum Ordinis* 2.
93. *Lumen Gentium* 6; *Gaudium et Spes* 38; 45; 32.
94. *Presbyterorum Ordinis* 16.
95. *Lumen Gentium* 48.
96. *Gaudium et Spes* 39.
97. *Lumen Gentium* 14.

6. Members of the Church and Sacraments of Christ's Servant–Headship

1. *As One Who Serves,* (Washington, D.C.: United States Catholic Conference, 1977), p. 11.
2. Joseph Bernardin, *Called To Serve, Called To Lead: Reflections on the Ministerial Priesthood* (Cincinnati: St. Anthony Messenger Press, 1981), p. 1.
3. *The Priest and Sacred Scripture,* (Washington, D.C.: United States Catholic Conference, 1972), p. 28.
4. *As One Who Serves,* p. 7.
5. John Krol, Chrism Mass Homily, April 4, 1985.
6. *The Priest and Sacred Scripture,* p. 47.
7. Ibid., p. 28.
8. *Spiritual Renewal of the American Priesthood* (Washington, D.C.: United States Catholic Conference, 1973), p. 41.
9. Ibid., p. 42.
10. *Spiritual Renewal of the American Priesthood,* p. 41.
11. Raymond Hunthausen, Chrism Mass Homily, 1981.
12. P. 21.
13. Victor Balke, Ordination Homily, March 15, 1986.

14. John Quinn, Ordination Homily for the Jesuit Community, June 16, 1984.
15. *As One Who Serves*, p. 11.
16. *The Priest and Sacred Scripture*, p. 5.
17. National Conference of Catholic Bishops, *The Program of Priestly Formation*, 3rd ed. (Washington, D.C.: United States Catholic Conference, 1981), p. 20.
18. *The Priest and Sacred Scripture*, p. 5.
19. *The Priest and Sacred Scripture*, p. 28.
20. "You Are a Royal Priesthood," *Origins* 18 (August 18, 1988): 179.
21. Victor Balke, Ordination Homily, May, 1983.
22. John O'Connor, Chrism Mass Homily, 1986. No reference given for the quote.
23. "You Are a Royal Priesthood," p. 168.
24. Victor Balke, Ordination Homily, August 28, 1982.
25. James Malone, "Vatican II and the Postconciliar Era in the U.S. Church." A Report to the Vatican's Synod Secretariate. *Origins* 15 (September 26, 1985): 232.
26. William Borders, "The Bishop as Builder of Community," Address to the Bishops' Assembly for Prayer and Reflection on Episcopal Ministry, June 1982, p. 5.
27. "Statement on Celibacy," November 14, 1969, in *Pastoral Letters of the United States Catholic Bishops*, vol. 3 (Washington, D.C.: United States Catholic Conference, 1983), p. 203.
28. *As One Who Serves*, p. 3.
29. Howard Hubbard, typewritten manuscript of a newspaper article, May 1985.
30. *The Program of Priestly Formation*, p. 10.
31. Ibid., p. 15.
32. *As One Who Serves*, p. 9.
33. Ibid., p. 6.
34. *Spiritual Renewal of the American Priesthood*, p. 2.
35. Howard Hubbard, Clergy Retreat Homily, September 1985.
36. John Roach, "The Priesthood: Yesterday and Today." An Address to a Serra Convention. No exact date was available, but 1981 was suggested by a member of the archbishop's staff.
37. Lawrence Welsh, "The Desert Will Blossom: Vocation Statistics, Research and Action-Plans," An Address to the Bishops' Assembly for Prayer and Reflection on Vocations, June 12, 1986, p. 7.

38. "The Quality of Candidates for the Priesthood," *Origins* 13 (August 18, 1983): 186.

39. Joseph Bernardin, "And Now, What Next . . ." Address to the Bishops Assembly for Prayer and Reflection on Vocations, June 16, 1986, p. 4.

40. Ibid., p. 12.

41. Thomas Murphy, "An Agenda for Confronting the Vocations Statistics," *Origins* 13 (December 22, 1983): 470.

42. James Malone, "Vatican II and the Postconciliar Era," p. 232.

43. Lawrence Welsh, "The Desert Will Blossom," p. 21.

44. Joseph Bernardin, "And Now, What Next," p. 11.

45. John Dearden, "Collegial Sharing in Ministry," Address to the Bishops' Assembly for Prayer and Reflection on Episcopal Ministry, June 1982, p. 3.

46. *Fulfilled in Your Hearing: The Homily in the Sunday Assembly* (Washington, D.C.: United States Catholic Conference, 1982), p. 4.

47. Op. cit., p. 22. The references given to Paul are Phil 2:1, 1 Cor 1:9, 2 Cor 13:13, and Phlm 6.

48. *The Report of the Bishops' Ad Hoc Committee On Priestly Life and Ministry,* (Washington, D.C.: United States Catholic Conference, 1974), p. 27.

49. *As One Who Serves,* p. 15.

50. Raymond Lucker, "Vocations to Lay Leadership in the Church and the World," Address to the Bishops' Assembly for Prayer and Reflection on Vocations, June 11, 1986, p. 8.

51. *As One Who Serves,* p. 19. Quoted from "A New Dogmatic Outlook on the Priestly Ministry," in *Concilium,* vol. 3, n. 5 (March 1969) (British edition), p. 14a.

52. *The Report of the Bishops' Ad Hoc Committee,* p. 23.

53. Joseph Bernardin, "In Service of One Another," *Origins* 15 (August 1, 1985): 136.

54. Rembert Weakland, "The Spirituality of the Priest: An Overview," An Address to a Pastoral Conference for Priests, June 29, 1980.

55. *The Continuing Formation of Priests: Growing in Wisdom, Age and* (Washington, D.C.: United States Catholic Conference, 1985), p. 9. This is a quote from *The Spiritual Renewal of the American Priesthood,* p. 22. The significance of the statement is underlined by the fact that it is cited in a document issued eleven years later.

56. Robert Sanchez, "The Bishop as Evangelizer," Address to the

Bishops' Assembly for Prayer and Reflection on Episcopal Ministry, June 1982, p. 4.

57. *Spiritual Renewal of the American Priesthood,* pp. 25–26.

58. John Sullivan, "A Vision for the Diocese," November 24, 1980.

59. *Spiritual Renewal of the American Priesthood,* p. 26. The reference is to *The Catholic Priest in the United States: Psychological Investigations.*

60. *The Continuing Formation of Priests,* p. 3.

61. *Spiritual Renewal of the American Priesthood,* pp. 26–27.

62. *The Continuing Formation of Priests,* p. 6.

63. Matthew Clark, "The Priest as a Man of Dialogue," *Origins* 13 (April 19, 1984): 748.

64. Thomas Murphy, "An Agenda for Confronting the Vocations Statistics," p. 471.

65. *Pastoral Letters,* vol. 3, p. 205.

66. *As One Who Serves,* p. 64.

67. *The Report of the Bishops' Ad Hoc Committee,* p. 34.

68. Daniel Pilarczyk, "Vocations to Ordained Ministries." Address to the Bishops' Assembly for Prayer and Reflection on Vocations, June 14, 1986, p. 22.

69. Op. cit., p. 24.

70. Joseph Bernardin, *Called To Serve,* p. 49.

71. Daniel Pilarczyk, "Vocations to Ordained Ministries," p. 23.

72. James Niedergeses, Chrism Mass Homily, April 15, 1976.

73. *Human Sexuality and the Ordained Priesthood* (Washington, D.C.: United States Catholic Conference, 1983), p. 35.

74. Op. cit., p. 37.

75. *As One Who Serves,* p. 64.

76. "Statement on Celibacy," *Pastoral Letters,* vol. 3, pp. 206–207.

77. Paul Dudley, "A Prayer for My Brothers." A Holy Thursday Pastoral Letter to Priests, March 27, 1986.

78. Op. cit., p. 9.

79. Ibid., p. 7.

80. Joseph Bernardin, *Called To Serve,* p. 42.

81. *As One Who Serves,* p. 16.

82. Sylvester Treinen, A Letter to Priests, April 15, 1974.

83. *The Continuing Formation of Priests,* p. 32.

84. Robert Sanchez, "Spanish-Speaking Catholics/The Difference Is a Value," *Origins* 7 (September 1, 1977): 174.

85. Robert Sanchez, "The Bishop as Evangelizer," p. 11.

86. Joseph Francis, "Keeping the Bread Fresh," *Origins* 14 (August 23, 1984): 171.
87. Patrick Flores, "The Opportunity Hispanics Provide for the Church," *Origins* 10 (September 11, 1980): 202.
88. *The Continuing Formation of Priests,* p. 7.
89. *Spiritual Renewal of the American Priesthood,* p. 1.
90. *The Continuing Formation of Priests,* p. 7.
91. Francis Stafford, "A Bishop Views the Presbyteral Council," *Origins* 15 (January 9, 1986): 504.
92. *Fullness in Christ: A Report on a Study of Clergy Retirement* (Washington, D.C.: United States Catholic Conference, 1979), p. 17.
93. *Pastoral Letters,* vol. 4, p. 418.
94. *The Program of Priestly Formation,* p. 4.
95. National Conference of Catholic Bishops (Washington, D.C.: United States Catholic Conference, 1979), p. 76.
96. *Fulfilled in Your Hearing,* p. 9.
97. John Quinn, Address to the Priests of the Archdiocese of San Francisco, December 14, 1983.
98. John Quinn, "At the Beginning of Lent . . ." A Pastoral Letter to Priests, February 25, 1980.
99. Daniel Pilarczyk, Ordination Homily, June 8, 1985.
100. *As One Who Serves,* p. 22.
101. Daniel Pilarczyk, Ordination Homily, June 11, 1983.
102. Joseph Ferrario, Chrism Mass Homily, March 21, 1986.
103. John Roach, Ordination Homily, May 25, 1985.
104. "You Are a Royal Priesthood," p. 177.
105. Daniel Pilarczyk, "Vocations to Ordained Ministries," p. 17.
106. James Hickey, Ordination Homily, June 29, 1985; Hickey, Ordination Homily, May 26, 1984.
107. Ordination Homily, 1979.
108. Joseph Bernardin, *Called To Serve,* 5.
109. Ordination Instruction, February 22, 1986.
110. John O'Connor, Chrism Mass Homily, 1985.
111. "The Mystery of the Priestly Vocation." *Origins* 18 (November 10, 1988): 355. Quoted from Pope John Paul II. *Dominicae Cenae* 8.
112. John Dearden, Chrism Mass Homily, March 20, 1978.
113. Homily for Malavern Workshop for Priests, November 10, 1977, in *The Church: Life-Giving Union with Christ* (Boston: St. Paul Editions, 1978), p. 538; Homily at the 50th Anniversary of

Msgr. Mondzelewski, March 13, 1983; Homily at the Chrism Mass, April 4, 1985.

114. John Whealon, Ordination Homily, June 24, 1983.

115. Chrism Mass Homily, 1979.

116. Raymond Hunthausen, Ordination Homily for Ott Hyatt and Anthony Bawyn, no date given.

117. John Quinn, Ordination Homily for the Jesuit Community, June 11, 1983.

118. Rembert Weakland, "The Bishop as Sanctifier." An Address to the Bishops' Assembly for Prayer and Reflection on Episcopal Ministry, June 1982, page 12.

119. Roger Mahony, "A Focus for Priestly Ministry." A Pastoral Letter to Priests, *Origins* 15 (March 13, 1986): 639–640.

120. Daniel Pilarczyk, "Vocations to Ordained Ministries," p. 14.

121. Ibid., p. 17.

122. Sylvester Treinen, "The Ordained Priesthood." A Pastoral Letter to Priests, 1986.

123. Joseph Bernardin, *Called To Serve*, p. 5.

124. John Krol, Chrism Mass Homily, April 4, 1985.

125. Sylvester Treinen, "The Ordained Priesthood."

126. Victor Balke, Ordination Homily, May 23, 1981.

127. John Dearden, Chrism Mass Homily, March 20, 1978.

128. John Krol, Toast to the Holy Father at the North American College Alumni Reunion, May 8, 1968, in *The Church*, p. 496.

129. Paul Dudley, "A Prayer for My Brothers."

130. *Spiritual Renewal of the American Priesthood*, p. 60.

131. *The Report of the Bishops' Ad Hoc Committee*, p. 25.

132. James Niedergeses, Chrism Mass Homily, 1984.

133. Joseph Bernardin, *Called To Serve*, p. 30.

134. John Quinn, "At the Beginning of Lent . . ." *Fullness in Christ*, p. 24.

135. Daniel Pilarczyk, "Vocations to Ordained Ministries," p. 17.

136. Thomas Murphy, "The Quality of Candidates for the Priesthood," p. 186; *Sharing the Light of Faith*, p. 52.

137. Daniel Pilarczyk, "Vocations to Ordained Ministries," p. 15.

138. John Quinn, Ordination Homily, June 11, 1983.

139. Howard Hubbard, typewritten manuscript of a newspaper article, May 1985.

140. Daniel Pilarczyk, "Vocations to Ordained Ministries," p. 18.

141. Rembert Weakland, "Lenten Pastoral Letter to All Priests of the Archdiocese of Milwaukee," 1981.

142. *The Program of Priestly Formation,* p. 22.

143. Op. cit., p. 18.

144. John Quinn, "Eucharist, Holy Orders and Apostolic Church Structures," *Origins* 13 (September 15, 1983): 234; John Krol, Chrism Mass Homily, March 27, 1986.

145. Sylvester Treinen, "The Ordained Priesthood"; *The Program of Priestly Formation,* p. 48; John O'Connor, "First Impressions and Initial Observations," Letter to the Priests of the Diocese of Scranton, September 1983.

146. "Vocations to Ordained Ministries," p. 13.

147. Rembert Weakland, "Lenten Pastoral to All Priests," 1981.

148. *The Priest and Sacred Scripture,* p. 12.

149. Francis Hurley, "Heroes and Holy Men," *The Catholic Bulletin,* August 3, 1986, p. 15.

150. "Archbishop's Homily at Priest Convocation."

151. Peter Gerety, "We Have Become a Pilgrim People." Homily for the Convention of the National Federation of Priests' Councils, *The Advocate,* May 1, 1985, page number not indicated in reprint.

152. John Quinn, Address to the Priests of the Archdiocese of San Francisco, December 14, 1983.

153. "Called and Gifted," in *Pastoral Letters,* vol. 4, p. 421.

154. Howard Hubbard, *We Are His People* (Albany, New York: The Evangelist, 1978), p. 1.

155. John Sullivan, "A Vision for the Diocese," November 24, 1980.

156. *The Continuing Formation of Priests,* p. 8.

157. Joseph Francis, "Vocations to Religious Life in the Church," Address to the Bishops' Assembly for Prayer and Reflection on Vocations, June 13, 1986, pp. 18, 25.

158. *The Continuing Formation of Priests,* p. 7.

159. *As One Who Serves,* p. 66.

160. Ibid., p. 35.

161. Joseph Bernardin, "And Now, What Next . . ." pp. 16–17.

162. John Dearden, "Collegial Sharing in Ministry," p. 25.

163. "Statement on Celibacy" in *Pastoral Letters,* vol. 3, p. 203.

164. William Borders, Chrism Mass Homily, 1977.

165. Victor Balke, "Conference Eight," A Priests' Retreat.

166. "Ministry to Priests," *Origins* 11 (June 17, 1982): 77.

167. Daniel Pilarczyk, "Vocations to Ordained Ministries," p. 12.

168. Ibid., p. 14.

169. Sylvester Treinen, "Praying and Studying the Scriptures," A Pastoral Letter to Priests. July 23, 1973; Victor Balke "Conference Nine," A Priests' Retreat.
170. Rembert Weakland, "The Bishop as Sanctifier," pp. 9–10.
171. John Krol, Homily at the Mass of the Holy Spirit, September 9, 1969, in *The Church,* p. 506.
172. Francis Stafford, "A Bishop Views the Presbyteral Council," p. 503.
173. Sylvester Treinen, "A Time for Building." A Pastoral Letter to Priests, April 13, 1969.
174. Address to the Duluth Presbytery, May 22, 1983.
175. Ibid.
176. John Quinn, Address to the Priests of the Archdiocese of San Francisco, June 7, 1985.
177. Op. cit., p. 21.
178. Daniel Pilarczyk, "Vocations to Ordained Ministries," p. 13.
179. Ibid., p. 14.
180. Chrism Mass Homily, 1986.
181. Joseph Bernardin, "In Service of One Another," pp. 136–137.
182. Aloysius Wycislo, "The Priest Today," Chrism Mass Homily, 1983.
183. Joseph Bernardin, *Called To Serve,* p. 3.
184. *Spiritual Renewal of the American Priesthood,* p. 15.
185. *As One Who Serves,* p. 24.
186. Ibid., p. 23.
187. *The Continuing Formation of Priests,* p. 8.
188. *As One Who Serves,* p. 28.
189. *The Continuing Formation of Priests,* p. 17.
190. John Quinn, Address to the Priests of the Archdiocese of San Francisco, December 14, 1983.
191. Address to Priests, January 15, 1986.
192. James Niedergeses, Chrism Mass Homily, 1980.
193. Op. cit., p. 40.
194. *The Program of Priestly Formation,* p. 6.
195. *The Continuing Formation of Priests,* p. 23.
196. Joseph Bernardin, Opening Address at the Overnight with Chicago Priests, November 5, 1984.
197. *A Shepherd's Care: Reflections on the Changing Role of Pastor* (Washington, D.C.: United States Catholic Conference, 1987), p. 20.
198. *The Continuing Formation of Priests,* p. 10.
199. Rembert Weakland, "The Bishop as Sanctifier," p. 12.

200. Francis Stafford, "A Bishop Views the Presbyteral Council," p. 503.
201. *As One Who Serves,* pp. 21, 61.
202. Joseph Bernardin, Overnight with Chicago Priests, November 5, 1984.
203. Matthew Clark, "The Priest as a Man of Dialogue," p. 749.
204. Ibid.
205. Victor Balke, "Conference Nine."
206. Victor Balke, "Conference Eight."
207. Victor Balke, "Conference Seven," A Priests' Retreat; Balke, Ordination Homily, March 15, 1986.
208. *As One Who Serves,* p. 21.
209. "You Are a Royal Priesthood," p. 178.
210. Pp. 40–41.
211. "A Vision of Future Ministry," *Origins* 13 (January 26, 1984): 553.
212. John Whealon, Chrism Mass Homily, 1984.
213. "The Bishop as Evangelizer," p. 8; *Evangelii Nuntiandi* 46.
214. Kenneth Untener, "A Vision of Future Ministry," p. 555.
215. *As One Who Serves,* p. 33.
216. Thomas Murphy, "The Local Community and the Future Priest," *Origins* 12 (December 16, 1982): 430.
217. Joseph Bernardin, Ordination Homily, May 19, 1984.
218. Kenneth Untener, "A Vision of Future Ministry," p. 556.
219. *The Continuing Formation of Priests,* p. 9.
220. Op. cit., p. 4.
221. Ibid., pp. 6–8.
222. Roger Mahony, "A Focus for Priestly Ministry," p. 640.
223. Philip Hannan, Holy Thursday Homily to Priests, March 22, 1986.
224. Aloysius Wycislo, "The Priest Today."
225. *Fulfilled in Your Hearing,* pp. 9–10.
226. Ibid., p. 20.
227. John Krol, Address at a Clergy Conference, April 1968, in *The Church,* p. 491.
228. *The Priest and Stress* (Washington, D.C.: United States Catholic Conference, 1982), pp. 7–8.
229. Joseph Bernardin, *Called To Serve,* p. 46.
230. Kenneth Untener, "A Vision of Future Ministry," p. 556.
231. *As One Who Serves,* p. 44.
232. "Called and Gifted," in *Pastoral Letters,* vol. 4, p. 419.
233. "A Bishop's Vision of Priests," *Origins* 12 (June 24, 1982): 78.

234. *The Program of Priestly Formation,* p. 49.
235. "Called and Gifted," in *Pastoral Letters,* vol. 4, p. 420.
236. Michael Begley, "Tensions Over a Priest's Time Off," *Origins* 12 (January 20, 1983): 506.
237. *Spiritual Renewal of the American Priesthood,* p. 16.
238. Op. cit., p. 46.
239. *A Shepherd's Care,* p. 9.
240. Joseph Ferrario, Chrism Mass Homily.
241. Patrick Flores, "The Opportunities Hispanics Provide for the Church," p. 203.
242. Howard Hubbard, *We Are His People,* p. 4.
243. Francis Quinn, "Golden Age of the Priesthood," *Origins* 15 (March 13, 1986): 645.
244. Daniel Pilarczyk, Ordination Homily, June 8, 1985.
245. Kenneth Untener, "A Vision of Future Ministry," p. 556.
246. *A Shepherd's Care,* p. 32.
247. Aloysius Wycislo, "The Priest Today."
248. *The Continuing Formation of Priests,* pp. 11, 14.
249. Op. cit., p. 13.
250. Ibid., p. 22.
251. *As One Who Serves,* p. 72.
252. "Golden Age of the Priesthood," p. 644.
253. Roger Mahony, "A Focus for Priestly Ministry," p. 640.
254. *Called To Serve,* p. 15.
255. Rembert Weakland, "The Spirituality of the Priest: An Overview."
256. *Spiritual Renewal of the American Priesthood,* p. 14.
257. *The Continuing Formation of Priests,* p. 21.
258. *Spiritual Renewal of the American Priesthood,* p. 11.
259. Matthew Clark, "The Priest as a Man of Dialogue," p. 748.

7. *Servants of the Poor and Witnesses to the Kingdom of God*

1. *Economic Justice for All* (Washington, D.C.: United States Catholic Conference, 1986), p. vi.
2. "The Bishop as Evangelizer," p. 5.
3. Ibid. The quotation is from the address of Pope John Paul II to the Barrio of Santa Cecilia, January 30, 1979.
4. Ibid., p. 6.
5. Robert Sanchez, "Spanish-Speaking Catholics," p. 175.
6. *As One Who Serves,* p. 8.
7. "The Priest Today," *Chicago Studies* 13 (Summer 1974): 131.

8. Joseph Bernardin, Letter to the Priests of the Archdiocese of Chicago, Corpus Christi, 1984.
9. Raymond Hunthausen, Chrism Mass Homily, 1981.
10. John Quinn, Ordination Homily for the Jesuit Community, June 16, 1984.
11. Rembert Weakland, "Lenten Pastoral Letter to All Priests of the Archdiocese of Milwaukee," 1981.
12. John Sullivan, Closing Address for the Emmaus Year for Priests, June 5, 1984.
13. Rembert Weakland, "The Spirituality of the Priest: An Overview."
14. *Spiritual Renewal of the American Priesthood*, p. 41.
15. John Dearden, An Excerpt from a 1969 Talk as Recorded in the 1980 Memorial Booklet "In the Midst of His Flock."
16. *As One Who Serves*, p. 11.
17. *The Priest and Sacred Scripture*, p. 21.
18. It is noteworthy that in underlining the significance of women in society the bishops state that our "tradition has always honored the Mother of God and recognized Mary as the one in whom, next to Jesus himself, human nature is expressed most perfectly." National Conference of Catholic Bishops, *To Live in Christ Jesus: A Pastoral Reflection on the Moral Life* (Washington, D.C.: United States Catholic Conference, 1976), p. 25.
19. "Toward a Theology of Vocations: The Mission of the Church in the United States," Address to the Bishops' Assembly for Prayer and Reflection on Vocations, June 10, 1986.
20. Ibid., pp. 8–9.
21. *As One Who Serves*, p. 8.
22. *The Priest and Sacred Scripture*, p. 3.
23. James Hickey, Ordination Homily, May 26, 1984.
24. Joseph Bernardin, Letter to the Priests of the Archdiocese of Chicago, Corpus Christi, 1984.
25. Op. cit., p. 3.
26. *The Priest and Sacred Scripture*, p. 7.
27. Howard Hubbard, Clergy Retreat Homily, September 1985.
28. Joseph Bernardin, Letter to the Priests of the Archdiocese of Chicago, Corpus Christi, 1984.
29. John Krol, "To Live the Mystery of the Priesthood," Notes for Remarks to U.S. Bishops, September 9, 1983.
30. *Spiritual Renewal of the American Priesthood*, p. 6.
31. Op. cit., pp. 3–4.
32. Ibid., p. 2.

33. John Quinn, Chrism Mass Homily, April 2, 1985.
34. Joseph Bernardin, *Called To Serve,* pp. 34–35.
35. Matthew Clark, Letter to the Clergy of the Diocese of Rochester, January 15, 1986.
36. Joseph Bernardin, *Called To Serve,* p. 40.
37. John Krol, Statement for "Labor, 1972," in *God—The Cornerstone of Our Life* (Boston: St. Paul Editions, 1978), p. 272.
38. John Krol, Address at the Acceptance of the 25th Anniversary Gold Medal Public Service Award, May 27, 1970, in *To Insure Peace Acknowledge God* (Boston: St. Paul Editions, 1978), pp. 118–121.
39. Robert Sanchez, "Spanish Speaking Catholics," p. 175.
40. Howard Hubbard, *We Are His People,* pp. 9, 15.
41. *As One Who Serves,* p. 14.
42. Joseph Bernardin, Opening Address at the Overnight with Chicago Priests, November 5, 1984.
43. *Spiritual Renewal of the American Priesthood,* pp. 6–7.
44. *Minneapolis Star and Tribune,* December 25, 1986, p. 10A.
45. "The Goal: Renewal and Reconciliation." A Pastoral Letter to Priests, December 1, 1973.
46. Address to the Priests of the Archdiocese of San Francisco, June 7, 1985.
47. *Spiritual Renewal of the American Priesthood,* p. 49.
48. Ibid., pp. 45–46.
49. Ibid., p. 47.
50. Closing Address for the Emmaus Year for Priests.
51. Sylvester Treinen, "Praying and Studying the Scriptures."
52. Ordination Homily, January 17, 1980.
53. *As One Who Serves,* pp. 18–19.
54. Letter to the Priests of the Archdiocese of Chicago, Corpus Christi, 1984.
55. Kenneth Untener, "A Vision of Future Ministry," p. 556.
56. Francis Quinn, "A Bishop's Vision for Priests," p. 77.
57. Raymond Hunthausen, "Developments in Ministry: Looking to the Future," Address to the University of Notre Dame Continuing Education Program, June 21, 1985.
58. Statement to the Synod of 1974, October 23, in *To Insure Peace,* p. 180.
59. *As One Who Serves,* p. 13.
60. *We Are His People,* p. 11.
61. National Conference of Catholic Bishops (Washington, D.C.: United States Catholic Conference, 1973), p. 17.

62. Howard Hubbard, *We Are His People,* p. 12.
63. "Vocations to Lay Leadership in the Church and the World," p. 12; *Apostolicam Actuositatem* 5.
64. Ibid., p. 11.
65. Ibid., p. 12. He quotes Pope Paul VI, "Evangelization in the Modern World," #70.
66. National Conference of Catholic Bishops, *The Challenge of Peace: God's Promise and Our Response* (Washington, D.C.: United States Catholic Conference, 1983), paragraph 58, p. 18.
67. Ibid., paragraph 56, p. 18.
68. Ibid., paragraph 339, p. 103.
69. *As One Who Serves,* p. 12.
70. *The Continuing Formation of Priests,* p. 16.
71. *As One Who Serves,* p. 12.
72. "A Vision for the Diocese."
73. Op. cit., p. 9.
74. National Conference, "Statement on Celibacy," p. 204.
75. *As One Who Serves,* p. 16.
76. Chrism Mass Homily, March 18, 1986. The image is from St. Gregory the Great (no reference given).
77. *The Priest and Sacred Scripture,* p. 14.
78. John Quinn, "Eucharist, Holy Orders and Apostolic Church Structures," p. 234.
79. *As One Who Serves,* p. 11.
80. "A Focus for Priestly Ministry," p. 642.
81. Ibid., p. 642.
82. *Spiritual Renewal of the American Priesthood,* p. 51; *As One Who Serves,* p. 71.
83. *Spiritual Renewal of the American Priesthood,* p. 49.
84. *As One Who Serves,* p. 73.
85. John Quinn, Ordination Homily, November 16, 1985.
86. Letter to the Priests of the Archdiocese of Chicago, Corpus Christi, 1984.
87. Ibid., quoted from *On the Mystery and Worship of the Holy Eucharist,* #6.
88. Clergy Retreat Homily.
89. Address to the Priests of the Archdiocese of San Francisco, June 7, 1985.
90. Chrism Mass Homily, March 27, 1986.
91. Ibid. The cardinal paraphrases a speech of Pope John Paul II given at the Philadelphia Convention Hall in 1979.
92. "A Focus for Priestly Ministry," p. 640.

93. *Spiritual Renewal of the American Priesthood,* p. 5.
94. *Called To Serve,* p. 16.
95. Ibid., pp. 16–17.
96. Address at the Beginning of the Emmaus Year for Priests, September 27, 1983.
97. *Montana Catholic,* March 6, 1985. No page number included with the reprint.
98. Op. cit., p. 12.
99. John Krol, Homily at the 50th Anniversary of Msgr. Mondzelewski.
100. "The Bishop as Builder of Community," p. 11.
101. Chrism Mass Homily, April 10, 1984.
102. John Quinn, "The Ministry of Reconciliation," A Pastoral Letter to Priests, March 4, 1981.
103. "A Focus for Priestly Ministry," p. 641.
104. Paul Dudley, "A Prayer for My Brothers."
105. Op. cit., p. 72.
106. Ibid.
107. Op. cit., p. 33.
108. "Golden Age of the Priesthood," p. 645.
109. "The Priesthood: Yesterday and Today."
110. Sylvester Treinen, "The Priest: A Beloved Disciple," A Pastoral Letter to Priests, April 11, 1971.
111. *As One Who Serves,* p. 42.
112. *The Continuing Formation of Priests,* p. 16.
113. Op. cit., p. 25.
114. Ibid., p. 15.
115. Address to the Priests of the Archdiocese of San Francisco, December 14, 1983.
116. "A Bishop's Vision for Priests," p. 78.
117. Op. cit., pp. 31–32.
118. Address at St. John's Seminary Centennial Dinner, Brighton, Massachusetts, October 11, 1984.
119. "Lenten Pastoral Letter to All Priests of the Archdiocese of Milwaukee."
120. Ordination Homily, May 26, 1984.
121. "The Priest Today."
122. Ordination Homily, May 26, 1984.
123. John Quinn, Ordination Homily, November 16, 1985.
124. National Conference, "Statement on Celibacy," p. 204.
125. *Spiritual Renewal of the American Priesthood,* p. 21.
126. Edward Szoka, "Ministry to Priests," p. 77.

127. Ordination Homily for the Jesuit Community, June 16, 1984.
128. Ibid.
129. Chrism Mass Homily, March 18, 1986.
130. Daniel Pilarczyk, "Vocations to Ordained Ministries," p. 23.
131. John Whealon, Homily at Mass for the Emmaus Program for Priests, April 27, 1982.
132. Op. cit., p. 48.
133. Ibid., p. 39.
134. Homily at the Conferral of Candidacy, November 4, 1977, in *The Church*, p. 534.
135. *The Priest and Stress*, p. 18.
136. "The Spirituality of the Priest: An Overview."
137. Ibid.
138. John Quinn, Chrism Mass Homily, March 18, 1986.
139. Paul Dudley, "A Prayer for My Brothers."
140. Chrism Mass Homily, April 4, 1985.
141. "Heroes and Holy Men."
142. *As One Who Serves*, p. 69.
143. "Praying and Studying the Scriptures."
144. Spiritual Convocation of the Priests of the Archdiocese of Newark, June 18, 1984.
145. Opening Address at the Overnight with Chicago Priests, November 5, 1984.
146. Letter to the Priests of the Archdiocese of Chicago, Corpus Christi, 1984.
147. "At the Beginning of Lent . . ."
148. John Quinn, Address to the Priests of the Archdiocese of San Francisco, December 14, 1983.
149. John Quinn, Address to the Priests of the Archdiocese of San Francisco, June 7, 1985.
150. John Quinn, "At the Beginning of Lent . . ."
151. Spiritual Convocation of the Priests of the Archdiocese of Newark.
152. *The Continuing Formation of Priests*, p. 16.
153. Chrism Mass Homily, March 18, 1986.
154. John Krol, Homily at St. Charles Seminary, October 23, 1973, in *The Church*, p. 518.
155. Letter to the Clergy of the Diocese of Rochester, January 15, 1986.
156. Address to the Duluth Presbytery.
157. Opening Address at the Overnight with Chicago Priests, November 5, 1984.

158. "A Bishop's Vision for Priests," p. 76.
159. Chrism Mass Homily, March 27, 1986.
160. Daniel Pilarczyk, Ordination Homily, June 8, 1985.
161. Op. cit., pp. 19–20.
162. Spiritual Convocation of the Priests of the Archdiocese of Newark.
163. Address to the Priests of the Archdiocese of San Francisco, December 14, 1983.
164. "A Focus for Priestly Ministry," p. 639.
165. Ibid., p. 642.
166. Op. cit., pp. 57–58.
167. Homily at the 50th Anniversary of Msgr. Mondzelewski.
168. John Krol, Chrism Mass Homily, March 27, 1986; John O'Connor, Chrism Mass Homily, 1986.
169. Ordination Homily, November 16, 1985.
170. *The Priest and Sacred Scripture*, pp. 7–8.
171. "First Impressions and Initial Observations," Letter to the Priests of the Diocese of Scranton, September 1983.
172. "The Priest Today," p. 131.
173. *Called To Serve*, p. 19.
174. Ordination Homily for Frs. Ott Hyatt and Anthony Bawyn.
175. "Witnesses to Christ," Homily at the Bishops' Assembly for Prayer and Reflection on Episcopal Ministry, June 17, 1982.
176. "Conference Twelve," A Priests' Retreat.
177. Ibid.
178. Joseph Bernardin, Letter to the Priests of the Archdiocese of Chicago, Corpus Christi, 1984.
179. Op. cit., pp. 32–33.
180. Address at the Beginning of the Emmaus Year for Priests.
181. Ordination Homily, November 16, 1985.
182. Ordination Homily for the Jesuit Community, June 11, 1983.
183. "Heroes and Holy Men."
184. Op. cit., p. 9.
185. *As One Who Serves*, p. 51.
186. Ibid., p. 51. The footnote reference given is to the *Declaration, 1974 Synod of Bishops*, paragraphs 12, 13.
187. P. 166.
188. *Spiritual Renewal of the American Priesthood*, p. 19.
189. Op. cit., p. 52.
190. *Spiritual Renewal of the American Priesthood*, p. 19.
191. Ordination Homily, March 15, 1986.
192. Op. cit., p. 22.

193. Ibid., p. 49.
194. *Economic Justice for All,* p. 166.
195. Daniel Pilarczyk, "Vocations to Ordained Ministries," p. 19.
196. "Statement on Celibacy," pp. 205–206.
197. Ibid., p. 205.
198. "A Prayer for My Brothers."
199. "Vocations to Ordained Ministries," p. 21.
200. "The Spirituality of the Priest: An Overview."
201. Victor Balke, Ordination Homily for the Benedictine Community, November 23, 1979.
202. Opening Address at the Overnight with Chicago Priests, November 5, 1984.
203. "Vocations to Ordained Ministries," p. 21.
204. *Spiritual Renewal of the American Priesthood,* p. 38.
205. Chrism Mass Homily, April 2, 1985.
206. "Vocations to Ordained Ministries," pp. 24–25.
207. Rembert Weakland, "Lenten Pastoral Letter to All Priests of the Archdiocese of Milwaukee."
208. National Conference, "Statement on Celibacy," p. 204.
209. *Called To Serve,* p. 47.
210. "Vocations to Ordained Ministries," p. 23.
211. Op. cit., p. 45.
212. Joseph Bernardin, *Called To Serve,* pp. 47–48.

8. An Ecclesial Spirituality for American Priests

1. For a description of this post-conciliar phenomenon, giving pertinent historical background and liturgical rites for emerging ministries, see David Powers, *Gifts That Differ: Lay Ministries Established and Unestablished* (New York: Pueblo Publishing Company, 1980).
2. For a detailed interpretation of the development of American Catholicism see Jay Dolan, *The American Catholic Experience* (Garden City, New York: Doubleday, 1985). Special attention is given to lay ministry on pp. 438–440.
3. The evolution of the church in the United States is elaborated by James Hennesey, *American Catholics: A History of the Roman Catholic Community in the United States* (New York: Oxford University Press, 1981). The new burst of enthusiasm is graphically described on p. 331.
4. This commitment to and ownership of the American church by the laity is emphasized by Eugene Kennedy, *The Now and Future*

Church: The Psychology of Being an American Catholic (Garden City, New York: Doubleday, 1984). See especially pp. 152ff.

5. For documentation of the movement toward a more aggressive and involved laity having new and challenging expectations of their church see David J. O'Brien, *The Renewal of American Catholicism* (New York: Oxford University Press, 1972). Especially pertinent are pp. 259ff.

6. The complex nature of presbyteral ministry as "a sacrament within a sacrament" is considered by Bernard Cooke, *Ministry to Word and Sacraments* (Philadelphia: Fortress Press, 1976), pp. 643–656.

7. The distinctive apostolic mission in which the ordained share is ordered to serving the church in living the apostolic faith. Severino Dianich, *Teologia del Ministero Ordinato: Una Interpretazione Ecclesiologica* (Rome: Edizioni Paoline, 1984), pp. 221–228.

8. The distinctive identity of the ordained as representatives of Christ, the head of the church, is treated by Edward Schillebeeckx, *Christ the Sacrament of the Encounter with God* (London: Sheed and Ward, 1963), pp. 169–172.

9. For a thorough treatment of the church as sign and the interrelationship of signs in the witness of the church, see René Latourelle, *Christ and the Church: Signs of Salvation* (Staten Island, New York: Alba House, 1972), pp. 65–73.

10. An extensive treatment of the interrelationship between the laity and the clergy operative in the contemporary church is found in Yves Congar, *Lay People in the Church* (Westminster, Maryland: Newman Press, 1967), especially pp. 28–54.

11. The distinctive service offered by the ordained in the context of a ministerial church is reflected on by Juan Esquerda Bifet, *Teologia del Sacerdocio: Historia de la Espiritualidad Sacerdotal* (Burgos: Ediciones Aldecoa, 1985), pp. 48–51.

12. The difficulties are faced and an appropriate context is constructed by Karl Rahner, *Theological Investigations*, vol. 12 (London: Darton, Longman & Todd, 1974), pp. 31–38; also see Edward Schillebeeckx, *The Church with a Human Face: A New and Expanded Theology of Ministry* (New York: Crossroad, 1985), especially pp. 125–203.

13. For a lengthy discussion of the significance of baptism, confirmation and eucharist in deepening participation in Christ, and the importance of the sacrament of orders in giving a stable and visible character to a particular expression of the spiritual

life, see Charles A. Bernard, *Teologia Spirituale* (Rome: Edizioni Paoline, 1983), especially pp. 287–326.

14. A treatment of sacramental character in a liturgical context is given by David Power, *Ministers of Christ and His Church: The Theology of the Priesthood* (London: Geoffrey Chapman, 1968), pp. 115–126.

15. The importance of the ecclesial context of ministry is underlined by Thomas O'Meara, *Theology of Ministry* (New York: Paulist Press, 1983), especially pp. 134–172.

16. A concise summary of the implications of the theology of Vatican II for the development of an appropriate presbyteral spirituality can be found in Juan Esquerda Bifet, *Teologia del Sacerdocio*, pp. 185–191.

17. The traditional teaching on sacramental character is discussed by Jean Galot, *Teologia del Sacerdozio* (Florence: Libreria Editrice, 1981), pp. 207–230.

18. The end of an immigrant church in which the clergy were idolized, seldom criticized, unquestionably respected and cared for has passed according to Eugene Kennedy, *The Now and Future Church*, pp. 3–26.

19. An approach called "sacramental realism" is used to bring together the ontological and functional aspects of the sacraments by Coleman O'Neil, *Sacramental Realism: A General Theory of the Sacraments* (Wilmington, Delaware: Michael Glazier, 1983); see especially pp. 192–197.

20. The tension between theological formulations and cultural preferences is discussed by Thomas O'Meara, *Theology of Ministry*, pp. 3–24.

21. Office and sanctity are related to one another since together they form the ecclesial commission. "This (sacramental) character gives a priest an intimate union in grace with Christ as Head of the Church, in such a way that his priestly ministration shows forth the holiness of the leader of God's people, Jesus Christ." Schillebeeckx, *Christ the Sacrament*, p. 174.

22. The essential connection between priestly ministry and holiness is underlined by Juan Esquerda Bifet, *Te Hemos Seguido: Espiritualidad Sacerdotal* (Madrid: Biblioteca de Autores Cristianos, 1986), especially pp. 100–108.

23. For an articulation of an authentic presbyteral spirituality arising from the nature of the priestly mission, see Agostino Favale, *Spiritualità del Ministero Presbiterale* (Rome: LAS, 1985), especially pp. 51–89.

24. An understanding of the presbyterate as found in the decrees of Vatican II is found in David Powers, *Ministers of Christ and His Church,* pp. 150–154.

25. This leadership is directed to the building up of the church by encouraging and enabling the ministry of all the members. Albert Altana, "La Vocazione al Ministero Ordinato," in *Vocazione Commune e Vocazioni Specifiche,* ed. Agostino Favale (Rome: LAS, 1981), p. 325.

26. The primary assembly of the faithful as church is the eucharist. Thus the "priestly character" is ordered directly to the eucharist. Coleman O'Neill, *Sacramental Realism,* p. 196.

27. The vocation to imitate Christ and to be conformed to him is common to all Christians, even in strict theological terminology, although it is specified differently in various members of the church. Charles Bernard, *Teologia Spirituale,* pp. 50, 132–133.

28. A theologically focused appreciation of the relationship of the eucharist to the sacrifice of Calvary is essential. Richard McBrien, *Catholicism,* 2:763–765.

29. The sacrament of orders makes Christ present in a specific way, as the one who saves the Church as its head. Alberto Altana, *Vocazione Commune e Vocazioni Specifiche,* p. 313.

30. The ordained do not take Christ's place, but they make Christ present; their words and actions are simultaneously those of Christ. "It seems safe to say that no interpretation allows for a more immediate involvement of Christ himself in the action of eucharist than to see the minister's function as *sacramental* in the strict sense." Bernard Cooke, *Ministry to Word and Sacraments,* p. 647; the discussion on pp. 644–649 is a very important one.

31. Priestly activity is the sacramental visibility of "the 'theandric' initiative of Christ." Thus, priests act *in persona Christi* in a strict sense. Piet Fransen, "Orders and Ordination," in *Encyclopedia of Theology: A Concise Sacramentum Mundi,* ed. Karl Rahner (London: Burns and Oates, 1975), p. 1144.

32. Although the role of making the eucharistic sacrifice present belongs to the ordained priest alone, it is not their sacrifice, but belongs to Christ and the church. Karl Rahner, *Theological Investigations,* vol. 3 (London: Darton, Longman & Todd, 1974), pp. 248–250.

33. Thus, the "renewal" of the initial grace of the sacrament of

orders is a powerful aspect of presbyteral spirituality. Karl Rahner, *Theological Investigations*, 3: 171–176.

34. I am particularly indebted to my own teachers for a broader vision in this regard, especially to Fr. James Moudry of the St. Paul Seminary School of Divinity faculty and Fr. John Gilbert of the Center for Priestly Growth, both in the archdiocese of St. Paul and Minneapolis. The bishops' document *A Shepherd's Care* brings together much of the experience of the pastor today, but little attention is given to the theological underpinnings of its vision of parish life.

35. The distinctive role of the bishop as enunciated by the council is treated by Severino Dianich, pp. 237–247.

36. The historical development of the relationship between the episcopate and the presbyterate is summarized by Nathan Mitchell, *Mission and Ministry: History and Theology in the Sacrament of Order* (Wilmington, Delaware: Michael Glazier, 1982), pp. 151–158, 241–250.

37. The common role of priests and bishops as representatives of Christ and animators of the Christian community is emphasized by Alberto Altana in *Vocazione Commune e Vocazioni Specifiche*, p. 312.

38. The way in which priests are related to the bishop as his collaborators flows from a plurality which is theologically and practically necessary in the exercise of pastoral ministry. Lack of clarity in this regard has created a lessening of morale among priests. Maurice Vidal, "Presbytérat après Le Concile de Vatican II," in *Dictionnaire de Spiritualité* (Paris: Beauchesne, 1986), vol. 12, part 2: 2103.

39. Sacrosanctum Oecumenicum Concilium Vaticanum Secundum, *Schema Decreti De Presbyterorum Ministerio et Vita: Textus Recognitus et Modi* (Typis Polyglottis Vaticanis, 1965), p. 45.

40. *Lumen Gentium* 28; *Presbyterorum Ordinis* 5.

41. Sacrosanctum Oecumenicum Concilium Vaticanum Secundum, *Schema Constitutionis Dogmaticae de Ecclesia: Modi III* (Caput III: De Constitutione Hierarchica Ecclesiae et in Specie De Episcopatu) (Typis Polyglottis Vaticanis, 1964), p. 52.

42. A presbyter's relationship to his bishop must never be confused with his relationship to Christ, since as a pastor the priest represents the Lord as one ordained to do so. David Power, *Ministers of Christ and His Church*, p. 186.

43. While the consecration and mission of priests is based on that

of Christ as head and pastor of the church, it is joined by its very nature to that of the bishops. Agostino Favale, *Spiritualità del Ministero Presbiterale,* p. 53.

44. The presbyterate is a *"fraternité sacramentelle,"* that is, an efficacious sign of sanctification and evangelization which flows from the sacrament of orders. Juan Esquerda Bifet, "Presbytérat a Le Concile de Vatican II," in *Dictionnaire de Spiritualité,* vol. 12, part 2: 2097.

45. Co-responsibility and solidarity are important aspects of the post-conciliar renewal of presbyteral ministry. Alberto Altana, in *Vocazione Commune e Vocazioni Specifiche,* p. 317.

46. A proper understanding of human weakness enters into an authentic appreciation of ecclesial relationships. For a helpful expansion of the usual application of 1 Corinthians to the life of the church see Jerome Neyrey, *Christ Is Community: The Christologies of the New Testament* (Wilmington, Delaware: Michael Glazier, 1985), pp. 200–213.

47. Eschatology is an essential dimension of ordained ministry, creating a necessary tension which gives a distinctive tone to presbyteral activities. Severino Dianich, pp. 228–233.

48. For a treatment of the theological identity of priests with an emphasis on their prophetic role, see Karl Rahner, *Theological Investigations,* 3:239–262.

49. In the post-conciliar period there has been a temptation to remove the understanding of priesthood from a theology of grace and to recast it in that of an "organization man." John Sheets, *To Believe Is To Exist* (Denville, New Jersey: Dimension Books, 1986), p. 174.

50. For a further consideration of the relationship between the presbyteral office and priestly spirituality, see Karl Rahner, *Theological Investigations,* vol. 19 (New York: Crossroad, 1983), pp. 122–138.

51. It is important that presbyteral activity be placed within the framework of a proper understanding of the priestly office. Walter Kasper, "A New Dogmatic Outlook on the Priestly Ministry," in *The Identity of the Priest* (Concilium vol. 43) (New York: Paulist Press, 1969), pp. 20–33.

52. Since the spirituality of religious priests is always ecclesial in nature, both the universal and the diocesan contexts of their ministry is important. Agostino Favale, *Spiritualità del Ministero Presbiterale,* pp. 48–50.

53. An authentic presbyteral spirituality is focused on the church

as a whole and on the fundamental relationship between priests and bishops in fulfilling an essential service to the ecclesial community. John Sheets, pp. 173–184.

54. The gospel demands that priests be present to the struggle of humanity both as members of the church and as a distinctive leaven in the community. Juan Luis Segundo, *The Community Called Church* (New York: Orbis, 1968), pp. 78–91.

55. Followers of Jesus are to separate themselves from all that would isolate them from the needy. Freely chosen apostolic poverty witnesses to the new humanity which is possible in Christ. Virgilio Elizondo, *Galilean Journey: The Mexican American Promise* (New York: Orbis, 1983), p. 93.

56. The lack of clarity in the ecclesial role of priests was often mentioned at the 1985 Synod of Bishops. In a particularly troubled situation, attention was focused on the need to elucidate the distinctive presbyteral mission to the poor by Cardinal Miguel Obando Bravo in *Il Sinodo Dei Vescovi,* ed. Giovanni Caprile (Rome: Edizioni "La Civiltà Cattolica," 1986), pp. 161–162.

57. Priests are to have an effect on the people of God which is much like leaven in bread; thus, it is the interaction between priests and those they serve which reveals the kingdom of God. Jacques Leclercq, *Où Va l'Église d'Aujourd'hui* (Tournai, Belgium: Casterman, 1969), p. 30.

58. Priests are no longer to be separated from the world by their spirituality, but to be united with the Christian people and the world itself in its struggle. This challenges priests to a rethinking of their ministry. Severino Dianich, pp. 33–36.

59. Since the eucharist is ordered toward the service and mission of the entire ecclesial community, the ministers of the eucharist fulfill their distinctive role by bringing the people of God to this sacramental source of their activity. George Tavard, *A Theology of Ministry* (Wilmington, Delaware: Michael Glazier, 1983), pp. 50–54.

60. The unity between office and charism is something to be striven after for the good of the church. The correspondence between leadership and charism is often close in the charismatic renewal. Francis Sullivan, *Charisms and Charismatic Renewal: A Biblical and Theological Study* (Ann Arbor, Michigan: Servant Books, 1982), pp. 81–82.

61. One of the most important tasks of contemporary ecclesiology lies in the area of working out the relationship between the

Spirit and the church in greater detail. Jerome Hamer, *The Church Is a Communion* (London: Geoffrey Chapman, 1964), p. 187.

62. The relationship between the Holy Spirit and the ministry of the apostles is treated by Yves Congar in *The Mystery of the Church* (Baltimore: Helicon Press, 1960), pp. 147–186.

63. The notion of authority which prevailed in the earliest period of Christianity was directly related to exemplary holiness. In this light, the church presented candidates for ordination. David Power, *Ministers of Christ and His Church*, pp. 60–61.

64. The family remains a primary place for the development and discernment of such charisms, as does the total life of the parish community. See Delores Curran in *Laborers for the Vineyard*, pp. 116–122, and Philip Murnion, pp. 122–132 in the same work.

65. Adequate discernment is important since "this grace (charism) cannot be ordained in advance by the official organs of the church and is not administered through the sacraments. . . ." Laudislaus Boros, "Discernment of Spirit," in *Charisms in the Church* (Concilium vol. 109), Christian Duquoc and Casiano Floristan, eds. (New York: Seabury Press, 1978), p. 78.

66. The priesthood is a permanent participation in the unique mission of Christ which demands continued growth in the imitation of his pastoral love. The four essential dimensions of this growth are service, evangelization, communion and witness. Juan Esquerda Bifet, *Teologia del Sacerdocio*, pp. 213–217.

67. Since the church is by definition a twofold reality, embracing the human and the divine, both must be maintained simultaneously. Henri de Lubac, *The Church: Paradox and Mystery* (Shannon, Ireland: Ecclesial Press, 1969), pp. 23–29.

68. Bernard Häring, *The Healing Power of Peace and Nonviolence* (Middlegreen, Slough, England: St. Paul Publications, 1986), pp. 7–34; Häring, *Healing and Revealing* (Middlegreen, Slough, England: St. Paul Publications, 1984), pp. 4–8.

69. Requests that Archbishop Roach, president of the National Conference when the pastoral was approved, speak on the subject had declined substantially two years after it was issued, as had requests for educational materials directed to the peace and justice education office of the archdiocese of St. Paul and Minneapolis. The director of the office comments: "We have a little bit of frustration at the parish level that people have kind

of dropped it." "Pastoral on nuclear arms loses impact," *Minneapolis Star and Tribune,* May 3, 1985, p. 18C.

70. The need of "breakthrough" releasing new life-energies is forcefully addressed by Rosemary Haughton, pp. 89–128. The promise by God of himself in Jesus "is always and everywhere the fundamental energy and force of the world and its history." This kingdom, "which can no longer be stopped," is the heart of the Christian message. Karl Rahner and Karl-Heinz Weger, *Our Christian Faith: Answers for the Future* (New York: Crossroad, 1981), p. 103. Henri de Lubac quotes abbot Joannès Wehrlé as saying: "We cannot even dream of untying the vital knot which binds together in an indissoluble unity the act of the mind, and the transport of the heart, knowledge and confidence, intelligence and will." *The Christian Faith* (Ignatius Press: San Francisco, 1986), p. 294.

71. Avery Dulles, "The Gospel, The Church and Politics," in *Origins* 16 (February 19, 1987): p. 643.

72. Since prayer and ministry come together as two interrelated aspects of presbyteral life, the priest is one who acts in response to the "voice of the Spirit" heard in many ways, but especially in those who suffer. Alberto Altana, in *Vocazione Commune e Vocazioni Specifiche,* p. 329.

73. Dulles, p. 638.

74. Since grace, by definition, is ecclesial and social, every effective actual grace has a certain "charismatic character" to it making the line between the ordinary and the extraordinary very fluid. Karl Rahner, *Theological Investigations,* 12: 90.

75. Joseph Bernardin, "And Now, What Next . . ." Address to the Bishops' Assembly for Prayer and Reflection on Vocations, June 16, 1986, pp. 8–9 (National Conference of Catholic Bishops, private publication).